About this book

The central purpose of this book is to re-establish the relevance of anthropological (and indeed sociological) approaches to development processes and, *pari passu*, persuading anthropology to recognise that the study of contemporary development ought to be one of its principal concerns. Professor Olivier de Sardan argues for a socio-anthropology of change and development that is a deeply empirical, multi-dimensional, diachronic study of social groups and their interactions, combining analysis of social practices and consciousness. It has, in his view, simultaneously to be a political anthropology, a sociology of organizations, an economic anthropology, a sociology of networks, and an anthropology of conceptions and belief systems.

The author also intends to make English- and French-speaking anthropologists and students much more aware of each other's contribution to understanding development and social change.

The Introduction provides a thought-provoking examination of the principal new approaches that have emerged in the discipline during the 1990s. Part I then makes clear the complexity of social change and development, and the ways in which socio-anthropology can measure up to the challenge of this complexity. Part II looks more closely at some of the leading variables involved in the development process, including relations of production; the logics of social action; the nature of knowledge, including popular knowledge; forms of mediation; and 'political' strategies.

Following its successful publication in French (where it has run through several printings), this important book will provoke much thoughtful debate about appropriate theory and practice within Anthropology, Sociology and Development Studies. It is also particularly appropriate as an advanced text for students in these fields.

About the author

Jean-Pierre Olivier de Sardan is Professor of Anthropology at the École des Hautes Études en Sciences Sociales in Marseilles and Director of Research at the Centre National de la Recherche Scientifique in Paris. Holding dual nationality in France and Niger, he was educated at the Sorbonne, and currently lives and works in Niamey. His long and distinguished research career has involved a huge number of different projects and activities, as well as long spells teaching at the University of Paris and other French universities, as well as in Africa. Between 1991 and 1996 he served as President of the Association Euro-Africaine pour l'Anthropologie du Changement Social et du Developpement. Since 1965 he has authored seven books in French, as well as contributing to numerous scholarly volumes and authoring many scholarly journal articles in French. He has also published articles in English language journals including *Africa*, *Current Anthropology*, *Critique of Anthropology*, *Visual Anthropology*, and the *Journal of Modern African Studies*, as well as chapters in several English language scholarly works.

Anthropology and Development

UNDERSTANDING CONTEMPORARY SOCIAL CHANGE

Jean-Pierre Olivier de Sardan

Translated by
Antoinette Tidjani Alou

ZED BOOKS
LONDON & NEW YORK

Anthropology and Development:
Understanding Contemporary Social Change
was first published in 2005 by
Zed Books Ltd, 7 Cynthia Street, London N1 9JF, UK and
Room 400, 175 Fifth Avenue, New York, NY 10010, USA.

www.zedbooks.co.uk

Cover designed by Andrew Corbett
Set in 11/13 pt Garamond by Long House, Cumbria, UK
Printed and bound in Malaysia by Forum

Distributed in the USA exclusively by Palgrave Macmillan, a division of
St Martin's Press, LLC, 175 Fifth Avenue, New York, NY 10010.

A catalogue record for this book
is available from the British Library

US Cataloging-in-Publication Data
is available from the Library of Congress

ISBN   Hb 1 84277 416 6
       Pb 1 84277 417 4

Contents

1

Introduction

The Three Approaches in the Anthropology of Development[1]

This work was originally published in France in 1995 and had several objectives. Its primary aim was to develop a specific perspective, in the form of a non-normative approach to the complex social phenomena linked to development actions, grounded in a resolutely empirical (nonspeculative and based on enquiry) and 'fundamental' (situated upstream of 'applied' anthropology) practice of anthropology. A secondary objective was to take simultaneous account of works in English and in French dealing with the anthropology of development.

It is remarkable, on one hand, that the works published in English that approach the anthropology of development from one angle or another are, as a rule, completely oblivious of the works that exist in French, despite the fact that French-speaking Africa is as much a region where development policies and operations prevail as Anglophone Africa.[2] Conversely, most of the works published in French bear witness to a very unequal and impressionistic knowledge of the literature in English.[3] Thus, in France, the present work provided a linkage between two frequently disconnected scholarly universes. Its translation into English now offers the same opportunity to readers from English-speaking countries.

However, the main aim of this book is more general. I wish to propose a point of view on development that reintegrates development into mainstream anthropology as an object worthy of attention, a perspective that engages in a minute exploration of the various types of interactions which take place in the world of development, bringing into play conceptions and practices, strategies and structures, actors and contexts. This is therefore a project that intends to steer clear of both apology and denunciation, to avoid both prophecies and caricatures. However, another characteristic of the literature on development, in English and French alike, is that it is permeated with normative judgements arising from a variety of ideologies and meta-ideologies (see Chapter 5).

The literature is the source of an endless stream of value judgements on development. Anthropologists are no exception to this rule: despite the fact that they readily denounce the ideologies in other people's work (especially those that are popular among development professionals), they fail to recognize those that abound in their own work – populism, for instance (see below and Chapter 7), or post-modernism and the 'politically correct' (see below). Contrary to this, my conception of anthropology is that it is an empirical social science, but of course not a positivist one like the classic natural sciences. Social sciences have nothing to do with Popper's notion of falsification: their logic is based on plausibility on a basis of natural reasoning. But they are not hermeneutic sciences in the sense that epistemological relativism or radical subjectivism give to this term. Their hands are tied by the search for an empirical foundation.[4]

As far as this is concerned, my interest in development does not aim either at saving or condemning, deconstructing or reforming. It is rather a question of understanding, through development, a set of complex social practices: from this point of view, development is simply a set of actions of various types which define themselves as constituting development in one way or another (whether in the ranks of 'developers' or of 'developees'), notwithstanding the variations in their definitions, meanings and practices. The very existence of a 'developmentalist configuration'[5] (see Chapter 2) – that is, a complex set of institutions, flows and actors, for whom development constitutes a resource, a profession, a market, a stake, or a strategy – is enough to justify the existence of a socio-anthropology[6] which takes development as an object of study or as a 'pathway'.

In fact, anthropology of development is merely a way of going about anthropology and sociology, that is, a way of carrying out empirical field enquiries leading to new ways of understanding social phenomena, based on contemporary objects. Development is just one of a range of topics, but one that presents some specific characteristics: in countries of the South, and in African countries in particular, it is omnipresent and inevitable.[7] It comprises considerable social stakes at the local and national levels, and is interwoven with interactions between actors originating in particularly heterogeneous social and professional worlds (see Chapter 9).

Anthropology of development is not an autonomous or independent discipline. Moreover, it is not necessarily 'applied' anthropology: the question of the relationship between research and action, whether in terms of the *relevance* of research to action, which is one thing, or of the *integration* of research into action, which is another, constitutes a different problem, which is certainly important, but different (I will make brief mention of this in Chapter 13).[8] Anthropology 'applied' to development stands in need of what we may call *fundamental* anthropology of development, which provides it with problematics, concepts, methods and results. Our first step is to take into account some social realities of great importance to Africa such as development projects, the financing of development, development brokerage, and development associations, all of which intervene on a daily basis in even the smallest village, and to use these realities as pathways into political, economic, social and cultural anthropology, by making investigations into the practices and conceptions of the actors concerned, the interplay of the pragmatic and cognitive relationships, and the structural and institutional contexts in which all this occurs. If this type of research objective is pursued appropriately, we might be able to play a role in possible action, whether the role in question be operational, reformatory or critical, depending on the situation in question or on the options available. Hence, this work makes the appeal that development should be embraced by fundamental anthropology as an object that deserves scientific attention, methodological vigilance, and conceptual innovation.[9]

This perspective implies a break from or discrepancy with certain works dealing with the relationship between anthropology and development (especially the 'deconstructionist business'; see below), and with a certain type of populist ideology encountered in the works of anthropologists and of development specialists alike (see below and Chapter 7). But I have also encountered many convergent viewpoints, not only during the writing of this book, but also in the years following its publication in French. Independently of my own work, various authors, mostly from English-speaking countries, have developed research positions similar to mine in many regards, despite some differences of opinion. Other authors, mainly writing in French, have gone further afield or have opened up new perspectives. Consequently, I believe it will be useful to review the works in English and French that have appeared since the publication of the French version of the present work.[10]

Three main sets of writings can be distinguished: discursive approaches, populist approaches and entangled social logic approaches to development.

The discourse of development

The fact that the social sciences observe a certain reserve regarding the vocabulary, ideologies and conceptions that are the order of the day within the developmentalist configuration is normal: on one hand there are deciders, politicians, technicians, idealists, managers, militants and prophets, who have their own particular type of rhetoric, while on the other there are professional researchers who conceptualize on a routine basis and make rational use of language. Hence all anthropologists inevitably arrive at a point when they turn a critical eye to the 'development discourse', or at least to its most prominent forms (often symbolized by the neo-liberal orientation of International

Monetary Fund economists). This criticism can also take a more systematic or diversified form (see my own, in Chapter 5). Even anthropologists, such as Horowitz or Cernea, for example, who have collaborated on a continual, long-term basis with development institutions have no qualms about attacking developers' unjustified dogmas.[11]

Two elements no doubt explain this situation.

First, in the development universe, there is a wide gap between discourses and practices: what is said about a development project when it is a matter of conception, establishment, formatting, shaping, financing, or justifying the project has little in common with the project itself as it exists in practice, once it gets into the hands of the people to whom it is destined. Thus anthropologists play a permanent role which consists in 'calling people back to reality': 'you announced that, but this is what is happening, which is quite another matter …'. They diagnose and describe sidetracking (see Chapters 9 and 13), which gives the lie to official declarations.

Second, the development universe is one of 'political' action, in the broad sense, that is, in the sense of an intention of transforming reality by voluntarist means. This is therefore a universe which, just like the political universe in the strict sense of the word, resorts to the use of clichés (see Chapter 11). Furthermore, development institutions are input-oriented: they must convince donors of their capacity to furnish resources. To obtain this effect, rhetoric is of vital importance. But this required stereotyped language mobilizes an enormous amount of set expressions. It would appear that the transformation of reality calls for thinking based on simple notions. This is one thing to which the anthropologist has a professional allergy (which, to my mind, is perfectly normal). The anthropologist's competence has to do, precisely, with a subtle knowledge of complex situations. This is why he so readily pinpoints the clichés and stereotypes of development professionals as signs of their ignorance of what is going on.

But anthropologists' criticism of development rhetoric has several limitations. One is that development professionals are not equally naive (though it is true that they have neither the possibility nor the competence to carry out serious enquiries on their own).[12] For example, there is a great difference between the public discourses of development officials and deciders in Northern countries and the private conversations of experts and operators in the field, who are aware of the complexity of real-life situations. Another is that the social sciences themselves are not immune to clichés (they have their own, while making vigorous criticisms of other people's) or to stereotypes, especially scholarly stereotypes (hence, in Chapter 5, my analysis of various common stereotypes includes those of the social sciences as well as those of development professionals). The last is that there is a particular social science ideology, commonly referred to as 'post-modernism', 'post-structuralism' or 'deconstructionism', which, having taken on the theme of development, itself has specialized in the analysis of the 'development discourse' and has even proclaimed itself as the only form of 'anthropology of development'.[13]

In recent years a series of works has appeared (Escobar, 1984, 1991, 1997; Ferguson, 1990; Roe, 1991, 1995; Sachs, 1992; Hobart, 1993a; Crush, 1995; Moore and Schmitz, 1995; Gardner and Lewis, 1996; Rahnema and Bawtree, 1997; Marcussen and Arnfred, 1998; Mills, 1999; Fairhead, 2000) which attack the 'development discourse' in one way or another, with the aim of 'deconstructing' it. They tend to produce a caricature or *reductio ad absurdum* of the developmentalist configuration, which they present as a 'narrative' of Western hegemony bent on denying or destroying popular practices and knowledge. Grillo (1997: 20) rightly pinpointed that 'there is a tendency, illustrated for example, by Hobart, Escobar and to a lesser degree Ferguson, to see development as a monolithic enterprise, heavily controlled from the top, convinced of the superiority of its own wisdom and impervious to local knowledge, or indeed commonsense experience, a single gaze or voice which is all powerful and beyond influence'. This diabolical image of the development world pays little attention to incoherences, uncertainty and contradictions, which are nonetheless structurally inscribed in development institutions. Moreover, these works do not take continuous shifts in strategy and policy into account (thus the 1990s saw a generalization of so-called 'participatory' or 'grassroots' approaches, and not only in alternative non-governmental organizations). In other words, these works seem to adopt an ideological approach to development, perceived *a priori* as an entity in itself, and, to be precise, as a negative entity at that. Their approach is not based on unbiased empirical enquiry into the real processes of various types of development action.

Approaching development through 'discourse' leaves the door open to this type of risk-free generalization. Moreover, authors tend to choose only those aspects of the 'discourse' that support their theses. Conflation is a common practice, which is moreover facilitated by the fact that terms like 'discourse' and 'narrative' are vague and have hardly benefited from any empirical mapping. In fact, it suffices to select one public rhetoric or another, one type of cliché or another, and to proceed to its deconstruction. Escobar's book is an obvious example of this type of procedure. The reader will not be surprised to find the recurrent use of terms such as 'discursive regimes', 'regimes of discourse', 'discursive formations', 'language of development', 'discursive analysis', 'regimes of representation', 'discursive field', 'development discourse'... Escobar's endless references to Said and Foucault (and occasionally to Derrida) are, moreover, the touchstones of the deconstructionist enterprise, as far as development (see Escobar, 1984, 1997) and other topics are concerned.[14]

The political correctness that this work exudes is unsurprising too: for example, Escobar's placing of positive value on Sachs's *Development Dictionary*

(1992), because it is 'a dictionary of toxic words in the development discourse' (Escobar, 1995: 227). Moreover, Escobar calls for 'the needed liberation of anthropology from the space mapped by the development encounter' (ibid.: 17). By dint of 'toxic words' and damaging discursive constructions, development is made out to be a fundamentally perverse Western creation (the West having 'created' the Third World in the same way it 'created' orientalism), whose aim is to enslave the people, destroy their competences and prevent them from taking their destinies into their own hands. Fairhead (2000) considers development to be a triple process of 'decivilisation', 'depoliticisation' and 'depossession', in support of which viewpoint he quotes Hobart, Ferguson and Roe respectively. Arnfred, having maintained without reservation that 'imperialism has been renamed "development"' (1998: 77), presents the 'five characteristics of development discourse' as follows: (1) its '"they-have-the-problem-we-have-the-solution" approach'; (2) 'immunity to adverse facts'; (3) 'the development expert as the agent'; (4) 'the development agent as male'; (5) 'the exclusion of indigenous experience and knowledge' (ibid.: 81–4). These categorical statements are presented without qualification, and without paying the slightest attention to possible counter-examples.

Of course, there is power behind aid (when it is not overt), and, of course, development aid came into existence in the Cold War period, which was a favourable context for all kinds of hypocrisy. It is also true that dependence on subsidies from the North is a reality and that the high-and-mighty attitudes of Western experts combined with their ignorance of the field is an endless source of exasperation for Africa's civil servants. But it is also true that the latter are experts in the use of double speak, while manoeuvres, intrigues, power struggles, appropriations, rhetoric and manipulations are initiated from all sides. Actors of the South, like those of the North, are on the hunt for power and advantages; moreover, all the actors concerned have elbow room at their disposal and are therefore never reduced to the state of simple agents or of mere victims of a totalitarian system. For example, 'dissuasion' of the strong by the weak is apparent in the development universe, both at the governmental and at the peasant levels …

Nevertheless, it would be unfair to put all the analyses of the 'development discourse' in the same bag. Numerous nuances exist within the 'discourse of development' business, and some of these are important. If Escobar is beyond doubt the most radical and the most ideological of all, Ferguson represents a subtler version, and one that has better empirical documentation, if only because of his solid case study of a Canadian project supported by the World Bank in Lesotho (Ferguson, 1990). In fact, there are two parts to Ferguson's work: on one hand, he carried out a *bona fide* field enquiry, which is exemplary in many ways, on a particular development operation, an enquiry in which he showed interest, over and beyond 'discourses', in the 'sidetracking' to which the project was subjected and in local power relations (an approach closed to the entangled social logic approach; see below). But, on the other hand, he readily resorts to deconstructionist jargon and also makes 'anti-development' elisions.[15]

Other works have also succumbed, as far as rhetoric is concerned, to post-modern ideology, while developing other analyses that are not directly in keeping with this trend, or that stand aloof at one point or another. We could mention, for example, the precautions of Gardner and Lewis in their general overview of anthropology of development,[16] which on one hand acclaims what they consider to be the accomplishments of post-modern, critical deconstructionism, and associates themselves with these, but which also points to certain limitations of this approach: 'Development agencies ... plans, workers and policies are all objective entities. We cannot simply will them into non-existence by insisting that they are constructs, however questionable the premises on which they are constructed may be' (Gardner and Lewis, 1996: 2). And in a similar vein: 'development discourse is more fluid and liable to change than many analyses allow' (ibid.: 75). The intention of Gardner and Lewis is to reform development from the inside, by promoting an 'alternative' development and by 'breaking down the barriers which exist between the "developer" and the "developed"' (ibid.: ix). In fact, they associate the deconstructionist approach with what we could call the 'populist' approach (see below).

Mills provides another example of the ambivalence to be found in some deconstructionist works: on one hand, he deplores the narrow interpretation of Foucault's works by various more or less post-modern authors as well as the simplistic character of radical 'anti-development' positions (Mills, 1999: 98, 111), but, on the other, he makes an attempt at rehabilitating the deconstructionist heritage, if only partially, through three 'intellectual models of interpretation of development': development as 'discourse', development as 'commodity'; and development as a 'performance'. Hence, he remains trapped by the object he criticizes: 'part of the problem comes from the development word itself, and the images and relations it invokes. We are inevitably trapped by the weight of the word' (ibid.: 99).[17]

As for Cooper and Packard, their collective work comprises texts that oscillate between certain deconstructionist and/or radical-criticism analyses of development orientations and other types of analysis which show a higher degree of subtlety and better documentation. But their introduction reflects an evident reservation concerning the post-modern perspective on development: 'this group sees development as nothing more than an apparatus of control and surveillance' (Cooper and Packard, 1997: 3); 'it is thus too simple to assert the emergence of a singular development discourse, a simple knowledge–power regime' (ibid.: 10).

Finally, certain analyses of the 'development discourse' can be qualified neither as post-modern nor as post-structural, and reject these elisions and caricatures (see Gasper, in Apthorpe and Gasper, 1996). They could be classified as 'methodological deconstructionism', as opposed to the 'ideological deconstructionism' in Escobar's work and in the works of those who take him as a reference (on the 'methodological/ideological' opposition, see below apropos populism and also Chapters 4 and 7). These authors, following Apthorpe's lead (1986; see also Apthorpe and Gasper, 1996), are receptive to the variety of discourse internal to the development universe (see also Grillo and Stirrat, 1997).[18]

Other works are content to pinpoint, in one area or another, the clichés and stereotypes with which developmentalist arguments are interspersed (on the environment, see Leach and Mearns, 1996). Some of these do not avoid a certain hint of populism.

Populism, anthropology and development

In the introduction to a book published under his editorship,[19] Hobart (1993a) closely associates deconstructionism and populism: 'The relationship of the developers and "those-to-be-developed" is constituted by developers' knowledge and categories…. The epistemological and power aspects of such processes are often obscured by discourses on development being couched predominantly in the idioms of economics, technology and management…. Knowledges of the peoples being developed are ignored or treated as mere obstacles to rational progress' (ibid.: 2). Hobart acknowledges in the same breath Foucault and Bourdieu, post-structuralism and post-modernism (ibid.: 17), and takes development to task, while expressing the intention to rehabilitate local knowledge. He describes a radical opposition between 'western knowledge' and 'local knowledge' (though a few less general and more balanced comparisons of these two types of 'knowledge', in the field of agronomy to be precise, can be found in Chapter 10), but various chapters in his book (by Richards, by van Beek and by Cohen) provide a subtler analysis of specific aspects of local knowledge.

Hence, we can note that a populist posture, defending 'indigenous knowledges' or encouraging a close study of these, is liable to run the gamut of a wide variety of scientific attitudes, which can be more or less 'ideological' (like post-modern deconstructionism) or 'methodological' (exemplified by documented descriptions of a specific local knowledge).

Chapter 7 of my book deals in a systematic manner with populism in the social sciences and in development, and takes particular pains to distinguish between 'ideological populism', which should be abandoned (Chambers's

1983 book is a classic example of this), and 'methodological populism', which is essential to anthropological enquiry. Ideological populism paints reality in the colours of its dreams, and has an romantic vision of popular knowledge.[20] As for methodological populism, it considers that 'grassroots' groups and social actors have knowledge and strategies that should be explored, without commenting on their value or validity.[21] The first is a bias which disables scientific procedure, while the second, on the contrary, is a positive factor which opens new fields of investigation. The problem, of course, is that both are often thrown together in the works of a given author, or in a given book. Nevertheless I remain convinced that, despite the difficulties involved, distinction between the two is necessary, as can be illustrated by a number of recent works constructed around local knowledge or the agency of 'grassroots' actors, along the same lines as Hobart's. On reading them, we observe that one can simultaneously succumb to ideological populism, through a systematic idealization of the competences of the people, in terms either of autonomy or of resistance, while obtaining innovative results thanks to methodological populism, which sets itself the task of describing the agency and the pragmatic and cognitive resources that all actors have, regardless of the degree of domination or deprivation in which they live.

A few years ago, Chambers co-authored a new book (Chambers, Pacey and Thrupp, 1989) based in large part on his earlier positions (Chambers, 1983). The latter, while stressing the agency of 'grassroots' actors and their innovative abilities (a point of view that could be categorized at first sight as methodological populism) is essentially dominated by the valorization and systematic inflation of this agency and of these capacities (which is tantamount, in other words, to ideological populism). Ideological populism authorizes participatory methods of quick research ('participatory rural appraisal', PRA), which supposedly draw their inspiration from anthropology, based on various techniques of 'animation' developed by Chambers and his disciples. Their aim – which I consider to be illusory and naive, if not downright demagogic – is to promote research on peasants to be carried out by the peasants themselves, in which researchers would play the role of mere facilitators.[22] Ideological populism maintains itself on the opposition that, it declares, exists between classic 'extractive' research and alternative 'participatory' research. Yet this opposition does not make sense in the context of the rigorous anthropology of development advocated here, and ignores the fact that anthropology invariably combines fieldwork focused on actors' points of view and actors' strategies (a process that is by definition 'participatory') with an 'as-objective-as-possible' analysis of their contradictions and contexts (a process that is by definition 'extractive').[23]

Three more recent works present a relatively complex combination of ideological populism and methodological populism, namely the works of Scoones and Thompson (1994), Scott (1998) and Darré (1997).

Scoones and Thompson in their introduction reconsider the work of Chambers, Pacey and Thrupp, expressing a strange mixture of praise and reservations. While associating themselves with Chambers's research (the latter is the author of the foreword to the book), they have no qualms about marking their distance in referring to the 'populist perspective' contained in the 'farmers first' proposition, and in insisting on the need to go beyond this perspective, both by replacing the simplistic binary 'local actors versus outside interveners' with an analysis of the diversity that characterizes the actors in confrontation, and by arguing against a systematic opposition between peasant experimentation and scientific enquiry, for instance. The phase of devalorization of peasant popular knowledge (linked to theories of modernization; see for example, Chapter 3), was supplanted by a phase of 'populist' revalorization. Scoones and Thompson rightly remark that we have now entered a third phase of the relationship between research and development, characterized by interest in complex, nonuniform interactions, in conflicts and bargaining, in processes of transaction (which takes us back to the third approach to development presented below, the entangled social logic).

As for Scott, to whom we owe the earlier and productive conceptualization of 'everyday peasant resistances' (Scott, 1985), and who subsequently (Scott, 1990) developed an increasingly 'resistance-centred' point of view, which could be interpreted as a particular form of populism (the systematic praise of anything that bears the slightest resemblance to 'resistance' by the people; see Olivier de Sardan, 2001a),[24] he has recently reverted to the praise of practical knowledge, the Greek *metis* (see Détienne and Vernant's classic work, 1974), to be precise.[25] This *metis*, which is always embedded in a local context, is supposed to be the basic underlying structure on which popular practices around the world repose. The constant failure of global centralized schemes of planned social transformation (whether urbanist, revolutionary or developmentalist) results from the fact they do not take this phenomenon into account. This explains Scott's plea: 'throughout the book, I make the case for the indispensable role of practical knowledge, informal processes, and improvisation, the face of unpredictability' (Scott, 1998: 6). Though Scott errs at times in making the type of oversimplification that typically arises from the fusion of deconstructionism and populist ideology ('a certain understanding of science, modernity and development has so successfully structured the dominant discourse that all other kinds of knowledge are regarded as backward, static traditions, as old wives' tales and superstitions'; ibid.: 331), his work also contains methodological populism. Thus, he invites scientists to describe and analyse the multiple processes of 'sidetracking' and the myriad 'gaps' that separate projects as produced by planners from local reality.[26]

Finally, there is Darré (1997) who proposes (based on case studies carried out in France) that we move beyond the simple recognition of the fact that peasants have the capacity to use strategies (*metis*) or that they possess a stock of their own peculiar knowledge. This recognition is, to his mind, insufficient as it admits the fact that norms of excellence and competence are produced by the outside world and imposed on peasants. On the contrary, his intention is to demonstrate that cultivators and animal rearers are constantly in the process of producing local norms, which allows for the evaluation of innovations that extension services provide: hence 'les éleveurs n'appliquent pas les techniques nouvelles, à proprement parler ils les construisent' ('cattle rearers do not apply new techniques, in fact, they construct them') (Darré, 1997: 57), since they produce, based on the local network of discussion, the norms that enable them to reject, modify or adopt the technical improvements.

In fact, empirical field analyses carried out by anthropologists provide the best illustrations of methodological populism in action, as well as a minimization of the biases due to ideological populism. Richards, for example (1993), also breaks away from the conception of popular agronomic knowledge as 'stocks of knowledge' and demonstrates that it is essentially a matter of contingent and approximate adaptations, based on 'performance skills'.

Hence, populism in anthropology of development assumes various hues:

- it is more 'methodological' and empirical in authors like Richards who stick to concrete forms of indigenous and technical knowledge

- it is more 'ideological' and is sometimes mixed with deconstructionism in authors who, like Hobart, systematically valorize indigenous knowledge over and against scientific knowledge

- it appears as a complex combination of methodological populism and ideological populism in original theoreticians like Darré or Scott

- finally, it is not only ideological but also quite rudimentary and 'applied' in the case of 'participatory rural appraisals' promoted by Chambers, which, in keeping with the general expansion of 'participatory' development projects, assume an ever-increasing importance on the market of 'rapid appraisals'.

The entangled social logic approach

Instead of focusing exclusively on popular knowledge, as in the populist approach, or on denouncing the developmentalist configuration and its discourse, as in the deconstructionist approach, the entangled social logic approach, centred on the analysis of the embeddedness of social logic, studies the relationship between both universes, or rather between the concrete segments of both, through empirical enquiry, particularly around their points of intersection.[27]

We could also refer to this as 'methodological interactionism' (as opposed to 'ideological interactionism'), in the same way that we make reference to methodological deconstructionism (as opposed to ideological deconstructionism) and to methodological populism (as opposed to ideological populism). Interactionism (see the Chicago School of sociology or Blumer's symbolic interactionism or Goffman) has a long scientific history behind it; we may use the term 'methodological interactionism' to designate the analyses that take social interaction as a privileged empirical 'pathway' while refraining from taking it as an object in itself, that is, without reducing it to the dimensions of a prison. Interactionism has sometimes been considered as a formal set of rules governing interactions, or as being restricted to situations of interaction. These pitfalls are well illustrated in research based on an ethno-methodological orientation. The works we group together under the 'entangled social logics approach' label share a common aversion to the fixation on interaction *per se*; instead they use interaction as a useful analyser of phenomena of broader import, examined on a variety of scales.[28] Interactions are therefore treated in the same way as the classic 'case study': as productive pathways into social reality, as means of deciphering concrete social situations, both in terms of actors' strategies and contextual constraints, and as means of approaching practices and conceptions, of pinpointing conjunctural and structural phenomena.

In the field of anthropology proper, the interesting thing about this approach is that is breaks away from the culturalist ideology that formerly predominated in this field, and underlines the transactions linked with consensus production and norms (resulting from negotiations, if only informal and latent). It is all the more relevant to anthropology of development to the extent that the social facts of development have the specific tendency to produce a great number of interactions, and, what is more, interactions between actors who have various statuses, heterogeneous resources, and dissimilar goals. Hence the use of the 'arena' metaphor (Bierschenk, 1988; Crehan and von Oppen, 1988; Bierschenk and Olivier de Sardan, 1997a; Dartigues, 1997; and below, Chapter 12). As far as the entangled social logic approach in anthropology of development is concerned, two independent sources can be identified: an Anglophone pole around Norman Young in the Netherlands;[29] and a Francophone pole, around APAD.[30]

Norman Long and rural anthropology of development
Long occupies an original position which justifies a few background details. A pioneer in his field, he is in the tradition of the Manchester School, and has developed over the last twenty years a 'school' of anthropology of development

based at the Agricultural University of Wageningen, where he recruits his disciples and collaborators (see, in particular, the collective works that set forth and illustrate this perspective: Long, 1989, Long and Long, 1992, Arce and Long, 2000). His orientation is essentially centred on the interfaces between different social worlds, and is defined by himself as 'actor-oriented', a term that has served as a label for his school of thought.[31] Thus Long and his collaborators define their work in terms of an 'actor-oriented paradigm' (Long, 1992b; Long and van der Ploeg, 1989), or in terms of an 'actor-oriented perspective' (Arce and Long 2000), which is supposed to revitalize the conventional approaches to development: their paradigm has been 'enthusiastically taken up in applied fields such as agricultural extension and communication studies, participatory rural appraisal (PRA) and stake-holder analyses' (Arce and Long, 2000: after page 27). The 'guiding concepts of the actor-oriented approach' are 'agency and social actors, the notion of multiple realities and arenas where different life-worlds and discourses meet, the idea of interface encounters in terms of discontinuities of interests, values, knowledge and power, and structured heterogeneity' (Long and van der Ploeg, 1989: 82; see one presentation of these concepts, among many others, in Long, 2000).

Many worthwhile monographic studies originating from Wageningen set forth these concepts in a variety of empirical contexts (see, among others, Arce, 1993; Mongbo, 1995; Breusers, 1999). As far as theory is concerned, there is hardly anything to object to in Long's orientation: it has to do with a dynamic, nonculturalist approach to anthropology, which is field-enquiry-oriented, makes judicious use of case studies, and takes an understandable interest in conflicts, negotiations, discords and misunderstandings. In this respect, Long's perspective is complementary to the one presented in this work.

However, I have reservations about the narrow and repetitive character of Long's system. His primary concepts (enumerated above) have been established since the mid-1980s, and have been cited, commented on and paraphrased, by Long himself and by his disciples, in articles and books for over fifteen years with hardly any modification. This very abstract system of interpretation (see its 'guiding concepts' mentioned above) has gradually evolved into an almost hermetically closed loop, while its empirical studies sometimes give the impression of being tailored to illustrate or to justify its 'guiding concepts' instead of producing innovative local or regional interpretations or of opening new perspectives. The restriction to rural development certainly does not facilitate intellectual renewal: the types of interaction liable to occur between the world's development agents and its peasants are relatively limited in number, and hardly encourage scientists to produce grounded interpretative innovation once they have settled into the comfort of Long's conceptual system. Notwithstanding, this system remains a touchstone in anthropology of development.

The works produced by APAD

The approach adopted in the present work, which is part of this entangled social logic approach developed in the 1980s, comes out of a French theoretical tradition that was linked for a long time to Marxist structuralism and Marxist populism (I acknowledge my own involvement), but also to Balandier, who made the works of the Manchester School known in France. The approach is related in various ways to the constitution of APAD. However, this book is not a direct presentation of research results, and is situated somewhere between state-of-the-art theoretical proposals and research programme. The articles by Elwert and Bierschenk (1988) and Chauveau (1994, 2000a) are situated in a similar register.

An important step forward has been made through the publication in recent years of a variety of works on French-speaking Africa, by African and European authors who all have the merit of *practising* the entangled social logic approach, and who therefore present empirical results on a variety of topics, all related in one way or another to the interactions that occur between a wide variety of actors involved in the terrain where development institutions are active. The interesting thing about this output is that it does not propose a singular or closed theoretical system. However, the authors concerned share a similar methodological position which allows them to produce new interpretations 'close to the field'. They show a common distrust of ideologies (be they scientific or developmentalist) and have a common aim: to apprehend development facts in all their remarkable complexity. This empirical quest after complex issues is perhaps the primary characteristic of the type of methodological interactionism practised by APAD, and stands in stark opposition to most 'discourse of development studies' and populist approaches.

Thus the field of African anthropology can now make use of fresh, innovative analyses on a series of important themes, including: peasant associations (internal cleavages, supervisors' strategies, bargaining with development institutions);[32] public health (systemic dysfunctioning of modern health structures);[33] relationships between local power and development (including the interventions of the modern state and decentralization);[34] land problems (the increasing number of stakes and strategies they mobilize);[35] and local development brokers (forms of 'capture' and redistribution of the 'development rent').[36]

Not only do these works constitute a corpus of concrete analyses on the embeddedness of various social logics, but they also address new objects, and issue, in part, from development alone (and from rural development alone). Their aim is to break new ground in fields where political and development operations straddle the political, economic and local administrative practices commonly encountered in Africa. In fact, it has become increasingly difficult to isolate interactions related to the developmentalist configuration alone from those related to the 'state apparatus' or to the 'civil society'.[37] From this point of view, anthropology of development has increasingly became a sociology and an anthropology of contemporary Africa, which of course integrates the social facts of development but goes significantly beyond them, in the direction of embracing the multiple forms assumed by the changes that are occurring across the board. Conversely, there is no field that remains unaffected, to one degree or another, by development interventions.

Another characteristic of these works is that they are often carried out in a systematically comparative perspective,[38] thus avoiding the risk of an endless accumulation of local monographs that interactionist studies incur (see Bowen, 1988; Booth, 1994). Even when the studies are carried out at the level of a single village, region or town, and this is sometimes necessary, the extra-local resources of local actors, or the intervention of actors from the outside into the local arena are treated with great attention, resulting in the production of a broad-scale analysis of transversal logics of action.

Using this perspective, many collective research sites have been opened, where work is still under way: corruption (see *Nouveaux Cahiers de l'IUED*, no. 9); decentralization (see *Bulletin de l'APAD*, numbers 14 and 16); health professions (*Bulletin de l'APAD*, no. 17); brokerage and intermediation (*Bulletin de l'APAD*, numbers 11 and 12). Administrative and professional subcultures and the local state are future topics to be addressed. This evolution does not imply the abandonment of development as an object, but rather its integration as one component, among others, of African modernity, studied with as great an empirical rigour as possible. This broadening and increasing variety of themes of enquiry, combined by flexible interpretations (see the 'grounded theory' of Glaser and Strauss, 1973) are perhaps the marks that distinguish these works from those situated in relatively close proximity to Long's school of thought.

Conclusion: the future of the entangled social logic approach and its work in progress (research in Africa and beyond)

Today's anthropology of development is, therefore, of great diversity and some-times entails antagonistic epistemological and scientific positions. 'Post-modern' and radical authors who denounce the very system of development on the grounds either of its discourse or its negation of indigenous knowledge seem to have little in common with the practitioners of 'applied' anthropology who willingly accept technocratic expertise, or populist 'participatory research appraisals'. Nonetheless, one sometimes observes surprising alliances or combinations of these two extremes.

However, the increase in the number of empirical studies, the diversification of development practices, the demise of the grand functionalist or structuralist systems of explanation have, beyond a doubt, opened the pathway into new spheres of research and interpretation.[39] The studies we refer to above, based on the entangled social logic approach, have all benefited from this, but they are not the sole beneficiaries, as many other types of studies originating in other disciplines illustrate (economic history comes to mind, with S. Berry, 1993, or political economy, with Bates, 1987, 1988b). Complementary relationships are in process between these disciplines and the entangled social logic approach in anthropology. In fact, the latter, which, for methodological reasons, places the emphasis on the 'micro-political level', has everything to gain from a collaboration with complementary scientific enterprises that adopt more panoptic and 'macro' perspectives (neo-institutionalism in economics, for example: see Colin, 1990).

I can agree with Bennett (1988), that anthropology of development has long since broken free from a traditionalist vision of society (having incorporated the analysis of 'peasant strategies', see Chauveau, 2000a), seen as a 'romantic egalitarianism'. Anthropology of development can be characterized, in contrast to traditional approaches, both by 'a recognition of adaptation as the key behavioural process in social change' (where adaptation supplants 'culture'), and by its taking into account of the 'coping-manipulative aspects of behaviour' (Bennett, 1988: 19–21), from either an offensive or a defensive point of view.[40] This evolution allows for a broader collaboration with neighbouring disciplines than was afforded by classical culturalism.

Let us take Africa as an example. This is a continent where the 'development rent' is most conspicuous and where its effects (intentional or not) are at their highest. This is also the place in which public administration and management encounter the greatest obstacles, and where informal practices, in politics as well as in economics, are prevalent and escape official controls.

The works mentioned above, most of them by French-speaking authors, shed new light on these phenomena by following a number of conceptual approaches grounded in empirical analysis. They lend a new degree of intelligibility to the situation that prevails on the continent as a whole, and to some of its particularities. The 'multiplicity' of norms is more remarkable here than elsewhere,[41] while intermediaries, brokers and suchlike, in development and in other areas, play a central role.[42] Successive forms of power are piled one upon the other without displacement or substitution taking place.[43] The norms and stakes of inhabitants of rural and urban areas are closely interconnected.[44] Rhetoric and neo-traditionalist 'performances' are important political resources.[45] Peasant strategies are particularly diversified and flexible.[46] The 'moral economy of corruption'[47] is a widespread and omnipresent phenomenon, the construction of a 'public space' comes up against numerous obstacles, and the borderlines between the 'private', the collective and the 'public' are permeable and uncertain.[48]

The social facts of development are thus taken into account and integrated into concrete analyses which also deal with the local forms of governance, strategies for capturing surpluses, power relations, close and distant social networks, so-called state apparatuses and the local state, professional norms and practices. These analyses cut across to the usual lines of division: economic resources are transformed into social resources and vice versa, the health sector contains processes similar to those encountered in rural development or in justice, there is an incessant back-and-forth movement between country and town, from the administrator to the administrated, while the dividing line between external aid and 'endogenous'[49] resources is erased.

Another opposition that becomes meaningless is the one between localized monographs and comparative multi-site analyses.[50] Without making detailed reference to the abundant and recent literature devoted to the question of 'locality', which is usually very abstract and integrated into broader (and characteristically vague and hold-all) problematics around 'globalization' and 'identities',[51] it is worth remarking that an increasing number of works, especially those marked by the entangled social logic approach, tend to combine localized research and general analyses, case studies and reasoned and regional comparativism.

Finally, there is another opposition, namely that separating the 'actor-centred approach' from the 'structure-centred approach', which falls into irrelevance on the practical rather than on the rhetorical level.[52] This is not the most insignificant result of the current renovation of anthropology of development, that is due in part to the entangled social logics approach. The chapters that follow represent the initial stage of a process that is still undergoing in-depth exploration. My hope is that this process will be rendered all the more fruitful by the mutual enrichment of works in French and in English.

Notes

1 This chapter, written in 2001, does not appear in the French original version. My thanks to T. Bierschenk, G. Blundo, J.-P. Chauveau, P. Geschiere, J. Gould, J.P. Jacob, Y. Jaffré, P. Lavigne Delville, C. Lund, P.Y. Le Meur, E. Paquot, and M. Tidjani Alou for their remarks and suggestions on different chapters of this book. I would like to acknowledge in particular the close collaboration that I had for years on these topics with Thomas Bierschenk and Giorgio Blundo, and on the fact that my analyses in this book have been helped and supported by theirs.

2 This is why French-speakers need to publish in English, and why a book like Colin and Crawford's (2000), which provides in English a sample of the work done in French on the African peasantry, is interesting.

3 There are rare exceptions, such as Jacob, 1989, 2000, Jacob and Blundo, 1997.

4 For an explanation of this neo-Weberian epistemology, see Passeron, 1991. Deconstructionist development anthropologists, in a Manichaean view of the social

sciences, systematically associate their own analyses with an alternative epistemology, and other people's analyses with a positivist epistemology (see Escobar, 1997, who considers anthropologists who do not make a radical critique of development, in other words who are 'associated with development', as following a 'realistic epistemology'. To the contrary, I believe that the (necessary and established) out-moding of yesterday's positivism does not mean that there is no means of escaping post-modern ideologies. Though its days of glory are over, post-modernism still exerts a strong influence on the literature of anthropology of development.

5 This term seems more neutral and more descriptive than the term 'field' (*champs*), which is preferred by authors like Lavigne Delville (2000), in reference to Bourdieu, and which implies an abstract and large system of power struggles and statutory positions. The term 'arena', on the contrary, evokes concrete interactions (see Chapter 12).

6 My use of this expression is meant to underline the convergence between anthro-pology and a certain type of sociology inherited from the Chicago School, often described as 'qualitative' (see Chapter 2).

7 In fact, this work concerns 'Africa and beyond', to borrow a phrase from the subtitle of the book edited by Fardon, van Binsbergen and van Dijk (1999): in Africa, the overriding importance and daily presence of development aid attain their peak, but the phenomena observed there also exist on other continents, albeit in different forms.

8 In his recent work (1998) on the process of monitoring, Mosse develops the same idea expressed Chapter 13: that follow-up-evaluation and feedback procedures are perhaps the best practical contributions anthropology can make to development action.

9 Considering that anthropology of development is capable of renewing classic anthro-pology (see Chapter 4, and Bennett and Bowen, 1988: ix) I agree with Bates (1988a: 82-83) who holds that anthropology of development makes four major contributions to academic anthropology: (a) it studies institutions and actors in real-life settings; (b) it does away with the vision of 'self-contained, autonomous, bonded communities'; (c) it opens the way for new themes of enquiry, including civil servants, elites, and administrators; (d) it provides linkages with other disciplines.

10 The chapters that comprise it were written between 1985 and 1993.

11 Michael Horowitz is the co-founder of the Institute of Anthropology of Develop-ment in Binghampton. One of his articles is significantly entitled 'On not offending the borrower: (self)-ghettoization of anthropology at the World Bank' (Horowitz, 1996). Michael Cernea is the best-known World Bank anthropologist. In the preface to a book published by the World Bank he writes, '[This] volume takes a firm stand against the technocratic and economistic biases in development work. It criticizes explicitly or implicitly the neglect of social or cultural dimensions, the rigidity of blue-print thinking in project design, the focus on commodities rather than on the social actor, the disregard for farmers' knowledge and the indifference towards people's grassroots institutions and organizations' (Cernea, 1991a: xii). Cernea, for his part, defends the idea that the World Bank can evolve, in particular thanks to the role played by anthropologists in World Bank activities (see Cernea, 1996).

12 Many administrators in charge of development will not identify with the very caricatured 'common assumption' that Marcussen and Arnfred (1998 :1) attribute to

them: 'planned intervention is expected to operate in a homogenous, conflict-free and perfectly predictable environment, rather than as establishing arenas of competition, conflict and struggle'. Besides, many development institutions now commission studies from anthropologists, some of them working on the basis of an 'entangled social logic approach' (see below), precisely because they consider development projects as 'establishing arenas of competition, conflict and struggle'.

13　Hence, in a recent paper, Escobar (1997) takes 'anthropology of development' to mean only post-structuralism (illustrated, according to him, by Crush, Ferguson or himself) to which he assigns the goal of 'déstabiliser les fondements mêmes sur lequel le développement s'est constitué, pour modifier l'ordre social qui régit le processus de production du langage' (destabilizing the very grounds on which development has constructed itself, with a view to modifying the social order which regulates the process of language production) (Escobar, 1977: 546). This very peculiar 'anthropology of development' has supposedly become a sub-discipline in its own right (other positions have been relegated to the status of applied anthropology, illustrated, he claims, by Cernea or Horowitz).

14　To recognize the pioneer and often stimulating role played by Foucault and, after him, by Said does not mean that we have to take their works as gospel truth or that our attitude to them should be one of praise alone, to the exclusion of any kind of critical analysis.

15　In the works that follow his book, Ferguson continues to fall into this type of oversimplification, which leads him to consider as obvious the existence of a 'knowledge/power regime of development' (Ferguson, 1994: 150), and to take over some of Escobar's rash judgements, devoid of any kind of empirical validation: 'as Escobar has argued, however, work in anthropology of development gradually came to be more and more adjusted to the bureaucratic demands of development agencies, at the expense of its intellectual rigor and critical self-consciousness' (ibid.: 164).

16　This overview is based on literature exclusively written in English, as is the case of other overviews originating in England and the United States (Bennett, 1998, Booth, 1994, Grillo and Stirrat, 1997).

17　The interest of this approach resides precisely in the fact that it drops the focus on the term ' development' (which Mills calls the 'D word').

18　See Jacob, 2000 : 233–36 ; Arce and Long, 2000 : 24.

19　This work is inserted in a series of books on anthropology of development which originated in the EIDOS seminars, held at regular intervals in Europe around a core of English and Dutch researchers (see also Croll and Parkin, 1992; Pottier, 1993; Fardon, van Binsbergen and van Dijk, 1999).

20　Primary health care strategies originating in Alma Ata, and the rehabilitation of 'tradi-practitioners', 'traditional birth attendants' and so on, are examples of ideological populism in practice in the field of development.

21　Thus, the knowledge that tradi-practitioners or birth attendants have might very well be ineffective or harmful from a clinical viewpoint, but they are nonetheless worthy of research documentation from an anthropological point of view.

22　See Chambers, 1991; 1994. For critical analyses of these methods, see Mosse, 1994; Bierschenk and Olivier de Sardan, 1997a; Lavigne Delville, Sellamna and Mathieu, 2000.

23　The moral or methodological lessons populists so willingly give are, from this point of view, absurd, and bear witness to a profound ignorance of the complexity of the research process : 'The extractive orientation must be reversed. The standard practice is for outsiders to come and do *their* research *on* people, after which they take away *their* data for analysis elsewhere. Ethically and methodologically, this practice is suspect' (Pottier, 1997: 205).

24 In one and the same criticism, Cooper and Packard (1997: 34) conflate Scott and Indian 'subaltern studies' (see Guha and Spivak, 1988): 'the autonomy of the "subaltern" or "the hidden transcript" of subaltern discourses is starkly separated from colonial discourse'.

25 Scott notes that the term *metis* is incorrectly translated into English as 'cunning' or 'cunning intelligence' (Scott, 1998: 313).

26 The remark that sidetracking is an inevitable aspect of development projects (a point which I underline in Chapter 9), and that it is not only the result of the 'popular reactions' emphasized by Scott, but is also due to the incoherence inherent in development institutions and in various strategies of actors and interveners, have long since been made by Hirschman, 1967 (see Jacob, 2000: 26–7; Bennett, 1988: 16–17). Other authors, situated on the inside of development institutions, have also made this point: 'contrary to the myth, it is a grievous misunderstanding to imagine that project interventions are a simple linear unfolding of a well-reasoned, time-bound sequence of pre-programmed activities with all but predefined outcomes. Beyond what is being planned and often despite it, development interventions occur as processes subjected to political pressures, social bargaining, administrative inadequacy, and circumstantial distortions. A host of necessary or unwarranted reinterpretations modify the intended outcome' (Cernea, 1991b: 6).

27 Obviously, the entangled social logic approach also entails elements of the deconstruction of development stereotypes (see Chapter 5), or analyses along the same lines as methodological populism (see chapters 8 and 10).

28 See Revel, 1995.

29 But this is not the only example: other authors adopt a similar point of view: see Bennett and Bowen, 1988; Booth, 1994; Gould, 1997.

30 APAD is the Euro-African Association for the Anthropology of Social Change and Development (apad@ehess.cnrs-mrs.fr); see the twenty-four APAD bulletins published to date.

31 Nonetheless, this has nothing to do with methodological individualism, and Booth is right when he maintains (1994: 19) that actors' studies 'may illuminate the micro-foundations of macro-processes. As Norman Long has argued (1989: 226–31), the use of micro-studies to illuminate structures does not imply radically individualist or reductionist assumptions.'

32 See Blundo, 1992, for Senegal; Gould, 1997, for Tanzania; Laurent, 1993, for Burkina Faso; Jacob and Lavigne Delville, 1994, for West Africa.

33 See Berche, 1998, for Mali; Jaffré, 1999, for West Africa.

34 See Bierschenk and Olivier de Sardan, 1998, Bako Arifari, 1995, 1999, Bako Arifari and Le Meur, 2001, for Benin; Blundo, 1991, 1998, for Senegal; Bierschenk and Olivier de Sardan, 1997b, for Central Africa; Fay, 2000, Bouju, 2000, for Mali; Ouedraogo, 1997, Laurent, 1995, 1997, for Burkina Faso; Olivier de Sardan, 1999a, Olivier de Sardan and Dagobi, 2000, for Niger.

35 See Lund, 1998, for Niger; Bouju, 1991, Laurent and Mathieu, 1994 for Burkina Faso;

Blundo, 1996, for Senegal; Chauveau , 2000b for the Ivory Coast; Lavigne Delville, Bouju and Le Roy, 2000, for West Africa.

36 See Blundo, 1995, for Senegal; Bierschenk, Chauveau and Olivier de Sardan, 2000, for West Africa.

37 The expression 'state apparatus' is taken here in a descriptive sense without the authoritarian or disciplinary connotations in Althusser (1970). As for 'civil society' we share the reservations and criticism that are usually expressed about this term (see, for example, Lemarchand, 1992; Comaroff and Comaroff, 1999). We submit to its use only by reason of its prevalence.

38 Rigorous 'qualitative' comparativism implies a certain number of methodological innovations: see, for example, the ECRIS canvas (Bierschenk and Olivier de Sardan, 1997a, presented in Chapter 12, which served as a methodological background for many of the works quoted above); see, at another level, Long's methodological annexes, in Long, 1989.

39 The demise of functionalism is at the centre of Booth's analysis; he insists that this is an effect of Marxism and is rather pleased with the current renaissance of 'development studies', its 'rediscovery of diversity' (Chapter 8 below proposes a more complex analysis on Marxism, but I agree with some of Booth's conclusions concerning the limitations of the Marxist approach).

40 See Yung and Zaslavsky, 1992, on offensive and defensive peasant strategies in the Sahel.

41 This is S. Berry's thesis (1993), which is often cited, especially by Lund, 1998, Chauveau, Le Pape and Olivier de Sardan, 2001. On the distinction between 'official norms' and 'practical norms' (in relation to corruption, favours and professional cultures), see Olivier de Sardan, 2001b.

42 In recognition of the pioneer works by Boissevain (1974), Long (1975), Schmidt et al. (1977), Eisenstadt and Lemarchand (1981), the relationship between clientelism and brokerage as related to development in Africa has been analysed by Blundo (1995) and by Bierschenk, Chauveau and Olivier de Sardan, 1999.

43 See Bierschenk and Olivier de Sardan, 1998.

44 See Geschiere and Gugler, 1998.

45 See Bierschenk, 1992.

46 Chauveau, 2000a.

47 See Olivier de Sardan, 1999b; Blundo, 2000; Blundo and Olivier de Sardan, 2000, 2001.

48 See Bako Arifari, 1999; Koné and Chauveau, 1998; Le Meur, 1999; Olivier de Sardan, 1999a; Olivier de Sardan and Dagobi, 2000. Empirical analysis of the prevalent community approach in development leads with the aid of the above works to interrogations of the public space and of collective action (see, in addition, Mosse, 1997, and Gould, 1997, who working along independent paths have arrived at relatively similar conclusions).

49 Though I can understand why Abram proposes a 'shift from international aid toward the organisation of development by either municipal or national governments for their own citizens' (Abram, 1998: 3), I believe that these two types of 'development' are hardly distinguishable and belong to the same analytical process. However, the irrelevance of analytical binaries like endogenous/exogenous, town/country or global/local does not imply that they are of no interest to anthropology of

development: to the extent that these oppositions remain strategic categories for certain social actors, we are still obliged to analyse their modes of reproduction and manipulation, without accepting their analytical validity wholesale.

50 See the comparativist, multi-site research canvas proposed by Bierschenk and Olivier de Sardan, 1997a (and here, Chapter 12).

51 See Appadurai, 1995, 1996; Miller, 1995; Long, 1996; Gupta and Ferguson, 1997; Binsbergen, 1998; and Meyer and Geschiere, 1999.

52 This is a much deplored opposition, but one that is easier to denounce than to abandon (see Booth, 1994: 17).

2
Socio-anthropology of development
Some preliminary statements

The matters dealt with in the present work can be summarized by a few simple theses.

- The processes and social phenomena associated with what is called development, development politics, development operations, development infrastructure, development projects, as regards countries of the South, constitute a specific domain within anthropology and sociology.

- In this field, in particular, anthropology and sociology cannot be separated, much less opposed. This is especially true in the case of a certain type of anthropology and a certain type of sociology, as long as we are willing to admit that these two closely related social sciences have nothing to do with essayism, philosophy, ideology or speculation, but are, on the contrary, the result of field enquiry, that is to say, the end product of rational procedures of empirical research.

- The dialogue and co-operation between operators and development institutions, on one hand, and anthropologists on the other, is necessary and useful, even though it is difficult and interwoven with almost inevitable mis-understandings, attributable to both parties. However, there is no 'applied' anthropology of development without 'fundamental' anthropology of development. Studies, evaluations and expert reports carried out at the request of development institutions should not be relegated to the ghetto of cut-rate research, to be dashed off simply to put bread on the table for researchers. They should be coupled, in ways yet to be invented, with anthropology 'in general' and with anthropology of social change and development in particular. In order to do this, their concepts, problematics and methodological requirements must be explored.

- 'Development' is just another form of social change; it cannot be under-stood in isolation. The analysis of development actions and of popular reactions to these actions should not be isolated from the study of local dynamics, of endogenous processes, of 'informal' processes of change. Hence, anthropology of development cannot be dissociated from anthropology of social change.

- Understanding development facts in their relation to facts of social change can contribute to a renewal of the social sciences. At any rate, anthropology of social change and development cannot exist as a separate discipline, truncated from sociology and anthropology as a whole. It calls on problematics situated at the heart of these disciplines, draws on the notions and concepts they provide, and makes use of their comparativist approach.[1] Anthropology of development focuses in particular on the analysis of interactions between social actors belonging to different cultures or subcultures. It attempts to inventory the respective constraints to which all actors are submitted, and to decode the strategies actors deploy according to the room for manoeuvre available to them. It describes the conceptions and sense systems mobilized by the groups in interaction, and it studies the dynamics of transformation of these conceptions and sense systems.

- The context of domination and inequality in which development processes occur activates various types of 'populist' ideologies, rhetorics and practices in operators and researchers alike. Anthropology of development is not impervious to this, yet it must break away from 'ideological populism', to the benefit of what we may call 'methodological populism', if it is to produce reliable knowledge.

Let us rest the matter here. This brief inventory of some of the themes to be developed in the following pages requires the use of a number of terms whose meanings are somewhat ambiguous. *Development*, of course, but also *anthropology, comparativism, action, populism.* … A few preliminary definitions must therefore be provided. The definitions proposed here are neither normative nor essentialist ones, aimed at defining the essence of things (for example what development 'really' is …), but rather definitions in keeping with norms of convention and clarity. Their sole ambition is to provide the reader with stabilized meanings of these terms as used subsequently by me, within the perspective to be developed in the present work (for example the purely descriptive use of the word *development*).

Development

I propose to define development, from a fundamentally methodological perspective, as a sum of the social processes induced by voluntarist acts aimed at transforming a social milieu, instigated by institutions or actors who do not belong to the milieu in question, but who seek to mobilize the milieu, and who rely on the milieu in their attempt at grafting resources and/or techniques and/or knowledge.

In a sense, and contrary to common opinion, development is not an entity whose existence (or absence) is to be sought for in the populations concerned. Instead, development exists based merely on the fact that there are actors and institutions who take development as an object or an end to which they devote time, money and professional competence. It is the existence of this 'developmentalist configuration' that defines the very existence of development.

I will give the name 'developmentalist configuration' to this essentially cosmopolitan world of experts, bureaucrats, NGO personnel, researchers, technicians, project chiefs and field agents, who make a living, so to speak, out of developing other people, and who, to this end, mobilize and manage a considerable amount of material and symbolic resources.

Let us sidestep the eternal debates on 'development and growth', on what 'real' development is, on whether development is an objective, a mystique, a utopia, good or evil, etcetera. …Whether development 'works' or not, whether it is positive or negative, profit-seeking or philanthropic, it exists, in the purely descriptive sense I am using, owing to the fact that there exists a whole range of social practices designated by this word. In the perspective of anthropology of development, development is neither an ideal nor a catastrophe, it is above all an object of study. Clearly, this resolutely non-normative definition of development does not mean that we should refuse moral or political judgements of the various forms of development – not at all.[2] But that is another problem. Anthropology cannot presume to *intervene* positively in the moral or political debates surrounding development, except by introducing new and specific knowledge. It must therefore take the preliminary pains of studying development as a social phenomenon like any other, in the same light as kinship or religion (this position was held by Bastide a long time ago: see Bastide, 1971). What happens when 'developers' induce a development operation among 'developees',[3] what are the social processes put into motion by the numerous actors and groups of actors who are either directly or indirectly concerned? How can we pinpoint, describe or interpret the numerous unintentional effects brought about by these daily multiform actions in African villages and towns that come under the term 'development'? A wide range of analytical tools is needed in order to answer such questions: it is important to understand how development agents (extension agents or nurses) act in the field – they are not mere transmission belts and have their own strategies – but it is equally important to analyse the real mode of functioning of an NGO or of the World Bank, to study the modes of economic action of a village population, to distinguish the local forms of political competition, or the role played by kinship, or to reveal the dynamics of the transformation of popular conceptions and sense worlds. In all these cases, only field enquiry provides description, comprehension, and analysis of practices and perceptions linked to development actions and the reactions they provoke. Hence, the role of the anthropologist does not consist in making public declarations about his opinion on development. On the contrary, he needs to be a very keen observer (and must therefore master the relevant conceptual and methodological tools). In the same way, he must, as far as possible, avoid ideological preconceptions and ready-made classifications.

The field of development is not impermeable to normative viewpoints, moral prejudices (on all sides), ideological rhetoric, noisy declarations, clichés and good intentions. It is saturated with all of these. The recurrent 'failure' encountered by development interventions is a topic of endless debate. Though the explanations suggested may vary, what remains constant is an abundance of moralizers on the topic of the crisis currently facing Africa, with its catastrophic economies and crumbling state apparatuses. There is no shortage of good advice and so-called new ideas. What is really lacking is an understanding of the real mechanisms at work and an analysis of the social processes at stake.

To paraphrase – and invert – a famous statement made by Marx in his 'theses on Feuerbach': the problem, as far as development is concerned, is to understand how the world changes, instead of claiming to change the world without first finding the means of understanding it.

Nowadays normative macroeconomic-type theories still enjoy pre-eminence as far as 'developmental thought', influence on policies, and the draining-off of funds for evaluation and research are concerned.[4] However, and to say the least, these theories are not founded on any in-depth knowledge of the life worlds of 'grassroots' social actors or their means of coping with their reality. On the other hand, closer to home, populist rhetoric, participatory ideologies and humanitarian goodwill, which all more or less propose themselves as alternatives, are hardly better informed. There is no way of cutting the cost of a more specific and more intense analysis, situated in greater proximity to 'real' social interactions. This is where anthropology comes, or should come, into play. The 'point of impact' of development policies on the populations concerned, that is, on the social space in which the interactions between development operators (development projects and development actions) and 'target groups' occur, is, in this respect, a strategic level of investigation, to which intensive anthropological field enquiry is particularly adapted. In this way, we arrive at a 'point of view' that is closer to the populations concerned, to the real or potential users of development, and that takes into account their reactions to the development operations carried out on their behalf. My insistence on this 'micro' and 'actor-oriented' level,[5] at which anthropology and 'qualitative' sociology[6] are particularly at ease, does not deny the importance of more structural and 'macro' studies. The interaction between developers and developees, under 'macro' type constraints (relations of production, the world market, national policies, North–South relationships, etcetera), is a privileged research space for understanding the 'real' logics of development institutions and the 'real' logics of the producers and populations concerned. Indeed, the supposition is (but this is a founding paradigm of the social sciences) that public speeches, declared policies, administrative or juridical structures do not always coincide, far from it, with effective practice, in development and in other spheres of social life.

Socio-anthropology of development

What I mean by 'anthropology' is the empirical, multidimensional study of contemporary social groups and their interactions, placed in a diachronic perspective, and combining the analysis of practices and of conceptions. It could also be called 'qualitative sociology' or 'socio-anthropology' because, thus defined, it distinguishes itself from quantitativist sociology, based on heavy enquiries through questionnaires, and from patrimonialist ethnology, which focuses on a favoured informant (preferably well initiated). It is the direct opposite of speculative essayism in sociology and anthropology. Anthropology combines the traditions of field sociology (the Chicago School) and field anthropology (ethnography) in order to attempt an intensive *in situ* analysis of the dynamics of reproduction/transformation of diverse social sets, taking into account actors' behaviour as well as the meanings they attribute to their behaviour.

We will limit ourselves to the term 'anthropology', as I have done on previous occasions. 'Anthropology' in this instance does not designate a so-called study of 'primitive' or 'simple' societies (which would correspond to the former meaning of 'ethnology'), but evokes, on the contrary, an approach that combines fieldwork and comparative studies, an intensive and society-wide approach to social reality, which is observable in part in a certain type of sociology.[7] This epistemological convergence obviously includes history (and the other social sciences, political science, and economics: see Passeron, 1991). However, historical research themes, properly speaking, as opposed to those of anthropology, call upon 'dead' material, as it were, which justifies my abandoning history – as a discipline – on the touch line. However, the historical perspective, the recourse to 'oral tradition', and historical contextualization constitute essential ingredients of any kind of anthropology worthy of the name. Development, as defined above, is a privileged field for anthropology. In fact, it requires the involvement of numerous social actors, belonging both to 'target groups' and to development institutions. Their professional status, their norms of action and competence vary considerably.

Development 'in the field' is the end product of these multiple interactions, which no economic model in a laboratory can predict, but whose modalities anthropology can describe and attempt to interpret.

This implies a level of competence that cannot be improvised. The confrontation of varied social logics surrounding development projects constitutes a complex social phenomenon which economists, agronomists and decision makers tend to ignore. In face of the recurrent gap between expected behaviour and real behaviour, in face of the deviations to which all development operations are subject, in consequence of the reactions of target groups, developers tend to resort to pseudo-sociological notions that bear a closer resemblance to clichés and stereotypes than to analytical tools. Consequently, the 'culture' or 'values' of the local populations are called upon to 'explain' their constant propensity not to do what one wants them to do, or to do it their way. This amounts to explaining the unexplained by the inexplicable. These particularly foggy notions, borrowed from a back-door anthropology, are characteristic of the do-it-yourself sociology of certain economists and agronomists.[8] Lackadaisical references to 'cultural factors' are more often than not oblivious not only of the existence of sub-cultures and internal cultural diversity within a given social group, but also of the influence of social cleavages (age, sex, social classes, among others) and of norms and behaviour. They lose sight of the fact that 'culture' is a construct subjected to continuous syncretic processes, and the object of symbolic struggles.

The analysis of the interactions between the 'developmentalist configuration' and local populations, like the analysis of the various forms of social change, demands certain types of competence, the very ones that sociology, anthropology and anthropology of development are determined to put to work. But can anthropology of development measure up to such demands? That is, does anthropology of development exist?

As demonstrated below, after a period of stagnation following pioneer works, recent studies have allowed us to answer in the affirmative. Nevertheless, this type of anthropology remains equally marginal in the world of development and in the world of the social sciences.

It is true that in the US, in particular, 'applied anthropology' has its place. There is a long tradition of social solicitation of sociologists and anthropologists (even prior to World War Two, they were called upon in all kinds of social questions, from the problem of the Indian reserves to that of urban gangs). However, as regards the world of development proper, as a general rule the problematics were still rudimentary, purely descriptive, often naive, and disconnected from major theoretical debates in the social sciences.[9]

In the francophone world, a quick inventory of the abundant literature devoted to development indicates that empirical anthropology of development facts constitute a rather marginal area that is largely ignored. The large majority of works classified under the headings of 'sociology' or 'anthropology' in fact deal with economy or ideology. As far as the latter is concerned, these works are based on normative or moralistic considerations – more or less legitimated by scholarly terms – about 'development in general' or about the need to take 'the cultural factors of development' into account.[10]

The label 'social sciences of development' is usually misleading, and anthropology of development (the type promoted here, based on solid field enquiry, using tried tools of investigation) is essentially nonexistent. For example, three recent works in French, which all claim to review, each in its own light, the relationship between social sciences and development, bear witness to a total ignorance of anthropology of development (see Choquet et al., 1993; Guichaoua and Goussault, 1993; Rist, 1994): neither those works in French belonging to the orientation defended here nor the works in English that come closest to this (Long, 1989; Long and Long, 1992; Elwert and Bierschenk, 1988) receive even the slightest mention in any of these books. This is all the more surprising as mention is made of the 'painstaking North American applied anthropology' in contrast with 'the rather modest anthropology of development' of the francophone world and its great 'theoretical poverty' (Guichaoua and Goussault, 1993: 103). Kilani's position (in Rist, 1994), which contests the idea that anthropology of development exists, is, for its part, founded on the most deplorable confusions. Anthropology of development is continually associated with applied anthropology. The deficiencies Kilani so abruptly denounces are related to the inevitable gaps between knowledge and action, and apply regardless of the field of study. These cannot be attributed to anthropology alone on the grounds that its interest in the social processes of development is misplaced. Besides, Kilani hastily accuses anthropology of development of yielding to the 'current trend' by rallying to development ideologies without taking the trouble of argumentation (Kilani, 1994: 29). He thus demonstrates his ignorance of the works accumulated over the last twenty years. He contends, moreover, that development is not a sociological concept, and that it has no other status than that of designating a reality outside anthropology, such as sports, towns, or old age (ibid.; 20). It is indeed true that 'development' is not a concept. But it is this very 'object' status that allows us to speak of anthropology of development without taking over conceptions held by 'developers'. Urban anthropology can be carried out even if 'town' is not a concept and without assuming an urbanist's ideology! Kilani criticizes the heterogeneous nature of development as an object for anthropology, which, he says, leaves no room for the 'general viewpoints ', or coherent theoretical developments, that are supposed to be the characteristics of real anthropology (ibid: 27). But it is the very heterogeneity of the facts of development that makes anthropology of development interesting. Is anthropology so without resources as to be interested only in coherent objects ? If this were the case, it would prove itself incapable of grasping the fundamental aspects of social life, which are just as heterogeneous!

Hence, the marginal status of the anthropology of social change and development on the public scene of development constitutes, at the same time, a marginalization on the public scene of social science research. Yet, in the same way that development institutions have everything to gain from collaborating with active anthropology, it is equally in the interest of social science research to take anthropology of development into account. It has long since been established that the various reactions of a society (or its various components) to an 'outside' intervention constitute one of the best indicators of the dynamism of its own structures, and allows for a particularly good analysis of social behaviour.[11] It is simply a matter of exploiting the body of knowledge contained in the social sciences regarding the social facts of development, since the task assigned to the social sciences is to interpret apparently unintelligible behaviour or practices, without recourse to prejudices, ideologies or personal interest. Thus the analysis of the social practices effectively deployed in the context of a development project places the emphasis on the inevitable differences between the various 'interests' and 'rationalities' which regulate the reactions of the populations concerned.

It is not a matter of chance if many contemporary works in anthropology of development, despite academic or linguistic differences, have a certain air of similarity. Yet this is due neither to discussion among their authors nor to their association as disciples of a common school of thought. One would be hard put to find ready-made standards of interpretation, either functionalist, systematic, liberal, Marxist or otherwise. In this respect, anthropology of development has no set paradigm. However, here and there, the same questions are often asked: how can we explain the discrepancy between a development project and its execution? How are constraints and elbow room articulated?

Many current anthropological works on development start off with the same postulates: popular practices have a meaning which needs to be discovered. These works share a common suspicion: they consider the ideological explanations and general theories advanced by development institutions to be unsatisfactory. They are organized along the same lines: researching on differences, cleavages, contradictions, seen as privileged analysers of social reality. They make the same attempt at reconciling the analysis of the structures that constrain action and the identification of the logics that found actors' behaviour and conceptions.

In the face of the simplifications encountered in all development ideologies, founded on consensual preconceptions,[12] anthropology of development affirms, from the very outset, that the social sphere is very complex, that the interests, conceptions, strategies and logics of the various partners (or 'adversaries') that development puts in relation with each other diverge. Conversely, the everyday life of development comprises compromise, interactions, syncretisms, and (mostly informal and indirect) bargaining. These are the kinds of notions – which, obviously, do not exclude power struggles – that must be explored in order to explain 'real' effects of development actions on the milieus they intend to transform. That implies breaking away from dualist explanatory 'patterns', structuralist frameworks and culturalist references alike.

Comparativism

Does this mean that each local situation or development operation requires a specific analysis and that no *law* can be derived from the infinite variety of concrete contexts? Yes and no. Yes, in the sense that each 'field' is a unique combination of constraints and strategies, which only specific analysis can decipher. No, in the sense that certain constraints are common or similar: typologies can be constituted based on ecological conditions, modes of integration of the world market, relations of production or political regimes. In the same way, beyond individual cases and contexts, economic logics (for example the minimization of monetary 'outflows'), social logics (for example networks of solidarity) or symbolic logics (such as codes of ostentatious consumerism, or modes of status identification, based on redistribution) frequently intersect.

A decisive progress of anthropology of development will, in all likelihood, result from rigorous comparative analyses, encouraged by an increase in the number of studies. Mutually compatible field material,[13] in other words material resulting from an identical research problematic, as opposed to the descriptive monographs of yesterday's ethnographers, would finally be available and subjectable to abusive generalizations, to hasty explanations and to 'broad' theories, which single out interesting 'illustrations' and ignore counter-examples.

In the interest of this desired progress, a few common or related concepts must be found. But it is not a question here of concept theories, integrated into hard paradigms, which function on the mode of verification or confirmation (the inevitable Marxist concept of 'modes of production', for example). What we propose instead are exploratory concepts, allowing for the production of new and comparable data which have nothing to do with pre-programmed overinterpretations. Popular technical knowledge, logics, brokerage, arena, strategic groups are some of the exploratory concepts mentioned below, and which can ensure a more or less comparativist approach within anthropology of development.

This does not exclude reference to certain notions, that is, to certain more or less imprecise but prevalent terms, which have the merit of indicating fields of investigation, fragments of reality which can be conveniently mentioned, without any analytic pretensions. Innovation is an example of this necessary though ambiguous type of notion.

Moreover, the comparativist approach at the base of anthropology of development has two specific characteristics: the multiculturalist view of development situations, and the transversality of conceptions and practices of actors engaged in these situations.

Multiculturalism

Development situations bring two different worlds into confrontation with each other. On one hand, there is a basically cosmopolitan, international culture, the culture of the 'developmentalist configuration'. This is of course divided into (trans-national) sub-cultures, in the guise of various clans, based on ideology and/or profession, which all behave in more or less the same way, all around the world. On the other hand, there exists a wide variety of local cultures and sub-cultures.[14] Although the results of such confrontations are largely unpredictable, it is possible, nonetheless, to identify a number of constants and invariants. This is what we intend to accomplish with the aid of some of the exploratory concepts (for example, brokerage, popular technical knowledge and logics) mentioned above.

Transversality

We could of course imagine a division of anthropology of development into sub-disciplines, in keeping with the types of intervention which it studies: rural development, health, urban youth, etcetera. Indeed, all development operations pass through institutional and technical filters which place them in one professional field rather than another, however integrated the development operation in question might be. General rhetoric aside, development usually takes the shape of specialized experts, specialized organizations and specialized funding, be it in the area of health, environment, agricultural production, administrative reform, decentralization or the promotion of women. As far as competence, planning, financing or administration are concerned, development cannot avoid compartmentalization. Anthropology of development might have some good reasons for following the example of the developmentalist configuration in its specializations, if only by increasing the priority placed on the *material* aspects of interventions and on the *mechanisms* on which these rely: the constraints involved in a hydro-agricultural installation are different from those on a vaccination campaign. But other social factors 'at the base', and in particular the 'clients' of development institutions, are not pre-occupied with cleavages of this kind. Popular practices and conceptions escape sectoral cleavages: it is the same peasant who reacts to a co-operative project and to a community health centre, frequently (but not always) through the exercise of identical logics of action, or in reference to similar social norms. The inevitable compartmentalization of the institutions or interventions thus stands in contrast to the behaviour of the populations addressed.

Popular transversality also differs from developmentalist compartmentalization from a diachronic point of view. Seen from the viewpoint of its organizers, a development project occupies space–time entirely. It is central, omnipresent, unique. From the peasant viewpoint, it is temporary, relative, incidental – just another link in a chain of consecutive interventions. Project agents devote 100 per cent of their professional activity to a sector of activity that represents only a fraction of the time used by the producer or the consumer it targets. Many oppositions arise as a result of such radically different standpoints.

One might also examine the question of sectorization from an angle other than that of the cleavages that distinguish development institutions, namely the persistent cleavages that characterise the social sciences. Anthropology, for example, has (more or less latent or more or less explicit) sub-cleavages. Economic anthropology deals with relations of production, modes of production, small-scale commodity production, informal trade. Political anthropology reflects on power at the local level, patron–client systems, political conceptions. And so on. But here again, the argument remains the same. Social actors are engaged in constant back-and-forth movements between the political register and the economic register, to say nothing of symbolism, language or religion. Popular practices and conceptions, confronted with change in general and development in particular, mobilize all the registers at their disposal. None of these registers can be dismissed or disqualified a priori, neither the economic register (with its relations of production and modes of economic actions) nor the political register (with its relations of domination and power strategies) nor the social, symbolic or religious registers.

Anthropology of development cannot be broken down into sub-disciplines: the transversality of its object is an essential ingredient of its comparativist objective. *Anthropology of change and development is simultaneously a political anthropology, a sociology of organizations, an economic anthropology, a sociology of networks, an anthropology of conceptions and sense systems.* This is why both patient–nurse interactions and supervisor–peasant interactions are equally interesting objects, and why it is equally interesting to describe and analyse the conceptions of both, the institutions of both, the social relations of both, the systems of constraints in which both are involved.

Nonetheless, declaring the cohesion of a discipline or sub-discipline, which defines the comparative field it attempts to understand, is always ambivalent and always relative. It is also worth mentioning the fact that this kind of declaration is readily used to mark off boundaries, that it is also a professional strategy, sometimes implies corporate concerns and is liable to end up as a metaphysical debate. The comparative ambition of anthropology of social change and development, as defined here, is based on a relative autonomy of its object, and on a number of problematics at the interface between anthropology and sociology. My position is therefore somewhat different from Augé's, for instance. Augé asserts that anthropology (and only anthropology) is by principle indivisible, as opposed to the overspecializations of other social sciences, which create sub-disciplines defined by their object. It is on this basis that he refuses to recognize health anthropology (Augé, 1986) as a discipline in its own right. I would like to take a more cautious stand, which I consider to be more realistic. Even those who do not condone overspecialization or endless fragmentation, and who do not question the deep epistemological coherence of the social sciences or the profound methodological unity of anthropology, are obliged to acknowledge that objects exert a certain influence on the constitution of knowledge, on the relative autonomy of comparative fields (trans-disciplines or sub-disciplines) which spring from them. These comparative fields can be defined on many bases, usually regional or thematic. 'Cultural zones' – Africa, South East Asia or rural European societies – thus constitute one of the possible dimensions of this relative autonomy induced by the object. Thematic classifications – sociology of education, anthropology of religion or anthropology of development – constitute another. These two modes of 'semi-specialization arising from objects' are at the origin of all forms of contextualized comparativism (moreover, there is no incompatibility between them). However (and I agree with Augé on this point), the autonomy of these comparative fields can only be relative; independence would be both absurd and unproductive.

In the final analysis, the comparative approach on which the relative autonomy of anthropology of development is founded is, to my mind, a result of the link between three fundamental and indissociable components: (1) a specific and particular object (the social processes of change, simultaneously endogenous and induced); (2) a problematic fuelled by the contemporary debates in the social sciences (which extend beyond anthropology itself); (3) a methodology of data production grounded in the tradition of anthropology and 'qualitative sociology', and which takes into account all the dimensions of reality experienced by social actors (transversal to the usual thematic partitions of the social sciences).

Action

The present work does not provide in-depth reflections on problems related to action, that is on the 'application', properly speaking, of anthropology of development (this will only be mentioned in Chapter 13, seen from the angle of the relationships between social science researchers and development operators). This does not imply any contempt or underestimation of these problems, which concern the integration of anthropologists into development programmes, or their role in studies, evaluation or expertise. I do not share the high-and-mighty attitude of certain researchers towards 'development practitioners', and I consider that a project chief, an extension agent or a doctor is worth quite as much as a sociologist or an anthropologist.

I do not think that the role of the social sciences is merely one of protest or criticism. This does not mean that the social sciences have no pertinence whatsoever; the contrary is obvious. But the modesty entailed in reformism, in development as elsewhere, is as worthwhile as panache or denunciation. There is room for both. Improvement in the quality of the 'services' that development institutions propose to the populations is an objective that should not be disdained. And anthropology of development can contribute its part, which is modest but real, to this improvement.

But only the quality of its procedures and of the knowledge it produces is capable of ensuring its influence on action. This is why I have focused on the function of knowledge and its prerequisites: this is the 'entry ticket' that lets anthropology of development into the field of action; it is also the means of drawing its attention to the pitfalls of ideological pressures, of which populism is not the least.

A long time ago, Marc Augé wrote, 'development is on the ethnological agenda: the duty of ethnology is not to elucidate it, but to study it, in its practices, strategies and contradictions' (Augé, 1973). I agree as far as the imperative of study is concerned, but I do not share his *a priori* refusal of all efforts at 'elucidation', that is to say, of all attempts to contribute to action. The simple fact is that study constitutes, among others factors, the condition of a possible (and necessarily modest) elucidation.

Populism

What I mean by 'populism' is a certain relationship between intellectuals (associated with privileged classes and groups) and the people (dominated classes and groups): a relationship in which intellectuals discover the people, pity their lot in life and/or marvel at their capacities, and decide to put themselves at the disposal of the people and to strive for their welfare.

Hence my use of the term 'populism' does not correspond to the sense it currently assumes in contemporary political discourse (where it makes pejorative reference to the 'demagogic' behaviour of more-or-less charismatic politicians). I am reverting to the original sense of populism, that of populist Russians in the nineteenth century (*narodnicki*).

Populism is very much part of the development universe. In a sense, it is even inseparable from development. Isn't it true that the developmentalist configuration comprises 'elites' whose intention is to help the people (peasants, women, poor people, refugees, the unemployed ...), to improve their living conditions, to be at their disposal, to work towards their welfare, to collaborate with them? The proliferation of non-governmental organizations (NGOs), their practice as much as their rhetoric, reflect this developmentalist populism, constitute indeed its most recent and most massive form, even though there are many others. 'Developing countries', the 'wretched of the earth', the unemployed of 'black Brazzavilles', cultivators facing the risk of famine, victims of war, malnutrition, cholera or structural adjustment, are so many faces the 'people' wear in a developmentalist context, that is to say as far as the 'privileged' and the 'endowed' Westerners converted to its service are concerned. But populism also structures, to a great extent, the world of research, in sociology, anthropology and history alike. The rehabilitation of grassroots social actors, the narratives of the lifestyle of the lowly, the inventory of peasant competencies and ruses, the inventory of the 'vision of the conquered', the analysis of popular resistance: these are some of the central themes of the social sciences.

This latent ideology has various advantages and merits, and as many short-comings and disadvantages, which will be mentioned below (see Chapter 7). But it nonetheless corresponds to a certain methodological progress. Despite the difficulties the social sciences have as regards accumulation, the explana-tory models they propose (at the height of their progress and inventiveness, which is not always reflected in the media) are currently, in part, a lot more complex than those of the past. It is no longer relevant to consider social phenomena – which invariably involve a great many factors – in terms of crude determinisms, isolated hermeneutic variables or simplistic sets: mode of production, culture, society, the 'system' ... Rather, an investigation into the resources that 'grassroots' actors have at their disposal – the very object of the concerns and solicitude of development institutions – integrates this increasing complexity, which does not mean that social constraints are disregarded, far from it. Consequently, it is no longer possible to present the diffusion of a health message as a linear 'telegraphic' type of communication in which an 'emitter' (active) sends a 'message' to a 'receptor' (passive), a message that is more or less disturbed by 'parasites' (interference to be eliminated). The receptor does not receive sense passively, he reconstructs it, depending both on the context, and on the incessant negotiations in progress. The social actor 'at the bottom', dispossessed and dominated as he may be, is never a mere 'recipient' who only has the choice between submission or revolt.

A collective problematic

The keywords defined above (development, anthropology, comparativism, action, populism), are also used by others in identical or related senses. These comments, or more or less similar ones, have also been made by other scientists. The creation of an association like APAD (Euro-African Association for the Anthropology of Social Change and Development)[15] bears witness to such convergences. There exists a number of collective works which constitute so many milestones marking the intellectual dynamics connected with the early or recent history of APAD, and which may be cited as significant moments in the creation of a series of convergent problematics. The present work is partially concerned with providing an overview of these problematics. As far as these are concerned, it is interesting to note the obvious and astonishing complementarity of insights, research and propositions made by scientists of differing starting points. We might mention, among other publications, *Paysans, experts et chercheurs en Afrique noire* (Boiral, Lantéri and Olivier de Sardan, eds., 1985); the special issue of *Sociologia Ruralis* on 'Aid and Development' (Elwert and Bierschenk, 1988); *Sociétés, développement et santé* (Fassin and Jaffré, 1990); and *Les associations paysannes* (Jacob and Lavigne Delville, 1994).[16] This observation probably calls to mind the notion of an 'invisible college': 'an invisible college is an informal network of researchers who construct an intellectual paradigm in order to study common topics' (Rogers, 1983: xviii; see Kuhn, 1970). It would of course be inappropriate to speak of a paradigm in the strict, Kuhnian sense of the word. Nevertheless, the fact remains that there is a configuration of scientific affinities and a convergence of problematics that is worthy of note.[17]

Social change and development: in Africa or in general?

Most of the examples and most of the references used in the present work concern Africa (and rural Africa in particular). The African continent obviously has various specific characteristics, of which the omnipresence of development institutions is by no means the least. The growing crisis of African economies and African states has merely enhanced the influence of 'development aid' and 'development projects', whether small or large, and regardless of their initiators (international institutions, co-operating national bodies, NGOs from the North or from the South). 'Development' (its language, its funds, its agents, its infrastructures, its methods) is a fundamental aspect of contemporary Africa, in rural and urban areas alike.

Hence, the fact that anthropology regards development as an important object of study has more sense in Africa than elsewhere. In the case of the other continents, the voluntary attempts at inducing social change no doubt assume a greater variety of forms, forms which cannot all be subsumed under the term 'development'.

Nevertheless, the research perspectives proposed above go beyond the Africanist frame of reference. There is hardly a village or neighbourhood in the world in which one does not encounter 'actions for change', in other words, interventions originating from outside a given milieu, initiated by the state, activists or private operators who attempt to transform the behaviour of actors in the milieu by mobilizing them. For example, in France, agricultural development, local development, and urban development constitute so many themes and fields in which voluntarist policies for change, directed towards 'the base' and conceived 'in its interest', produce incessant interactions between interveners and target populations. Though the context, constraints, actors and themes involved here are far removed from Africa, the methods and concepts of observation and study employed in the field in France by the rural sociologist or the urban anthropologist, insofar as they take these multiple interventions into account, are closely related to those proposed in this work.

Let us take for example the 'development agents' one encounters around the corner in any African village: extension worker, livestock agent, nurse, co-operative manager, literacy agent … The difficulty of their social position, the contradictions inherent in their function, their unstable professional identity, tend to remind us, *mutatis mutandis*, of the problems encountered in France by social workers, educators, extension agents or supervisors of cultural activities, etcetera.

How do these propositions for change, induced from without, enter into confrontation with local dynamics? This minimal definition of the object treated in the present work might help us to understand why our remarks aim at being both specified (anchored in the context of rural Africa) and generalist (presenting conceptual tools that can function in other contexts). In this respect, the term 'development' serves essentially as a port of access into more general social processes: it is not an ivory tower.

Let me add a final comment on the structure of the present work. The question of the multiple factors of various types to be taken into account, if we are to procure the tools to allow us to understand social change in general, and the interactions of developers and developees in particular, will be incessantly raised. Technical, economic, institutional, political, social and symbolic logics, each with its system of constraints and its particular context, will be continually evoked. Consequently, the reader should not be overly surprised to find numerous interconnected themes which echo one another throughout the following chapters.

The first part of this work will explore, along various lines, the complexity of the phenomenon of social change and development, and will attempt to point out the ways in which anthropology can and should measure up to this complexity.

The second part will isolate some of the variables involved: relations of production, logics of action, popular knowledge, forms of mediation and 'political' strategies. An attempt will therefore be made to suggest some specific directions in which we might explore such complex phenomena. Others possibilities do, of course, exist.

I have avoided classifying variables in order of importance and have refrained from defining any given variable as a 'last resort' or in terms of an effect of 'over-determination'. There are no grounds on which we may possibly assert, a priori, that any one register has a greater explanatory value than another, at least not at the level of the type of anthropology that attempts to remain 'actor-close'. A long-term history of structures must dare to take the risk of going beyond such a priori assertions. However, when it comes to accounting for the micro-processes of change, or understanding how interventions from without are adopted, ignored, sidetracked, recomposed or refused, one cannot rightfully expect to find answers through any other means except field enquiry. Only enquiry can allow us to select from the variety of potential factors. Even so, enquiry must acquire the intellectual and conceptual tools in keeping with its ambitions. The objective of this work goes a little way in this direction. Though the perspective developed here is an empirical one, this empiricism owes nothing to naivety.

Notes

1 More than fifty years ago Malinowski noted: 'Unfortunately there still subsists in certain milieus a prevalent but erroneous opinion according to which applied anthropology is fundamentally different from theoretical and academic anthropology' (requoted in Malinowski, 1970 :23).

2 As for normative definitions, Freyssinet's work (1966) provides an already dated but well-furnished catalogue, which has since been enriched.

3 These useful expressions have their drawbacks: they can indeed lead us to believe that all 'developers' (or all 'developees') are being put in the same bag. The only interest of this type of general opposition is to underline an undeniable, massive cleavage seen from a 'broad perspective': developers, on one hand, and developees, on the other, do not belong to the same life world. But it is obviously not a matter of two homogeneous categories.

4 These theories are more and more tied nowadays to the different neo-liberal trends, in consequence of the collapse of trends formerly in competition (themselves normative and macroeconomic), in particular those connected to marxism and which advocate a breakaway from the world market.

5 The expression belongs to Long: 'The essence of an actor-oriented approach is that its concepts are grounded in the everyday life experiences and understandings of men and women be they poor, peasants, entrepreneurs, government bureaucrats or researchers' (Long,1992c: 5).

6 I borrow the epithet 'qualitatitive' from certain American sociologists (see Strauss, 1987, 1993) but not without some reservations. On one hand the term 'qualitative' has the merit of underlining that one can practise sociology without falling victim to statistical obsessions, polls, or questionnaires ('what cannot be quantified *does* exist, does have consequences, can be argued and made the subject of propositions and hypotheses', Bailey, 1973b:11). But on the other hand, 'qualitative' could lead one to believe that there is a certain casualness concerning problems of representativeness, or, worse, a lack of rigour. ... Obviously, the sociology or anthropology referred to as qualitative, at least in the mind of many researchers, makes an equal (or superior) claim to rigour as the sociology referred to as quantitative and, moreover, neither disdains figures nor the procedures of systematic surveys; indeed, quite the contrary (see Olivier de Sardan, 1995b). From this point of view, there is no epistemological difference between qualitative sociology and quantitative sociology, but rather a complementarity between methods of data production.

7 This is not, however, to deny the impact of disciplinary and academic idiosyncrasies which, regrettably, set up boundaries between sociology and anthropology. An example of this is the system of erudite reference particular to each, with a tendency to ignore the dynamism of research carried out on the other side of the fence.

8 Hence the irritation with economists displayed in a particularly polemical book by Polly Hill which is not lacking in truth (1986). The problem I am raising concerns the role of economists in the piloting of research on development, and their frequent disdain for the competence of an anthropological order, and not the role of the economic dimension of social phenomena linked to social change and to development, which anthropology can by no means ignore. Economic anthropology (including the type formerly or currently practised by various economists on the borderlines of their discipline) as well as economic sociology (which, in the US, brings together a number of economists who resist the econometric tidal wave) are the basic ingredients of the sauce with which anthropology seasons development.

9 This difficulty in defining clear lines of approach and unified problematics is evident in various 'state-of-the-art' works based essentially on North American literature: see Hoben, 1982; Chambers, 1987; Arnould, 1989; Ranc, 1990. One might also mention several collective works presenting various general reflections or personal experiences in applied anthropology: (Cochrane, 1971; Oxaal, Barnett and Booth,1975; Pitt, 1976; Green, 1986; Grillo and Rew, 1985; Horowitz and Painter, 1986; Cernea, 1991b; Hobart, 1993b). This stands in contrast with the existence, on the other hand, of American manuals and texts on applied anthropology (Partridge, 1984; as well as *Human Organization*).

10 A francophone bibliography bears witness to this (Kellerman, 1992). The works analysed, which are supposed to give an account of the 'cultural dimension of

development', are essentially essayism and make no reference to an empirical anthropology of development. The (already dated) bibliography produced by Jacquemot et al. (1981) made wide use of sociological references, but the approach, in that era, was very macro, as practised by sociologists, and very much 'on the outskirts of development, as far as anthropologists are concerned (see Chapter 2). The bibliography established by Jacob (1989) is, to date, the only francophone bibliography that makes room for reference to books and articles related to anthropology of development. It is also one of the rare works that, like the present one, attempts to bring together anglophone and francophone sources.

11 See Bastide (1971), or Balandier (1971).

12 Consensus, that is, at one level or another (village, class, nation, Third World, humanity …) and according to various legitimizations (moral, religious, political, scientific …).

13 The main advantage the evaluations commissioned by the short-lived Bureau of Evaluation of Co-operation and Development Services of the French Ministry of Foreign Affairs was that of having outlined such a body of work (see Freud, 1985, 1986, 1988); see also, as examples of the articles issued by these evaluations, Pontié and Ruff, 1985; Yung, 1985.

14 Foster had already underlined in his own way this multicultural dimension of the process of development: 'In developmental programs, representatives of two or more cultural systems come into contact… . Whether the gulf between two worlds is full-cultural or sub-cultural, it is significant. In either case the technician shares the cultural and social forms not only of the country from which he comes but also of the professional group he represents' (Foster, 1962: 5).

15 http://durandal.cnrs-mrs.fr/shadyc/APAD/APAD1.html
email: apad@eness.univ-mrs.fr

16 One might also note a clear convergence, in this instance an unintentional one (that is to say independent of any kind of joint action) with the work carried out in Norman Long's circle in Wageningen (see in particular Long, 1989; Long and Long , 1992). See Chapter 1.

17 The text that served as a type of platform for APAD at its creation bears witness to this. It was published in the *Bulletin de l'APAD* No. 1, 1991, under the title '*Pourquoi une Association euro-africaine pour l'anthropologie du changement et du développement social?*'.

3
Anthropology, sociology, Africa and development
A brief historical overview

Though sociology and ethnology were originally one and the same discipline in the days of their founding fathers at the beginning of the twentieth century, fieldwork in Africa came under the sole heading of ethnology and was thus cut off from sociology.[1] The study of modern and Western societies, towns and mass phenomena were reserved for sociology while 'primitive' and colonized societies, villages, fraternities and sects were devolved to ethnology. Africa was then perceived as a reservoir of customs, religions and traditions to be inventoried. As far as knowledge is concerned, this orientation gave rise to a wealth of highly interesting studies. But these acquisitions came at a cost. Ethnology was faced with the risk of descending into the patrimonialist and traditionalist ghetto.

French colonial ethnology

A common accusation brought against French colonial ethnology must be rebutted: ethnology was rarely used as an agent of colonial administration. In contrast to British colonies (though it would appear that ethnologists and civil servants were often at loggerheads), French colonies rarely called upon ethnologists as 'experts'. 'Knowledge of the milieu' was part of the responsibilities of the colonial administrators. The enquiries they carried out were considered sufficient backup for the exercise of their discretionary powers. Advice from the outside was not welcome. Nevertheless certain colonial administrators became interested in ethnology and produced some of the most outstanding 'fundamentalist' works of this period (see Monteil, 1932; Tauxier, 1932, and many others).

The enormous gulf separating colonial 'mise en valeur' (the forerunner of today's 'development') and anthropological research is not only a product of

42

the mode of administration of the French colonial territories. It is also a by-product of tendencies within French social science.

Indeed, during the period between the two world wars, the formerly dominant problematic of evolution from Morgan to Marx, from Auguste Comte to Tyler, was abandoned in favour of cultural relativism, the latter having discovered the irreducible specificity of each individual culture and the necessity of studying societies through fieldwork.

This undeniable advance progressed even further owing to another discovery of the same kind: African cultures, it was admitted, had their own inherent forms of rationality. At the beginning of the colonial era, the prevalent idea was that African peoples were 'primitive' and therefore motivated by deeply irrational impulses. The development of anthropology rejected this commonsense notion prevalent in Western countries. Despite certain appearances, Lévy-Bruhl, though he refers to a 'pre-logical mentality', while embracing the evolutionist approach in vogue at the time, made allowances for the existence of a certain form of logic in primitive peoples: 'archaic' and distinct from 'real' logic, but nonetheless real and worthy of interest (Lévy-Bruhl, 1931). The discovery of the complexity of the systems of African thought, of their extensive symbolic and cosmogonic construction, placed an emphasis, based on a culturalist perspective, on the specificity of the 'values' of African societies, thus opposing Western technical and economic rationality to a distinct African traditionalist rationality. This represented an onslaught on ethnocentric and Western prejudices.

But this unmistakable progress was made at the expense of a disregard for historical dynamics and resulted in a research orientation that was static and 'traditionalist'. Four strands can be identified within this orientation.

(a) The holistic problematic of the Durkheim–Mauss school of thought which puts the emphasis on social globality. The whole is more than the sum of its parts, society is more than the sum of its components. This point of view, despite its indisputable epistemological advantages, incurs the danger of 'fetishising' society, viewed as an almost supernatural entity,[2] thus drawing attention away from sectoral changes, progressive transformations and syncretic innovations.

(b) The French school of Africanist ethnology, led by Griaule, which directed its efforts towards the study of religious phenomena, rituals, symbolic systems. Their priority was the coherence of 'indigenous' values and mythical constructs, to the exclusion of both historical mutations and the interaction between religious and other social facts (including their political and economic dimensions). Their research on the specific knowledge and visions of African societies did serve to rehabilitate them by emphasizing their wealth and complexity. Unfortunately, it also strengthened a 'patrimonialist' and somewhat ahistorical vision of these cultures.

(c) The dominance of ethnic classification had similar results. It is now a known fact, since Barth (1975), that the ethnic group is a social construct, that ethnic identity is relative, fluctuating, in part situational and negotiated.[3] Obviously, ethnic reference is not merely a figment of the colonial administrator's imagination, nor is it an ethnological invention: those involved play the primary role in the process of its construction or naturalization, not to mention the linguistic aspects of the matter. However, the restriction of ethnological research within an ethnic context, under colonial rule, has doubtlessly helped to obscure the full extent of trans-ethnic, infra-ethnic and supra-ethnic processes, which are precisely those involved in social change.

(d) Structuralism gave an enormous impetus and a wide international audience to French anthropology in the 1960s. However, the intellectualist problematic specific to Lévi-Strauss and the themes of research which he imposed (kinship, mythologies) hardly allowed for any serious consideration of the socio-economic changes Africa was undergoing at the time.

The combined influence of various traditions of this kind resulted in a certain interpretation of African societies by French ethnologists. Seen from their perspective, African societies were based on a 'society–culture–ethnicity' trilogy, of which culture was the centre of gravity. Each ethnic group–society had its own culture, the cornerstone of its originality. This process endowed African societies with three broad characteristics: they were purportedly homogenous, resistant to history, composed of independent entities.

Being rather more sensitive to the differences between any African culture and Western society than to those existing within a given African society, classical ethnology often minimized contradictions and social and cultural rifts inherent in the groups they studied.

Being rather more sensitive to the permanence and traditional character of value systems and symbolic structures than to the conditions attendant on their production and reproduction, classical ethnological research has rarely considered history in the making except as posing a risk of destroying 'what already exists'.

Being rather more sensitive to the independence of cultural forms and ethnic entities, defined in terms of their articulation with external constraints, classical ethnological research often restricted itself to the context of the ethnic group or village, and to a monographic approach, incapable of grasping the interactions with macro-sociological phenomena.

However, a scientific analysis of the process of social change in general and of development facts in particular, of the impact of development action on target populations and of the reaction of the former to such actions, requires an understanding of internal diversity, of socio-cultural change and of external pressure. These three elements stand in need of a problematic in stark contrast to classical ethnology.[4]

Reactions: dynamic and/or Marxist anthropology

The works of Balandier heralded a breaking away from French traditional ethnology. The fact that Balandier introduced anglophone African studies to France is not fortuitous. By placing the emphasis on religious syncretisms, he oriented his work in a resolutely dynamic perspective. By introducing urban sociology into African studies, he broke away from a backward-looking approach focused on the rural milieu. His analysis of the effects of 'the colonial situation' took stock of the existence of a system of domination and reinserted ethnologized societies into a larger framework. Generally speaking, his intention was to 'réhabiliter l'histoire à l'encontre des présupposés fonctionnalistes et structuralistes' (Balandier, 1963 : VI).

Essentially due to his influence, and in the wake of Claude Meillassoux, who was something of a pioneer and the author of a seminal article in 1960 (published in Meillassoux, 1977), a social and economic anthropology of Marxist inspiration was developed. Its main focus was the analysis of internal cleavages in rural African societies, viewed in a historical light. Junior–senior and men–women relationships (Meillassoux, 1964, 1975a; Terray, 1972; Rey, 1971), pre-colonial trade (Meillassoux, 1971), slavery (Meillassoux, 1975b, 1986), the State and pre-colonial war (Bazin and Terray, 1982), constituted the major consecutive themes of this research. These themes were also approached in various monographic studies (for example, Olivier de Sardan, 1969, 1984; Pollet and Winter, 1971; Amselle, 1977; Copans, 1980; Dupré, 1982; Diawara, 1991).

But this did not reconcile social science with the changes in progress. The approach suggested by Africanist economic anthropology was in many respects far removed from the analysis of development facts.

For one thing, it was often general and very 'theoretical', owing to its Marxist tradition, preoccupied as it was with filling the conceptual vacuum on the question of African modes of production, to the detriment of a descriptive analysis of relations of production. The latter is still of scientific interest, despite the collapse of Marxism as a scientific ideology, and can be encountered in certain aspects of agro-economic analysis of systems of production. But it has often been neglected in favour of a combination comprising modes of production and a rhetoric centred on 'articulation',[5] which leaves no room for the taking into consideration of local situations or of effective economic behaviour. Analysis was thus limited to macro structures and phenomena of transition from one structure to another, with scant attention being paid to practical social strategies and to the immediate constraints they entail. As we are well aware, Althusser's 'Marxist structuralism' (as it was sometimes called) influenced this school of thought (see Terray, 1972).

Moreover, the scientific and empirical efforts of this Marxist Africanist anthropology focused primarily on the pre-colonial and colonial periods, to the detriment of the contemporary changes in progress. 'Development' was often considered to be unworthy of academic interest, especially since it was considered to be a long-since-familiar aspect of the dynamics of imperialism, no more, no less. It is true, however, that from time to time case studies were indeed conducted on the subject of the African peasantry, some under the influence of the above-mentioned school of thought, albeit of a more empirical character, especially those conducted by ORSTOM. Their main advantage was that of demonstrating the existence of specific rural African economic rationalities.[6] Peasant rationality, though distinct from developers' postulates and from the *homo economicus* pattern of neo-liberal theories, none-theless entailed rationalities of a specifically economic nature, which could be accounted for without any reference to the famous 'cultural impediments' or religious prohibitions.

From a sociological viewpoint: sociology of modernization and sociology of development

Let us take a few steps back into the past. At a time when ethnology was moving towards independence and breaking away from the evolutionist theory in favour of a view of the cognitive equality of cultures, sociology, especially so far as the Third World was concerned, remained faithful, on the whole, in the name of a certain theory of social change, to a revised and corrected version of the evolutionist perspective. From a theoretical point of view, Parsons's domination of American sociology contributed to the survival of the dichotomy between 'traditional societies' and 'industrial societies', main-tained in an archetypal opposition, the main concern being the creation of a process of interrelation between these poles.[7] There was, besides, a whole series of oppositions (see Parsons, 1976; Redfield, 1956; Hoselitz, 1962, and many others) which might be summarized as follows:

traditional societies	modern societies
ascription	achievement
community	individual
gemeinschaft	*gesellschaft*
homogeneity	heterogeneity
gift	money
patron–client relationships	bureaucratic relationships
routine	innovation
solidarity	competition

At the same time, in the aftermath of World War Two, modernist theories took pride of place in development economics (Rostow's famous 'stages of economic growth' comes to mind) and exerted considerable influence on related disciplines (see especially the developmentalist school in political science including Apter, 1963; Pye, 1966; Almond and Powell, 1966).

The reaction against all such neo-evolutionist conceptions of modernization, accused of advocating the generalization of Western liberal economy, gave rise to a new stream of thought, essentially of Latin American origin and under Marxist influence, and which can accurately be referred to as 'theories of dependence'.[8] In this analysis, the 'underdevelopment' of the South is neither a sign of its backwardness, nor a vestige of its 'traditional' nature, but rather the product of a historic spoliation to which they were subjected, the expression of their dependence, for which the world economic system (that is, imperialism), be it ancient or contemporary, is responsible. André Gunder Frank is probably the most important representative of this kind of theory within the field of sociology (Frank, 1972). He analyses the chain of successive dependencies that end up linking the lowliest Third World villages to the centres of Western capitalism. This is the 'development of underdevelopment' promoted in part by the system of 'unequal exchange' (see Emmanuel, 1972). Breaking away from world economy is thus seen as the only means of attaining the freedom that leads to 'true development'.

Samir Amin popularizes and adapts a personal interpretation of these theories to Africa, a blend resulting from a hasty reading of Marxist economic anthropology: the theory of the articulation of modes of production and the theory of dependence are reconciled in his work in an effort to account for 'stagnation' in Africa.[9]

The positive aspects of these theories is that they shed light on the processes of domination and exploitation, to the disadvantage of the Third World, which structured and continues to structure the world economy, which affected and still affect producers of the South. However, an obsessive focus on the mechanisms of domination, what Passeron calls 'domino-centrism' in a different context (in Grignon and Passeron, 1989), has obvious shortcomings. Not only does it fall into the trap of 'miserabilism' (people are reduced to the oppression to which they are subjected), but it also prevents research innovations, restricted as it is to the drawing up of an endless list of the forms of constraint, spoilage and domination to which the popular masses of the Third World fall victim. The sociology of dependence thus rapidly found itself at a loss, once knowledge of the mechanisms of external exploitation was acquired. The reality of these mechanisms should not be ignored. Nonetheless, the sociology of dependence found itself without resources as soon as the question of how much elbow room was left to dominated actors came up, or when asked to account for the complex and unpredictable aspects of a concrete situation.

In this regard, the theories of modernization and of dependence, though opposed to one another, are related. They consider development from the vantage point of the centres of power, based on 'a determinist, linear, and externalist view of social change' (Long, 1994: 15).

Systems analysis

The crisis of Marxism cannot be brushed aside as a mere turn or inversion of fashion, though this kind of effect is not entirely absent. It is also the dead end of the road of an excessively 'macro' and determinist problematic, whose productiveness in terms of results, though real, has progressively declined.

Systems analysis appeared and might still appear to be an alternative scientific ideology (or set of paradigms) from which politico-prophetic and dogmatic Marxist rhetoric have been removed, but which is still capable of interpreting complex social phenomena. However, we have to recognize the fact that the analysis of systems in the social sciences is in part a product of language. The vocabulary of cybernetics took over from earlier metaphorical systems (with vocabularies borrowed from biology, linguistics and economics). Old concepts were swept aside: systems, subsystems, interfaces, retroactions, thus became modern versions of structures, levels, links, influences…[10].

In fact, systems analysis can be considered both as a paradigm and as a metaphor.

Systems analysis as a paradigm?

There are two versions of systems analysis as a paradigm: in the maximalist version, reality is a system; in the minimalist version, reality appears to be a system. In both cases, in the disciplines in which systems analysis flourished – thermodynamics, of course, but also ecology and agronomy – the conceptual whole organized around the systemic problematic is both self-regulated and systematic. We are therefore dealing with a system, to remain within the systems analysis framework, but with a particular type of system, i.e. a conceptual system. Since Kuhn, this is readily defined as a paradigm.

Nonetheless, a number of serious problems arise as soon as an attempt is made to apply this conceptual system to other areas, and especially to human behaviour. Most social processes cannot be defined as systems in the strict sense of the word, except, at best, certain extremely specific areas in which human activities integrate natural cycles, in the form of a physical economy, and which can be taken as independent analytical entities: this is probably the case of traditional agro-pastoral systems of production. In social science in general, systems analysis can scarcely claim to be a paradigm, for reasons inherent in the very nature of social phenomena and of society. Social practices and cultural meaning have nothing to do with systems, either in the maximalist or in the minimalist sense of the word. That is a fact. Not only is it impossible to cut a systemic pattern out of actor strategies, ambivalent behaviour, ambiguous conceptions, but the former contradict the very notion of system, which connotes coherence and functionality. Neither society nor culture can be properly defined as systems, and to consider them as such would amount to ignoring the specificity of social phenomena, multiple actor strategies, human agency, power struggles, as well as the contradictions and incoherencies at the heart of thought and practice in general.

This is why anthropology is not a *nomos*, why history has no *laws* (strictly speaking), why the formal procedures peculiar to the natural sciences are only fleeting episodes in the life of social sciences, which are nonetheless obliged to use a 'natural language' (see Passeron, 1991, and among other comments on this work, Olivier de Sardan, 1993). The main register here is that of plausibility as opposed to the Popperian register of falsifiability.

Systems analysis as a metaphor?
Nonetheless, the systemic vocabulary is used constantly in social science. This is because it readily accommodates loose interpretations. We thus enter into the realm of metaphor, which is constantly used in the social sciences, even though berating other people's metaphors (see Passeron, 1991: 14–54) remains common practice. Metaphors are of course even more present in the language of common sense. If society is not 'really' a system, nor anything approaching a system, it is still possible to play with the idea of using terms that vaguely suggest that this is the case. The gap between what society is and what we may consider it to be leaves room for a nice semblance of precision. Instead of a hard paradigmatic system we are provided with a loose metaphorical system. This type of method is in fact quite productive. But there are dangers involved, as is usually the case with metaphors. The recourse to a new metaphorical system (imported into a field where it was not previously employed) always generates results in the beginning (see the organicist metaphor in early social science research, or Bourdieu's use of the market metaphor in expressions like 'symbolic wealth' and 'social capital'), but results gradually decline and sometimes degenerate into clichés. The projection of systems analysis on society does not get away from this law of declining productivity. Hence, when Easton first proposed that the 'political system' be perceived as a 'system' in the thermodynamic sense of the word (Easton, 1974), to be treated like a 'black box', and focusing on the analysis of inputs (support and demands) and outputs (decisions), he opened the path towards a new interpretation of certain phenomena linked to power; in other words, he produced new sense (see Cot and Mounier, 1974, 197–225). However, it may be observed that when used repeatedly the result is a rapid decline in productivity. Systems

analysis thus turns out to be 'ready-made' thought, an additional cliché which only goes to reproduce a simplistic reading of society. Three major difficulties then arise:

- a risk inherent in all metaphoric systems: the naturalization and reification of metaphors; that is, an artificial process is taken as a reality. One ends up believing, in the present case, that society is really a system.

- a risk inherent in the systemic metaphor, namely, the emphasis placed on system functionality. One ends up believing that all social systems are functional, with a tendency to reproduce their own coherence (Parsons's sociology and Radcliffe-Brown's anthropology, both termed 'structural–functionalist', both being pre-systemic, illustrate the point: see Parsons 1976; Radcliffe-Brown, 1972).

- a risk inherent in the systemic metaphor as applied to development, namely that of analysing interactions between a development project and its target population as if one were dealing with a systemic circuit. One ends up believing that the project is one sub-system and the 'milieu' another.

The systemic framework of analysis put forward by the AMIRA group (Barrès et al., 1981) for the analysis of development projects is an example of what we might call 'a systematic use of the systems analysis metaphoric system' (*sic*) in social science.[11] The distinctions that this text establishes between an 'eco-system', a 'project system', a 'peasant system' and an 'external system' (and the sub-divisions it establishes inside each category and within various sub-systems) can only serve as a pedagogical tool, and even then only on condition that we move rapidly beyond the formal classifications proposed. From a heuristic point of view, what interest is there in amalgamating, within the same framework, eco-system analysis (hard systemic analysis) together with the 'peasant system' (which is vaguely systemic, at best), and the 'sub-system of social organization and lifestyle' (which has nothing to do with systems, barring the vocabulary abusively applied to it)? How can one seriously maintain that the latter sub-system, 'like the others', has its own objectives, means and constraints (ibid.: 22)? This semantic exercise serves only to mask the variety of rationalities dependent on actors and circumstances. What these authors call the 'project system', which they break down into orderly symmetrical components, refers, in fact, to various, disparate levels of analysis which are not easily distinguishable when confined within systemic metaphors: the written project and its coherent arguments have nothing to do with the project as an institutional reality operating in the field, with its infrastructure, personnel, organization chart, nor, indeed, with the project as a system of action, that is, as the end product of the way actors behave. At this level of execution, we are faced with a range of problems which cannot be forced into a systems analysis pattern: the corruption of local civil servants, the career plans of project leaders, hierarchical antagonisms and conflicts between international experts and national civil servants, the race for material benefits, moralistic activism, political ideologies, etcetera.

Attempts have been made, within the systems analysis paradigm itself, to arrive at a more flexible type of systematization, capable of taking into account the 'non-system' aspects of social reality (soft system approach, critical systems analysis: see Mongbo and Floquet, 1994), such as conflicts, power struggles or symbolic resources. But why go to all this trouble? Wouldn't we save a lot of argumentative energy if we simply abandoned the systemic paradigm? It is interesting to note that two of the authors of the 1979 AMIRA text produced a new methodological text a few years later (Gentil and Dufumier, 1984) in which they abandoned systematization as a whole, in favour of a refined and more tempered analysis which reserves the term system, without excluding the use of other terms, to productive systems: agricultural system, cattle rearing system, productive system and agrarian system. But the definition of the latter as 'the series of relations between systems of production, social organization and data on external constraints' is evidence enough of the extent to which the meaning of the word 'system' tends to become vague, hence almost useless. The same phenomena can be observed in Friedberg, who attempts to keep the 'system' as a concept of central importance while at the same time draining it of all meaning, seeing that he limits the term either to the relational context of actions (Friedberg, 1993: 223) or to the observation of order and regularity of actions (ibid.: 226, 243). And he ultimately defines the system as 'an empty shell to which content and precision must be given (it is what actors make it out to be)' (ibid.: 225).

Hence, either the term is discredited, and becomes a kind of cliché that we all use distractedly – there is no concept and even less of a paradigm, and therefore no systems analysis – or one gives it credence, in which case the excessive levelling out and search for coherence operated by the 'systemic metaphor system', the exhaustive interpretation of communication flows that it aims at providing, enter into conflict with the practice of dialectical thought (to use an outdated expression which, however, has no modern equivalent), interactional analysis and the demonstration of multiple rationalities.

The current situation: multi-rationalities

Most researchers are convinced that a less pretentious approach is needed, one that is more empirical and which shows a greater awareness of the fragmentation characteristic of current social reality. This type of approach covers two complementary levels.

First, it is more localized, with a greater focus on the micro and even on the meso levels. Planetary and continental perspectives are abandoned. Its efforts at theorizing focus on the understanding, partial though it may be, of regional and sectoral phenomena, preferred over general theoretical viewpoints and dogmatic statements made out of context.

Second, the emphasis is placed on social actors or groups of social actors, their strategies, and the stakes they vie for. The elbow room available to individuals and groups within the series of constraints determined by structures is now a major object of study.

The fact that the analysis of patron–client relations or the study of social networks have regained favour since the 1980s is an important sign of this double adjustment of focus.[12] This can be read as the advent of a more interactionist kind of perspective, in that it brings the interactions between actors and groups of actors and the effects they produce, deliberately or unwittingly, into the limelight. The rediscovery of formerly classic themes in sociology and anthropology such as patron–client relations, mediators, new big men and 'brokers' is symptomatic of this interactionist tendency (see, for example, Boissevain, 1974; Schmidt et al., 1977; Rogers and Kincaid, 1981; Eisenstadt and Roniger, 1980; Bayart, 1989; Médart, 1992; Olivier de Sardan and Bierschenk, 1993). And when one sees J.P. Darré putting the study of networks at the centre of his anthropology of rural development in France, one might recall that Mitchell, one of the key figures of the Manchester School, was one of the first to study networks (Mitchell, 1969; Boissevain and Mitchell; 1973). The pieces of the jigsaw fall into place one by one. Studies in anthropology of development currently under way in Wageningen, under the direction of Long (Long, 1989; Long and Long, 1992), himself a former member of the Manchester School, also use networks analysis in their study of patron–client and brokerage relationships. As far as French Africanist studies are concerned, it is interesting to note that the new impetus given to anthropology of development was the work of former students of Balandier. In the 1950s Balandier's was the voice that opposed the invasion of Levi-Strauss's structuralism, by placing emphasis on social dynamics, diachronic thought, rifts and contradictions. He introduced the Manchester School and Anglo-American anthropology to French scientists (see Bailey, 1969).

The interactionist approach that I am defending here is a combination of the analysis of constraints and the analysis of actors' strategies, of structures and of individual or collective dynamics. The term 'interactionist' is liable to lead to two kinds of misunderstandings. First, the interactionism I refer to is not to be confused with symbolic interactionism and even less with ethno-methodology: it is more social and less generative, more polyvalent and less obsessive, more cautious and less pretentious. It takes into account interaction in general (social, political, economic, symbolic) between actors in a given field vying for given stakes (for example, related to the development process), as opposed to the grammatical and formal aspects of the definition of such-and-such a kind of interaction or such-and-such a situation existing between co-actors. On the other hand, power struggles and phenomena of inequality are not ignored; quite the contrary. The emphasis is placed on 'grass roots' actors and the room for manoeuvre available to them, without brushing aside the constraints that come to bear on them and that limit the elbow room at their disposal.

Giddens and his concept of 'agency', which may be interpreted as the capacity for action possessed by social actors or as their practical competences, come to mind (see Giddens, 1979, 1984, 1987). Long's work in particular provides a clear adaptation of Giddens's problematic to anthropology of development, which coincides at various points with the perspectives of the present work.[13]

This kind of interactionist problematic may also be seen as the result of a partial importation into anthropology of a certain type of strategic analysis produced by the sociology of organizations (Crozier and Friedberg, 1977; Friedberg, 1993)[14] or as an effect of a larger, massive, diffuse, contemporary tendency, sometimes referred to as a 'return of the actor' (Touraine, 1984; see Dubet, 1994). This return of the actor is not – in turn – guaranteed against fashion swings, semantic risks and clichés. The excessive and often unstabilized use of the word 'strategy' is one example among many others (this can be observed in Desjeux, 1987). Hence our primary objective is to work towards a conceptual clarification capable of highlighting the progress that has been made without denying the fact that many problems remain to be resolved.

Indeed, numerous obstacles still remain along the way. In particular, the problem concerning the articulation between levels such as 'macro/structures' and 'micro/social strategies' is still wide open: how are the dialectic interactions between systems of constraint (economic, political, ecological, symbolic…) and processes of adaptation, sidetracking, innovation, resistance, to be understood? Anthropology of development is still directly confronted with problems of this kind.

However, the multirationality of social actors, according to various renewable combinations, can henceforth be taken for granted. Social science has discovered or rediscovered multirationality and has restored cultural and symbolic rationalities to their rightful place alongside economic rationalities, whose importance are in no wise excluded. African societies, be they rural, urban or 'rurban', are also, perhaps even more so than some others, traversed by diverse rationalities. Their point of intersection is the best vantage point from which one may understand currently ongoing changes.

Of course, it is still normal in some respects to give priority to the logics that seem most relevant to one's particular field of investigation: economic logics when analyzing production strategies, symbolic logics when studying rituals or other religious facts. But we are well aware of the danger of overspecialization, which, from the outset, restricts the field of enquiry in the name of a pre-determined, Western-centred idea of what relevant logics are. Economic logics also come into play in rituals, and symbolic logics are also at the basis of economic behaviour. Lineage strategies, the pyramid of symbolic wealth, modes of social recognition, capitalization of power and norms of ostentation: these are examples of the recourse to rationalities which cannot be boiled down to economic strategies properly speaking, not that they abolish the latter, but they are in fact embedded in them and add to their complexity. Besides, the rationalities traversing a given rural society are not all identical, to the extent that homogenous rural African societies do not exist. Cleavages of age, gender and social status distribute economic as well as socio-political logics amongst members of a given social group. Over and beyond the variability of individual strategies, the systems of social norms vary widely from one social group to another, and not just from one 'ethnic' group to another. Such differences in the systems of norms within a given culture can in turn become the stakes around which inter-group confrontations are staged. This brings to mind the question of the ideological survival of slavery and the symbolic status of people of caste in the Sahel, and the recent opposition to this, even though the productive grounds and the relations of production to which they correspond have all but disappeared.[15]

Of course, the cumulative aspect of social science is still uncertain and contested. Though the great majority of scientists in anthropology of development take it for granted that African peasantries react, in the face of development projects, in accordance with their particular multiple rationalities and that the task of social science is to discover these, this does not mean that such a reaction is shared by all. The fact that many scientists have freed themselves from former persistent and widespread stereotypes does not mean that these have completely disappeared.

Viewed in the somewhat linear perspective of the 'history of ideas', Western conceptions of Africa – on the topic of rationality – passed through four stages: following an initial stage denying that Africans had any kind of rationality whatsoever, there was a second phase opposing African 'religious' rationalities to western 'economic' rationalities. This was followed by the discovery of technical and economic rationalities within the African peasantry, before the fourth and current phase of multirationality was reached. Nonetheless, the conceptions inherent in each preceding stage are still 'alive' today, and still structure the discourse of many actors in development (including scientists). Literary language (like that of Senghor, declaring 'emotion is black and reason Hellenic') apart, the everyday conversations (in private) of Western experts continue to repeat and to diffuse the idea that the Africans with whom they relate are, in one way or another, 'irrational'. The initial stage of Western conceptions of Africa, though currently outlawed and therefore censured in public speech, has not disappeared from the experts' mental reflexes. As for the second stage, that of the religious, cosmic, esoteric rationalities, which are supposed to be the 'essence' of the 'African mentality', these have significant outgrowths within the scientific community and serve to regulate a good number of everyday conceptions.

This rapid overview hesitates between two extremes. On one hand, a tempered optimism gives rise to a kind of history of ideas in which anthropology of development is seen as a progressive advance, albeit chaotic and uncertain, towards an increased awareness of the complexity of social phenomena. On the other, a disillusioned relativism observes the constant need to restage old battles which were supposed to have been won, and finds it deplorable that the pet exercise of the world of development and of research seems to be a constant reinvention of the wheel. After all, this kind of tension is probably inherent in the assessment of social science, and might just be the shape assumed by a combination of the 'pessimism of reason and optimism of will' evoked by Gramsci. The next chapter, for its part, will be a lot more in line with the optimism of will.

Notes

1 The term 'anthropology' replaced 'ethnology' among French researchers during the 1970s, mostly because of the colonial connotation of the latter.

2 Marx underlined this danger which he himself did not always escape: 'one must avoid making society out to be a rigid abstraction in relation to individuals' (in *Political Economy and Philosophy*).

3 See, in francophone literature, Amselle and Mbokolo, 1985; Chrétien and Prunier, 1989; Poutignat and Streiff-Fenart, 1995.

4 The term 'cultural uniformism' is sometimes used to express this ethnological tendency to underestimate sub-cultural differences: uniformism is 'a label for referring to the various descriptions and theories that are based on an idea of common, shared, homogenous culture, or on culture as *the* set of standards, rules or norms' (Pelto and Pelto, 1975: 1–2). From a methodological point of view, the recourse to 'privileged informants' incurs the risks of this kind of bias: see 'the strong tendency for key informants to assume greater homogeneity than actually exists' (ibid., p. 7).

5 Hence this sarcastic remark 'Thou shalt not articulate modes of production' (Clarence-Smith, 1985). It is possible that the concept of articulation of modes of production was meant to solve the problem of a logical contradiction in Marx's work: the dualism of social classes in the abstract analysis of a given mode of production, and their multiplicity in the concrete analysis of social formations. It had the added

advantage of finding a place within the capitalist world economy for 'noncapitalist' forms of production. Many attempts have been made to sum up Marxist economic anthropology (in its Africanist version, which is quite different from Godelier's work, for example): see especially, Bloch, 1975; Clammer, 1975; van Binsbergen and Geschiere, 1985; Jewsiewicki and Letourneau, 1985; Jewsiewicki, 1986; Copans, 1986, 1988.

6 Acknowledgement must also be made of the AMIRA group (mostly comprising economists) and certain geographers (Sautter, 1978; Pélissier 1979), whose work went along similar lines. The Ouagadougou seminar on 'Maîtrise de l'espace agraire rural en Afrique tropicale: logique paysanne et rationalité technique' (organized in 1979 by ORSTOM), is an appropriate landmark of this period of convergence.

7 A good criticism of structuralist–functionalist positions and their application to African peasantries, in terms of their resistance to change, can be found in Hutton and Robin, 1975.

8 For a general presentation of the theories of dependence see Long, 1977, and for a more detailed analysis of their Latin American forms (reformist and Marxist) see Kay, 1989.

9 See Amin, 1972. At the time this was published, I proposed a 'leftist' criticism of Amin's work, a critique at variance with the unilateral nature of theories of dependence (particularly present in Amin's work). My intention was to highlight the fact that Amin systematically ignored internal class relations in African countries and the responsibility of their dominant classes (Olivier, 1975). Though the Marxist vocabulary of this article is currently seen as outdated, even now I subscribe to the general contents, which seem in fact to have become common currency: the analysis of the role of leading classes in Africa and the mechanism of the accumulation of wealth cannot be bypassed (this is the stand taken by J.F. Bayart, 1989). External causes (to use the vocabulary of that era) act through the intermediary of 'internal causes'...

10 Hence it might be noted that Boukharine's [Bukharin's] pioneer work, which is largely unknown, written in the heat of the October revolution, already contains the germ of the contemporary systemic approach (Boukharine, 1971).

11 Röling (1987, 1991) also provides a systemic interpretation of rural development, understood in terms of communication and flow of information, an interpretation which Long (1992: 274) accuses of masking the discontinuities and the processes of transformation–reinterpretation at the centre of the results induced by agricultural extension services. Berche (1998), for his part, provides an empirical demonstration on an empirical basis of the pitfalls inherent in analysing project/population interaction in systemic terms (the case in point is a primary health project in Mali).

12 The resurgence of studies on patron–client relationships had already been remarked on, in 1980, as a sign of the decline of structural–functionalist analyses, which had exercised a hegemonic rule in anthropology, with the priority being placed on corporate, kinship and territorial groups, or in sociology with a taste for broad, universal generalizations and for theories on modernization (Eisenstadt and Roniger, 1980).

13 A work co-written by Long (Long and Long, 1992), a chapter of which has been translated into French (Long and Long, 1994, 17) bears out the point: 'Dans les limites dues à l'information, à l'incertitude et aux contraintes, (e.g. physiques, normatives, socio-politiques), les acteurs sociaux sont 'compétents' et 'capables' (Long, 1994:17);

according to Giddens, 'knowledgeability' and 'capacity' constitute the two forms of agency; see Giddens, 1984, 1–16). 'Action and power depend critically on the emergence of a network of actors who become partially, but never completely, engaged in the projects of one or several other people. The efficacy of the agency thus requires the strategic creation/manipulation of a network of social relations' (Long, 1994: 27). 'Local practices include macro-representations and are shaped by distant time-space arenas' (Long, 1992: 6–7). 'Rather than viewing intervention as the implementation of a plan for action it should be visualized as an ongoing transformation process in which different actor interests and struggles are located' (ibid.: 9). It is therefore a question of developing 'theoretically grounded methods of social research that allow for the elucidation of actors' interpretations and strategies and how these interlock through processes of negotiation and accommodation' (ibid.: 5).

14 'The behaviour of actors cannot be deduced from the surrounding structures. It is in fact the outcome of a personal "bricolage", an original agency which combines elements drawn from these surrounding structures, with considerations of strategic opportunity resulting from interactions and exchange processes in which the actors are involved locally' (Friedberg: 1993, 16).

15 One could of course gain from making formal distinctions (like those of Boltanski and Thévenot, 1991) between the various principles of legitimacy at work in the interactions and conflicts related to change and development, in the towns and villages of contemporary Africa, but, in my estimation, their conception of different 'cities', defined as conceptual, social and material worlds, each based on a specific legitimacy, is too rigid, abstract and systematic to be able to account for strategic interplay between rationalities and legitimacies staged in local arenas.

4
A Renewal of Anthropology?

This chapter is solely concerned with the 'fundamental' aspect of the anthropology of social change and development; it does not take 'applied' anthropology into account (this will be discussed in Chapter 13). Our opening hypothesis is as follows: *anthropology of social change and development represents an important stake for anthropology and for sociology in general, and even for social science as a whole.* In this context, I prefer to make specific reference to anthropology for two reasons. The first is that anthropology, whether academic or journalistic, appears at first glance to be less concerned than sociology with the processes of social change and with development facts. The second is that anthropology of development derives most of its methodological tools from general anthropology (to which the Chicago School of so-called qualitative sociology owes its inspiration). However, one could also make a more or less similar demonstration, along parallel lines, on the subject of sociology.

One might adopt one of two attitudes regarding the relationship between the anthropology of social change and development and classic anthropology. The first is a simple, defensive reaction begging for a rehabilitation of the anthropology of social change and development presented as the 'rejected branch' of academic anthropology. In this case, the appropriate reaction would be to criticize Lévi-Strauss's comments and the condescending distinctions that he establishes between 'pure' anthropology (his own) and 'diluted' anthropology, that is, anthropology of development (see Martinelli, 1987). One could then go on to demand that anthropological studies about the way villagers react to an irrigation programme, about conflict between herdsmen and cultivators or urban delinquency, be put on the same academic footing as studies on kinship or cosmogony … However, the danger incurred here is that of lapsing into the whining corporatism of a rejected sub-discipline. This reaction is doubtlessly understandable and certainly legitimate, but it is nonetheless most likely to amount to nothing.

The second solution, which is at the same time more startling and more complex, would be to consider anthropology of social change and development as a potential source of renewal of anthropology and social science.

To the rescue of social science?

I would like to propose the following three-point summary of a familiar situation, the details of which cannot be dwelt on at the moment.

(1) The crisis of social science is often discussed. It is possible to list its various symptoms, which do not all intersect and which fail to be equally convincing: the collapse of global systems of interpretation, delivered 'key in hand'; conflict between an endless pile of monographs and case studies, on one hand, and unbridled comparative essayism on the other; conflict between an exaggerated quantitative orientation and an excessively qualitative and/or speculative bent.

(2) Social science turns increasingly to anthropology as a *recourse* because of the heuristic and methodological qualities that anthropology has or is thought to have. These scientific demands made by various disciplines – sociology, geography, history, social science… – can be generally observed either as an 'anthropologization' of scientists from these fields or through an increase in the number of anthropological references to be found in related disciplines. Many historians now claim to practise 'historical anthropology', while political scientists interested in 'popular political action' seem to be a lot more familiar with ethnological literature than many ethnologists (see Bayart, 1989, 1992).

(3) Unfortunately, 'mainstream' anthropology, at least as it now stands, is not in a position to direct this kind of dialogue or to respond to such expectations. The most dynamic and innovative areas of this discipline are not necessarily those that determine the way anthropology is viewed from the outside: the weight of academic traditions, the permanence of culturalist traditionalism, the exaggerated hegemony of structuralism in France, the constant danger of 'exotic' deviations, the recent vogue of 'deconstructionist' and 'textualist' trends all come to mind as alternative influences.

Based on such evidence, we could propose the following hypothesis, which is, admittedly, a rather voluntarist one:

The processes of social change and development provide anthropology with new objects and new questions. By this means, they can contribute to a partial renewal of the problematics not only of anthropology, but also, through it, those of sociology and other social sciences.

In order to understand the processes of social change and development, anthropology must develop a number of new concepts, elaborate a couple of new strategies of investigation, create a new methodological apparatus. These, along with the many valuable tools anthropology has already acquired, are needed for an understanding of the phenomena of change. For example, neither the technique of the favoured informant nor structural analysis are appropriate methods for apprehending the processes of social change. On the other hand, so-called qualitative approaches or 'participatory observation' seem to be essential to the treatment of such questions.

But how can we be so optimistic about the heuristic capacities of the anthropology of social change and development? Could this optimism be due to the nature of its object of study?

The 'properties' of 'development facts'.

One can attribute four major 'properties' to the processes of social change and development which influence the very perception of the anthropologist himself:

First, the processes of social change and development inevitably involve relationships between *heterogeneous* norms, cultures and sub-cultures, heterogeneous value systems, heterogeneous structures of knowledge and conceptions, heterogeneous systems of action, heterogeneous logics and heterogenous social systems.

However, most of the objects of classic anthropology do not intersect in this manner. Classic anthropology picks out objects which highlight permanence, homogeneity and coherence.

On the contrary, such a confrontation of heterogeneous, divergent, dissimilar, contradictory elements is at the centre of the anthropology of social change and development. The latter is necessarily an anthropology of syncretism. The complex interaction between these heterogeneous elements is at the very centre of the object construction peculiar to the anthropology of social change and development. Anthropology of development is therefore obliged to take interest not only in 'local communities' and 'target populations', but also in frameworks of intervention, mediators and brokers, as well as external agents.

This is where phenomena of confrontation, negotiation, rejection, sidetracking, accommodation, subversion, power struggles, compromise and transaction come into play... Whether these phenomena are perceived on a cognitive, economic, political or symbolic level is of little importance: they tend to be unavoidable in the field of anthropology of development. They are not frequently encountered in classic anthropology.

Such notions are intrinsic to development facts in Africa, and are increasingly present at the centre of most contemporary social phenomena.

The second major property of the processes of social change and development is that they mobilize intermediary, informal, *transversal,* structures: networks, affinities, patron–client relationships, local, social, professional and kinship relationships … These cannot be studied on the basis of a more-or-less Durkheimian conception of institutions, on which basis anthropology has written many a chapter of its monographs: power, kinship, religion etcetera. Classic anthropological preference for corporate groups and villages leaves hardly any room for the description of the more fluctuating, ambivalent, adjustable social frameworks that come between actors and the established order. In this field, once again, a certain kind of anthropology and of sociology are indissociable. Indeed, interpersonal relationships, be they 'egalitarian' or 'hierarchical' do not disappear upon modernization – quite the contrary – and bureaucratic rationality is far from being a regulator of African administration.

Third, the processes of social change and development are *diachronic* by definition. This is one aspect of the matter that classic anthropology (functionalism, culturalism, structuralism, symbolism …) too often neglected, due to a marked tendency to throw away the baby of history with the bath water of evolutionism.

Fourth, the processes of social change and development are situated at the *interface* between anthropology and 'macro' sociology, on one hand, and ethnography and 'micro' sociography, on the other. That is to say, between structural contingencies and the action of social agents. The facts of social change and development highlight not only external constraints but also the autonomy or capacity for innovation (or resistance) of individuals and local groups.

Once again, classic anthropology tends, on the contrary, to stress the autonomy of cultural systems, thus erasing the effects induced by broader contexts and by the creative 'bricolage' of social actors.

Two heuristic points of view

These four properties which characterize social change and development throw light on the relationship between social sciences and two major 'heuristic perspectives' (often called, I would say misnamed, paradigms), between which they oscillate continuously. And it is perhaps owing to this that the anthropology of social change and development is able to play a part in clarifying certain recurrent epistemological debates, which go beyond anthropology itself. I would like to make a very brief reference to two dominant heuristic perspectives: holism and methodological individualism.

Anthropology as a holistic point of view

Within the realm of social sciences, anthropology is often credited with a holistic or global point of view. It is true that the feeling that society is more than the sum of its parts is also shared by the founders of sociology and by many of their successors. However, anthropology seems to bring its specific methods of fieldwork to the aid of holism. Intensive, long-term, real-life enquiries seem particularly appropriate for a proper grasping of reality in all its dimensions, and therefore in its globality.

Anthropology of social change and development draws on this holistic perspective. It pinpoints the fact that the multiple, conflicting logics involved in 'development' processes are not due simply to the existence of different groups of actors (and refer, in part, to conflicting collective rationalities), but also mobilize various registers of social reality, which have to be considered simultaneously. Practices and conceptions are always at one and the same time economic, social, political, ideological, and symbolic.

Anthropology of social change and development owes an important debt to Polanyi (1983), to the extent that he placed great emphasis on the notion of the embeddedness of the economy into social life as a whole.[1] This thesis has been developed in recent times through a variety of formulations, from Hyden's unfortunate attempts on the subject of the 'economy of the affection' (Hyden, 1980, 1983) to Thompson's (1971) and Scott's (1976) earlier and more prudent theses concerning the 'moral economy'.[2] Their common intention is to take into account, *simultaneously*, the various levels of social reality, as perceived by cultures, sub-cultures and social actors. Special emphasis is placed on the fact that the classic economic phenomena (production, exchange, and consumption of wealth and services) that are generally involved in 'development' processes cannot be arbitrarily isolated from their social dimensions (for example, cleavages of age, gender, status, condition, class), their cultural and symbolic dimensions (norms of respectability, modes of social recognition, criteria of prestige, solidarity and achievement), their political dimensions (patron–client relationships and factions, neo-patrimonialism) or their magico-religious dimensions (for example, accusations of witchcraft). This is therefore an obviously holistic and eminently positive perspective.

However, anthropology of development needs to break away from another type of holism: the type that considers society as a coherent and homogeneous whole, regardless of the characteristics attributed to this whole, that is, whether or not it is seen as despotic and 'totalitarian', or fraternal and egalitarian. This is the case with classic structural–functionalism and it is also the case with Marxism; both of these, for different reasons, hold that behaviour simply reflects the system, that positions are simply positions within a social structure. This is also the case with 'culturalism' which reduces all societies (along with their various groups and sub-cultures) to 'one' system of cultural values, or even to a 'national character' or 'basic personality', if not to a 'habitus'.

We are therefore confronted with two types of holism. The first is transversal and multidimensional. The second is a hypertrophied version of the social totality, of the structure of the system, of the whole. In order to differentiate between the two, one might speak in terms of 'methodological holism', in the first case, and of 'ideological holism', in the second.

Development facts dictate the use of methodological holism and the rejection of ideological holism.

Anthropology as a highlighting of actors' strategies

This second heuristic point of view is usually associated with what has been called 'methodological individualism'. It is found not only in sociology (see Schelling, 1973, 1980; Boudon, 1984, 1988, among others) but also in anthropology (Barth, 1981) and in a field that is very close to the one in which I am working at present, situated on the borderline between economic anthropology and political science (Schneider, 1975; Popkin, 1979; Bates, 1987). It is often a reaction against one aspect or another of the preceding point of view, which reaction could therefore be interpreted as a rejection of what we have just termed 'ideological holism'. Structural–functionalism or Marxism are thus blamed, and not without cause, for failing to take into account the existence and the importance of informal organizations (friendship, networks, alliances, coalitions), for overlooking the fact that social actors are entrepreneurs who manipulate personal relationships to arrive at their own ends, for neglecting the incessant material or symbolic 'transactions' that go on between individuals (see Boissevain, 1974: 3–33). The resulting research programme feeds on the insufficiencies of ideological holism and readily declares that 'social change should be analysed as the result of a series of individual actions' (Boudon, 1984: 39). But methodological individualism is neither monolithic nor univocal. It might be better to break down this expression, as has been done with holism, by differentiating between 'methodological individualism proper' and 'ideological individualism', with which it is abusively amalgamated under the term 'methodological individualism', as used by its defenders and its detractors alike, who combine and confuse these two dimensions.

Anthropology of social change and development is 'actor-oriented' (Long, 1977). It gives priority to the conceptions and actions of actors at the base and 'consumers' of development.[3] To this end, it tends to pinpoint their strategies, even under constraint, and the room for manoeuvre at their disposal, however minute, as well as their agency. It underlines the logics and rationalities that determine their conceptions and behaviour. It emphasizes the existence of real spaces of decision-making at all levels, as well as the choices that individuals make in their own name or in the name of institutions of which they consider themselves to be the delegates. This 'heuristic point of view' can thus be placed under the heading of methodological individualism properly speaking. It helps us to avoid taking the aggregates produced by social science (society, culture, ethnic group, social class, family system, mode of production, socio-professional category ...) for collective subjects, with a will of their own, and wards off the danger of reification and determinism inherent in the manipulation of such concepts.

However, the anthropology of social change and development does not presume that the social actor has only one single rationality, based either on the neo-liberal pattern or on several of its more circumspect versions (such as Simon's 'limited rationality', 1957), nor does it support the notion of a single formal principle at the centre of all logics of specific action. Actors' strategies are not just about 'mastering zones of uncertainty' or maximizing the relationship between ends and means. 'Real-life' actors, be they individuals or collectivities, navigate between several logics, choose between various norms, manage multiple constraints, are at the crossroads between several rationalities and live in a mental and material world woven with ambiguities and ambivalences, in the sight of other people, in quest of their recognition or in confrontation with their antagonism, and under their multiple influences. In this respect, anthropology of social change and development cannot accept ideological individualism, disguised as what its supporters refer to – incorrectly – as methodological individualism.

These two methodological points of view, holism and methodological individualism, are not at all incompatible; they are not opposed to harder research paradigms (or to paradigms in general) and can, to my mind, be combined with the former (unlike their respective 'ideological' counterparts). Other similarly complementary methodological perspectives could be added to these.[4] Methodological populism, which is particularly relevant to the anthropology of social change and development, will be examined later (in Chapter 7).

The anthropology of social change and development does not have a monopoly on the use of these 'heuristic points of view' which are obviously held in common by the social sciences in general. However, in the actual situation of the social sciences, it is particularly well placed to benefit in terms of innovation.

Anthropology of social change and development and the fields of anthropology

The advantages provided to the anthropology of development by its object can only be understood within the context of the anthropological patrimony whose multiple heritages can and must be assumed. The sub-divisions within the field of anthropology must, of course, be relativized (see above): oppositions like that between 'social' anthropology and 'cultural' anthropology, for example, are part of the history of anthropological ideas, but make very little epistemological sense at present. The boundary between anthropology and sociology must, of course, be disregarded. However, anthropology of social change and development is as much an heir as it is a pioneer. It inherits various layers of contributions which can be classified under four headings: religious anthropology, economic anthropology, political anthropology and symbolic anthropology.

Anthropology of social change and development and religious anthropology

In the same way that 'development', which represents a modern voluntarist method of inducing economic and social change in countries of the South, is only one of a number of simultaneous and interwoven channels through which economic and social change can pass, economic and social change are only two possible aspects of change in general, which is as much a matter of culture as of religion. Moreover, cultural and religious change also pass through more or less voluntarist and external channels (proselytism) or more or less spontaneous and internal ones (conversion). There are certainly privileged areas in which change is more visible and more impressive than in others. The religious domain, which is nevertheless the domain in which patrimonialist and backward-looking ethnology prospered, is also the field in which anthropology of social change was most massively and spontaneously involved. Religious change gave rise to countless anthropological works. Hence, religion is one of the major and most fertile sources of inspiration for the anthropology of social change and development. Missionary enterprises, new syncretic cults, prophetic movements, the transformation of traditional magico-religious systems (possession cults, masks, ancestor cults, etcetera), the recent arrival of Western and Eastern sects, the production of new clergies: these phenomena come to resonate with the processes of economic change and the facts of development. Similar if not identical processes can be brought to light. The actors of religious change are also the actors of economic change.

Anthropology of social change and development and economic anthropology

As mentioned above, economic anthropology left behind a great number of achievements, which we should not forget under the influence of new trends. Three heritages intersect, sometimes in terms of competition, sometimes in terms of mutual support: the 'open-ended' question of the articulation between economy and society, which, in the wake of Polanyi and the debates about 'moral economy', emphasizes the social and cultural norms that come to bear on economic behaviour; the analysis of 'peasant rationalities', which puts the priority on the search for specifically technical and economic logics and coherences; Marxist anthropology, of a more morphological order, which makes an inventory of social classes and articulates the modes and relations of production. These heritages must all be taken into account in the analysis of social change and development.

Anthropology of social change and development and political anthropology

Classic political anthropology frequently placed the priority on visible and institutional forms of power and on 'traditional' political structures, viewed in terms of stability, but it has also accumulated valuable knowledge on the means of acquiring notability, on village patron–client systems, on the relationship between seniority and authority or gender, on the interrelations between power and the supernatural, on the transformation of pre-colonial political structures, on the power struggles among kin and on related strategies of alliance, as well as other subjects of which we must be aware in order to understand how development action is integrated into the rural political game.

Anthropology of social change and development and symbolic anthropology

Finally, the anthropology of social change and development is to a great extent an anthropology of conceptions. Reflection on the cultural codes based on which the actions proposed and the actors who propose them are analysed, on the popular knowledge onto which technico-scientific knowledge is supposed to be grafted, on the semiological configurations that organize the fields in which change is projected is proof enough. While avoiding the exaggerations of ethno-science and of symbolic interactionism, it is essential to attach the utmost importance to 'emic' conceptions, 'modes of indigenous thought', 'local life-worlds', indigenous 'ways of thinking'. These are, in a manner of speaking, the stock in trade of anthropology, and the well from which knowledge about the way in which processes of social change are perceived and experienced by the actors concerned can be drawn. This is a prerequisite for their comprehension and interpretation.

An important precondition must be fulfilled, however, before we can come into this anthropological inheritance: the taking into account of all the actors involved in the interactions linked to change and to development, in other words, not only 'grassroots' actors and those originating in indigenous societies, but also external actors, regardless of their level of intervention, be they 'national' developers or foreigners, bureaucrats or technicians, agents of the state or agents of international organizations, enterprises or private economic operators, religious or lay missionaries. They are all involved in religious anthropology, economic anthropology, political anthropology and symbolic anthropology.

The various anthropological traditions must, of course, undergo some amount of renovation, and frequently need to be invested with a new dynamism and a sense of history. But they remain essential. It is by revising and re-evaluating them, rather than ignoring them, that a fruitful combination of empirical enquiry and 'heuristic viewpoints' can be achieved, and that the anthropology of social change and development might, owing to the material for analysis provided by the process of social change and development, thus make a small contribution to the renewal of anthropology and social science in general.

Notes

1 But Polanyi reserved the notion of embeddedness (incorrectly, I think) to pre-capitalist economies. Current works analysing the function of 'real' markets, quite distinct from the neo-liberal norm of abstraction (see Watts, 1994) merely extend Polanyi's intuition to modern economy (see also Granovetter, 1985).

2 On the extensive anglophone debate on the 'moral economy', see, among others, Popkin, 1979; Hunt, 1988; Lemarchand, 1989, as well as my criticism of Hyden's thesis in Chapter 5, below (see pp. 79–80).

3 It is obvious that actors, as considered here, are social actors and not abstract subjects, ethereal atoms, isolated and calculating individuals. They are socially situated and have unequal resources, they are integrated into special networks, and they are subjected to various contingencies.

4 This resolutely eclectic stand is obviously utterly different from Bourdieu's, whose intention is to 'go beyond' the antagonism between holism and methodological individualism, through the creation of a new system, his personal invention of a global theoretic construction which refuses to be dissociated, and demands instead to be accepted in its systemic coherence (Bourdieu, 1992: 21). I think, to the contrary, that it is impossible to 'go beyond' these two heuristic points of view. They can, however, be combined, on the condition that we are allowed to divide them into different components (methodological and ideological, for instance). The dissociation of aggregate sets or systems, including Bourdieu's, in social science as in development, is, to my mind, a healthy practice and should not be prohibited.

5
Stereotypes, ideologies and conceptions

We can begin this chapter with the following eye-opening observation: those who intervene in development, that is to say development agents in general (or 'operators'), regardless of their field of intervention or their origin (locals, expatriates ...), when applying in the field (in African villages) the technical methods acquired through training – and taking for granted that they are undeniably competent in their particular discipline (which is often the case) – are confronted with a shocking reality: the behaviours of the people with whom they enter into contact (their 'clients' in a sense, or their 'patients') do not coincide with their expectations.

This perception of the discrepancy between expected or desired attitudes and the 'real' attitudes of 'target populations' is an experience – often traumatizing and usually painful – to which, I think, all development practitioners have been subjected, to various degrees.[1] The problem resides less in the discrepancy itself (which is unavoidable, as we shall see) than in the way in which interveners react to it: how they adapt (or fail to adapt), how they integrate (or fail to integrate) it, how they explain (or fail to explain) it. I would like to dwell on this last point by putting the emphasis on the phenomena which enable us to understand this discrepancy, and so avoid 'false explanations' like 'they are backward', or 'it's because of their culture' (where 'culture' can be replaced by 'mentality', the explanation remaining the same, which is to say that there is no explanation). Such pseudo-explanations are all too often resorted to in an attempt to justify the routinization of development operators' practices, their resignation when confronted with certain realities that they consider to be much too complex, their constant repetition of the same mistakes, or their attitudes, which reveal a lack of inventiveness or an unwillingness to adapt.

This boomerang effect of 'reality' on development practitioners corresponds, in fact, to two causes which are very simple in their principle:

(1) People do not react as expected because the expectations regarding their behaviour are misguided. In other words, development agents have erroneous and 'biased' conceptions about African populations.

(2) People do not act as expected because they have good reasons for not doing so. In other words, the logics of 'clients' and those of 'sellers' do not coincide. Peasants make use of the services, opportunities and constraints supplied by development institutions according to norms that differ from those of these institutions. Nevertheless, their use of these services remains coherent.

This second point will be developed later on (see Chapter 9). This chapter will concentrate on the first point, which takes into account the conceptions of the actors involved in development, namely how they perceive development in general, how they perceive development projects in particular, and, finally, how they perceive the other actors involved. This is not only a question of ideology (see Dahl and Hjort, 1985). As soon as the question of development, and even more so that of 'development policy' is raised, the usual reaction is to put the emphasis on 'ideologies' – that is, on grand, explicit options (theories or policies, or even philosophies) on which diverse 'theories of development' are grounded and which guide or propose to guide current economic policies, or aim at generating alternative policies. The anthropology of development is interested in the more-or-less latent conceptions that predominate among the actors involved: the way in which land-holders see European experts, as well as the way in which extension workers involved in agricultural innovation perceive notables, or the way in which technical assistants view the local administration ... In fact, reciprocal social conceptions constitute the basic data needed for understanding individual strategies as well as their interaction, in other words, the 'policy game' that a project represents. The development configuration is shaped by conceptions that tend to conceal this 'policy' of interactions, and to make room for simplistic and mistaken images of 'target populations'.

Obviously, the same can be said about the conceptions that target populations have of development operators. Unfortunately, this is one area in which very little has been done by way of enquiry. Nevertheless, this type of approach is indispensable: one readily imagines that the reactions of a population (or certain sectors of a population) to an external intervention or to a 'development proposal' are partially structured by the way in which those concerned see interveners or proposers, by the suspicion they have concerning them, or by the hopes invested in them. Peasant clearly have very vivid 'recollections' of the preceding development projects carried out in their vicinity. These influence their reaction to subsequent development operations. On the contrary, development operators have less of a tendency to remember, and readily act as if they were arriving on unfilled ground. It is an acknowledged fact that the projects of the years directly following political independence, calling for 'human investment' and guided by a 'progressive' ideology based on 'participation', were seen by villagers as renewed forms of colonial forced labour. However, efforts must be made to avoid a romantic or dewy-eyed interpretation of popular conceptions about the developmentalist configuration. The way developers view developees is neither more accurate nor less biased than the way in which developees view developers. Numerous examples can be put forward to illustrate the misunderstandings, productive (Sahlins, 1989) or otherwise, that shape the perceptions that the various actors and social groups, placed in relationship by development action, have of each other.[2]

Nevertheless, this situation is not entirely symmetrical.[3] Popular conceptions of development operations are localized, by definition, and linked to specific contexts: it is difficult to sketch out a typology due the scarcity of case studies. Conversely, the conceptions existing within the developmentalist configuration are generally shared and relatively independent of the specific context. They are therefore well known and standardized. Thus, it is possible to attempt an interpretation of a few of their invariants. They are dominant and structure in part the orientation, conception and execution of development actions. However, they are not development *ideologies* in the classic sense of the word. These are expressed through a self-proclaimed 'rhetoric' and/or 'policy' of development: autocentric development, sustainable development, decentralization, structural adjustment, self-promotion, etcetera. But above and beyond such explicit ideologies, it is possible to point out the existence of a *meta-ideology* of development (that is, a latent common foundation, beyond ideological divergence), as well as *infra-ideologies* of development (that is, recurrent figures, which, when combined or opposed to each other, cut across ideologies). Meta-ideologies or infra-ideologies are so many preconceptions that are handed around within the developmentalist configuration, and which anthropology of development must avoid in order to produce new knowledge.

A meta-ideology of development

Two paradigms which appear to be intricately linked provide an overall justification of the professional practices of developers, regardless of their ideological, moral or political orientations:

(a) Development seeks the welfare of others (the altruist paradigm). Hence its strong moral connotation.

(b) Development implies technical and economic progress (the modernist paradigm). Hence its strong evolutionist and technicist connotation.

All development interventions are based, more or less, on these two paradigms. Everyone (whether World Bank expert or humble NGO activist) is convinced that his or her efforts serve the welfare of the populations, and everyone is convinced that the competence he or she employs in this noble task (be it in specialized tropical agro-forestry or in a somewhat vaguer and more nebulous domain like 'community development') is beyond the current capacity of these populations. Individual interpretation of these paradigms, the sauce with which they are served, the means by which individuals justify the particularity and originality of their personal policy, as opposed to those of their competitors, are all unimportant. The essential fact is that these paradigms are inescapable.

This is not the proper place to enter into a criticism of the above-mentioned paradigms. It will suffice us to observe that they do exist, without making any kind of value judgement. I would prefer to avoid the pitfalls of a certain kind of development sociology, which is characterized by a strong ideological and weak empirical bent, and which feeds on the vehement denunciation of the developmentalist ideology, thus setting itself up as a counter-ideology (see Latouche, 1986). The point to note is that what the altruist paradigm and the modernist paradigm – under various latent forms, of course – have in common is that both constitute an almost unavoidable reservoir of justifications. However, this meta-ideology partially overshadows the fact that development is both a market and an arena. It is a market in which goods, services and careers are put into circulation … It is a question of 'selling' projects, slogans, policies, hardware, software, careers … Humanitarian aid has obviously become a 'market' in which NGOs compete with and rival each other. Long before the present day, and on a smaller scale, 'development' was already a *market*. But it is also an *arena*. Various social actors, situated on the same stage, vie with each other for stakes of power, influence, prestige, celebrity and control. Altruistic and evolutionist visions of development incur the enormous risk of clouding this aspect of the matter. This does not imply that NGO activists do not have moral motivations or that we suspect promoters of self-development of hypocrisy and self-aggrandisement. However, neither the tree of altruism nor the tree of technical know-how – real and respectable though they may be – should be allowed to prevent the anthropologist from perceiving the forest of the market and of the arena.

Infra-ideologies: conceptions

'Infra-ideologies' of development, as observed in development actors, entail conceptions that shape real or projected world visions. Two series of complementary conceptions exist side by side: first, conceptions of societies as they are; second, conceptions of societies as they ought to be.

1. Conceptions about what societies ought to be are particularly explicit and normative. They are composed in part of development 'theories'. They are related to the sense infused into the word *development*. It is a projection of the objectives to be attained, of the society to be built: following either the American model of society, the 'socialist' models, or alternative models such as self-management, eco-development, 'African' development, etcetera. These conceptions sometimes refer to models already in existence, sometimes to models yet to be invented (utopia). But the outlines they provide about the means of developing the ideal society are more or less vague, more or less realistic, or desirable as far as development theoreticians or development experts are concerned. Development projects do not aim only at transferring technologies and know-how: these aims are combined with attempts to transfer and to create structures and modes of organization (or social technologies) based on a social ideal to be constructed. For instance, the emphasis placed, for more than half a century, on co-operatives, or the modern equivalent, the current vogue for peasant associations, is not based on technical reasons alone. The influence of socialist ideologies and of Western Christians is clear.

2. Another type of conception, more or less related to the first, has to do with the society to be developed as it is (or rather as it is imagined to be). Many of these conceptions are usually unspoken, but they are nonetheless important. They are often 'disconnected' from academic theories, that is to say that they continue to function even when the academic theories that lent them explicit justification fall out of favour or out of use. Thus the perception of African societies as 'primitive' and 'backward' is currently forbidden in public discourse, and no longer expressed in academic works, but it nevertheless continues to shape, implicitly, the conceptions of a number of development operators (locals and foreigners alike), even though their spoken words and their writings are at variance.

But many other types of 'active' conceptions do of course exist. Most of them remain legitimate (as opposed to the 'primitive and backward peasant' syndrome) and are therefore expressed as explicit arguments in development literature. Let's take, for example, the conceptions about the African peasantry and rural areas. Five particularly characteristic 'ideal-types', among others, can be distinguished. They constitute five patterns of stereotyped conceptions which can be encountered, in varying degrees, in the conversation and writings of rural development professionals. These patterns (sometimes encountered in combination) are all prevalent …. and all false! A rigorous anthropological approach allows us to demonstrate, case by case, that these stereotypes are based on the use of partial or even marginal data, leading to selective and abusive generalization, and ultimately to a biased conception of the peasantry, comprised of romantic and deformed images of reality.

Each of these patterns is relayed or theorized by social science researchers. They do not escape from biased or a priori conceptions. At times sophisticated arguments and references are the only factors distinguishing their work from commonsense notions; they share the same clichés and preconceptions, to which they lend support and legitimacy. The five models that we will now review are not only present in the development configuration but also occupy pride of place in various anthropological works, some of which will be cited as examples.

Five stereotypes

The consensual village community

Africa, seen from its villages, is supposed to be the continent where community is the order of the day, and consensus a general rule. The individual is believed to melt or dissolve into the community. This persistent and prevailing myth of 'traditional community spirit', which supposedly continues in today's day and age, and on which, presumably, development actions can lean, is well illustrated in works like those of Guy Belloncle (Belloncle, 1982, 1985). Many sociologists and anthropologists fall for this myth.[4]

The practice of intervention in the rural milieu, by the state (co-operatives, rural training), by parastatal organizations (projects based on village groups), or by non-governmental organizations (community projects), is receptive to preconceptions of this type. 'Community development' is only one of the shapes it assumes. It has been relayed by many others. From peasant groups to village pharmacies, from co-operatives to rural associations, the favoured levels of intervention of development organizations (public or NGO) coincide in fact with those of the former colonial administrators, who sought 'collective interlocutors'. Systematic valorization of the 'village community' level is in part profoundly ideological. Reference has been made above to the debt it owes to two Western traditions, Christianity and socialism. Others have pinpointed an ethnocentric projection of British 'community development' experiences (Foster, 1962: 183–5). It also coincides with a mythification of traditional village institutions, evident in the first missionary and colonial administrators, and often copied by intellectuals and African politicians, who overestimate former solidarities in the name of an image of Africa characterized by palaver, age group and mutual assistance. They forget that in the past Africa was also characterized by war, slavery and banishment. This exotic, 'community-centred' idealization of village solidarities has served to strengthen so-called 'African socialist' politics, discourses on 'authenticity' and the goodwill of NGO activists. Paradoxically, it falls in line with the prerequisites inherent in the choice made by colonial rulers and afterwards by independent states of massive recourse to collective organization in the rural milieu. Gentil (1984) reminds us that co-operatives in Africa are primarily a product of state intervention in relation to the peasantry. Regardless of the political and ideological affiliation of government, 'mass' control by development institutions and by administrators gives priority to aggregates, villages, associations, groups and co-operatives, above all else.

Reality, however, is another matter. As a smokescreen in the face of administration, a stepping stone for emerging elites or, conversely, a means of conserving power for long-standing 'notables', an illusion or an empty shell, the peasant association is rarely the living image of egalitarian consensus, and this type of consensus is generally short-lived. Fostering collective dynamism is certainly a worthwhile objective, but it should not overshadow the full extent of the difficulty entailed in this precarious and permanently menaced enterprise. Development reveals an overestimation of the collective functions attributed to 'peasant organizations', whether incited or appealed to as interlocutors, links or intermediaries (see Esman and Uphoff, 1984). This goes hand in hand with an underestimation of the divisions between members and leaders of these organizations.

The village consensus ideology overshadows the multiple divisions and antagonisms that shape African peasantries and the collective structures that originate in them, no matter how 'egalitarian' such structures may appear at first sight to an external observer: contradictions based on status (men/women, seniors/juniors, free persons/former slaves, indigenous people/newcomers), competition regarding factors of production (control of the workforce, control of land, conflicts between cultivators and herdsmen) or disputes about power (chiefdoms, co-operatives, parties, notabilities, etcetera), or even other more fluid types of informal, interpersonal networks of rivalry (neighbourhoods, kinship, friendship or camaraderie, clienteles, factions, etcetera).[5] On the eve of colonialization, most rural African societies were already strongly hierarchical (see their tributary relationships) and individualized (see their mercantile relationships). Thus external interventions, community-centred as they aspired to be, were promptly appropriated by existing groups and intermediaries, even if they did not always play into the hands of the powerful and sometimes managed to create new spaces (see Marty, 1986; Jacob and Lavigne Delville, 1994).

The peasant as an individual petty entrepreneur

The opposite stereotype is hardly better. It is often fuelled by a justified criticism of the former. In this case, one places one's stake on an individual entrepreneur, the kind of peasant motivated by the logic of profit now back in fashion thanks to neo-liberal influence, the kind of peasant desperately sought after by projects of the pilot-peasant variety. Rural sociologists have already underlined the discrepancy between such a conception and the history of the transformation of modern countrysides in the case of the West. Its inadequacy is reinforced by the multiple and tightly interconnected levels of decision-making characteristic of rural Africa (see Ancey, 1975). The farmer (or pilot-peasant) is only one level among others, like the village and the village association. Other levels include the junior brother, the wife or wives, mothers, fathers, lineage, the age group, the religious fraternity, etcetera. It is true that, contrary to community-centred ideology, most operational decisions in the economic (or health) domains are made by specific individuals, at levels other than that of the village or so-called 'community'. However, these decisions mobilize various sets of solidarities and appeal to a variety of interests. Increase in yield or maximization of the profit generated by exploitation do not necessarily take pride of place among the concerns of peasant decision-makers, whose modes of economic action cannot be reduced to an 'investment logic' such as that postulated by Popkin: 'There is a unifying investment logic that can be applied to markets, villages, relations with agrarian elites and collective action' (Popkin, 1979: 224).

This type of logic is a good example of the dead ends that this model runs into. Often convincing when it comes to attacking idyllic visions of the peasant 'moral economy' (see above), that is, when it comes to attacking the stereotypes produced by others, it is considerably less convincing when it comes to proposing its own conception of peasant rationality, which seems tantamount to a symmetrically inverted stereotype. The peasant is described as an 'investor', seeking after individual gains (economic and political), subjecting all collective actions to a personal calculation of the relations between advantages and disadvantages. 'Village processes are shaped and restricted by individual self-interest, the difficulty of ranking needs, the desire of individual peasants to raise their own subsistence level at the expense of others, aversion to risk, leadership interest in profits and the free-rider problem' (Popkin, 1979: 38). A categorical generalization like: 'the main motivation for assuming a leadership role is not prestige but gain' (ibid.: 58), underlines the fact that this is in fact a prefabricated model.

Generally speaking, the belief (for this is what it is) that peasants who integrate the modern economy, dominated by logics of gain and profit, become 'entrepreneurs' who have broken away from so-called 'traditional' solidarities is largely belied by actual facts. This is yet another consequence of the 'great division' between pre-capitalist and capitalist societies, traditional and modern economy, which continually biases commonsense and learned conceptions alike. From Durkheim (organic solidarities) to Weber (bureaucratic rationality) and Polanyi (the great transformation), contemporary society (as opposed to 'traditional' society) is seen as being regulated by strictly economic and organizational mechanisms, related to the market or to the state, mechanisms which supposedly bring independent, rational actors into relationship with each other, with a view to maximizing their profit on the basis of financial calculations, or of their efficiency evaluated through purely functional and abstract criteria. Yet everything points to the fact that even in the heart of the big multinational enterprises or Western administrative apparatuses personal relations, clientelism, ostentation, corruption, fashion swings or symbolic legitimacies have not disappeared. Economic factors are constantly confronted with non-economic factors, bureaucratic factors with non-bureaucratic factors, though it remains true that the rules of the official game (and this is not unimportant) concentrate on agent productivity, balance sheets and stock market rates. Moreover, the search for industrial profits, improved work organization and commercial advantages is manifestly not incompatible with these 'non-economic' and 'non-bureaucratic' dimensions, which come into play even at the very heart of the world economic system and the great modern metropolitan centres.

It is therefore necessary to take into consideration the fact that in Africa as well, 'modernization' is also combined with other factors such as the discrepancy between ongoing practice and the official model, among others. The premise, which is in fact fundamentally correct, according to which Africa must be analysed in the same way as the rest of the world, without community-centred illusions, as a continent possessing 'modern' actors no less rational than others (peasants included), leads to faulty conclusions (the model of the pilot-peasant or of the neo-liberal entrepreneur), because of an erroneous conception of modernity, which has since proved bankrupt elsewhere. Modernity, entry into the world economy, the search for profits, application of economic logic, maximization of comparative advantages, commodification, are in no wise incompatible with clientelism, the establishment of personal networks, conspicuous consumption, prestige investments and redistributive practices.[6] If the resulting cocktail seems to be rather less satisfying in Africa than elsewhere (this is not the case in all areas, as is well illustrated by the sturdiness of the so-called informal sector), this is not because there is a cocktail *per se* (these are to be found elsewhere), but doubtless because of the proportions, or the shortage of certain ingredients (the current erosion of the ethic of public service obviously comes to mind), in general explicable by reference to recent history, despite a common temptation to take refuge in tradition-based explanations.[7]

The peasantry and its traditionalism

Reference to a so-called ancestral past is incredibly frequent. By dint of searching for an elusive economic actor, one ends up blaming tradition for the fact that this actor cannot be found. Superstitions, customs, mentalities are repeatedly and routinely called upon to account for the 'backwardness' of peasant populations, their inertia or their resistance to development operations. Development operators are sometimes accused of neglecting this traditionalism (that is of paying insufficient attention to 'cultural factors'). The populations themselves sometimes serve as scapegoats. But in both cases, the fact that innovation, syncretism and borrowing have always existed in rural African societies (obviously in quite different shapes from those of modern scientific and technological innovation) seems to go unnoticed. What was already true in pre-colonial times is even more true today.

Let us take the example of a Sahelian village unexposed to foreign cultures: everything seems to indicate the existence of an immemorial tradition, millet cultivated with antiquated hoes, the district chief and his courtesans, spirit possession cults ... Nevertheless, relations of production have undergone change since colonial rule. Moreover, political power is now channelled through towns, probably the place of origin of the chief, whose prerogatives are not to be confused with those of the pre-colonial emir, whose descendant he happens to be. Moreover, spirit possession cults have seen their pantheons drastically changed and their rites transformed. The contrast with Western civilization is still real, but this should not lead us to believe, under the influence of exoticism, that everything that is different is 'traditional'. On the contrary, in town as in the remotest bush, transformation, adaptation and change are the rule.

It is now frequently recognized (this is a considerable improvement) that local societies possess knowledge as well as rich and complex cultures. But the tendency is immediately to confine this knowledge and these cultures to an ahistorical, backward-looking, patrimonialist interpretation. Let us take the example of 'indigenous' therapeutic practices: the new interest accorded to these readily interprets them as vestiges of ancestral knowledge. Isn't it common practice to apply the WHO's terminology of 'tradi-practitioners' to African 'healers'? However, the therapeutic steps recommended by these tradi-practitioners (regardless of their effectiveness, which is not our concern at present) and the knowledge on which they draw, are largely unrelated to 'tradition'. Without being 'Western', they have nevertheless undergone considerable change since the nineteenth century and colonial conquest. They have integrated (and transformed) a whole series of material and symbolic elements linked to European medicine. Numerous examples can be given, from peddlers who sell amphetamines, illegally produced in the workshops of Nigeria, in markets all over Africa, to healers' associations or 'indigenous' doctors', dressed in the bureaucratic finery and using the symbolic markers characteristic of the colonial and post-colonial public health apparatus (Dozon, 1987; Fassin, 1992).

This stubborn illusion of traditionalism can be imputed to two processes:

(a) Everything in Africa that is unrelated to what is considered to be 'modern' – in the Western sense of the word – is automatically attributed to African traditionalism and linked to a cliché of ancestral Africa which purportedly manages to weather contemporary storms.

(b) Everything belonging to what is taken to be 'modern' sectors (the state, the university, technical services …), but which fails to correspond to what we could call the Western economic or political norm, is also alleged to be cultural vestiges, belonging, despite 'modern appearances', to the same old patrimonial stock. Thus certain contemporary phenomena, like corruption or nepotism, which assume original expressions in their African forms, and are closely linked to the processes of elaboration of modern African elites and to the avatars of the construction and erosion of the post-colonial state (see Coquery-Vidrovitch, 1985; Bayart, 1989), are explained away by reference to strange cultural atavisms.

The submissive and passive peasantry

'Explanations' sometimes go off in the opposite direction. Reference to tradition is avoided and the 'backwardness' of rural areas is attributed, on the strength of convincing arguments, to the domination to which they are subjected. Subjugated and helpless under the yoke of power, rural societies are progressively crushed by contemporary economic mechanisms, victims of the world market. Even on occasions when they appear to stand aloof, this is yet another deliberate blow dealt by imperialism. Marxist analyses of imperialism, or analyses influenced by Marxism, feed essentially on such pathetic images and theories of the peasantry. This perspective has been particularly developed in anthropology by Meillassoux, especially regarding the relationship between rural domestic communities and the capitalist economy, seen through more or less temporary migrations in the direction of towns (Meillassoux, 1975a). These migrations, the importance of which is recognized in the African context, are supposed to be basically due to an imperialist will to 'appropriate' a local workforce (a modern and permanent form of primitive accumulation), off the back of the 'traditional' domestic subsistence-based rural economy, which assures the production and reproduction of insecure workers who can be used at low cost in the mining and industrial sectors. 'For the capitalist to be able to derive a rent from labour, he has to find a way of extracting it without thereby destroying subsistence economy and the domestic relations of production which make the generation of such a rent possible in the first place' (ibid.: 168). In the spaces in which migrants originate: 'paradoxically, the capitalist must prevent the expansion of capitalism into the rural areas from which the labour force is drawn' (ibid.: 175). In the capitalist spaces in which migrants work: 'the turnover of labour is ensured by the discrimination which, by depriving the migrant worker of welfare benefits or job security, forces him to return home' (ibid.: 182).

Two distinct assertions can be underlined: the first is a kind of empirical observation (there is purportedly a vast permanent sector of rural self-subsistence regulated by domestic pre-capitalist relations of production), and the second belongs to the more hypothetical register of causality (this permanence is allegedly a deliberate imperialist strategy). Both registers are at fault. Meillassoux (who paradoxically coincides with Lewis's classic dualism) underestimates in this particular case the transformations that have occurred in rural areas: he ignores both colonial and post-colonial efforts to develop cultures of exportation in these zones (including those areas in which temporary migrations are still massive) and undermines the fact that the refusal to accept such cultures has essentially been the work of peasants, acting against or outside colonial injunctions.[8] Similarly, migrations are for the most part produced by internal dynamics and usually result from the local strategies of peasant youths (see Chapter 8), often resorted to in opposition to state anti-migration policies.

This kind of argument, which interprets mechanisms of domination (whose concrete manifestations are real) as the product of an implacable machinery, or as the expression of an extremely sophisticated conspiracy elaborated by an economic system endowed, almost, with a will of its own, seems oblivious of the dialectic between the actor and the system, and fails to give justice to peasants' personal initiatives. It forgets the room for manoeuvre available to petty producers, and permanent or temporary migrants, as well as their capacity to adapt and to improvise, not to mention the myriad forms of 'passive resistance' and sidetracking to which they subject public policies (ever since the colonial period) intervening in rural spaces.

The uncaptured, restive, rebellious peasantry

This is once again an inversion of the preceding argument. Peasants supposedly refuse to enter the modern market and supposedly take refuge behind self-sufficiency and ancient solidarities, as a form of resistance to the state and to the modern economy. Several authors defending such a point of view are often amalgamated under the 'moral economy' or 'economy of affection' label, despite differences in their analyses which cannot be dismissed as mere details.

Let us take the example of the works of Hyden, who invented the term 'economy of affection' (Hyden, 1980, 1983). The evocative or provocative subtitle of his first book ('underdevelopment and an uncaptured peasantry') announces his central thesis: the African traditional peasant economy has resisted capture, domination, absorption and transformation by capitalism, despite the efforts of the latter, and, on the contrary, strongly resists it. The pre-colonial mode of peasant production, inscribed in a system of solidarities, exchanges, and moral obligations based on 'affectionate' ties of kinship, provides a 'safety net' and an insurance against risks. It is still currently based on a subsistence logic, and manages to shy away from state imposition and from the influence of development institutions which promote a logic of profit and accumulation: 'a peasant mode of production is still a prevailing force on the African continent. The words *peasant mode* refer to the fact that production continues to be guided by the law of subsistence rather than the law of value' (Hyden, 1986: 685).

Here again we encounter the coexistence of assertions belonging to the registers of observation and causality. The outlines of Hyden's assertions are identical to Meillassoux's: the permanence of a traditional mode of production (peasant in Hyden, domestic in Meillassoux) non-integrated into the capitalist economy (however, justice must be given to Meillasssoux for proposing a different and subtler image than Hyden's regarding relations in the traditional sphere and in the capitalist sphere, linked to the theory of articulation as opposed to a simple theory of incompatibility). Nonetheless, the causality proposed by Hyden goes in the opposite direction: where Meillassoux saw an imperialist strategy meant to delay integration, Hyden sees peasant resistance to the efforts of integration deployed by imperialism.

These arguments are also highly questionable. In fact, the extensive debate (see Geschiere 1984; Bates, 1986; Kasfir, 1986; Lemarchand, 1989) resulting from Hyden's work is an ample illustration of the shortcomings of this author's arguments. Not only do peasants fail to elude the grip of state and to lead self-sufficient lives, their integration into exchange circuits linked to the modern economy is partly of their doing. Peasants are not rebels who triumphantly resist entry into the modern economy. Nor are they conquered rebels. In reality, they collaborate with integration either out of interest or out of obligation. Mercantile logics, profit-seeking, and the use of modern institutions are broadly familiar to them.[9]

Compared to Hyden's, J. Scott's initial analyses (based on South West Asia, but having a global ambition) seem more complex (Scott, 1976). His 'moral economy' or peasant pre-capitalist economy leaves room for internal contradictions and socio-political cleavages. The social norms regulating social relationships in rural areas are far from egalitarian. Moreover, his main reference concerns a peasantry subjected to traditional clientele relationships (Scott, 1977). Patrons, lords, aristocrats and other notables who rule over rural areas, though they sometimes levy severe tributes, provide peasants with a minimum of guaranteed subsistence, furnish a number of collective guarantees, and observe the 'safety-first principle'. The loss of this safety net, due to a dissolution of patron–client relations, to the advantage of a capitalist economy, is thought to engender peasant resistance, in the name of values formerly respected by their patrons and lords, and which are currently held in derision by the new rural entrepreneurs.

Though Scott has the merit of mentioning the various 'everyday forms of peasant resistance' (see Scott, 1985, 1986), and especially their individual, concealed, diffuse character, we cannot subscribe to his imputing these practices to a refusal of the modern economy and of the state, owing to the persistence of a superstructure of normative values formerly associated with a infrastructure of reassuring patron–client relations which no longer exist (see Geschiere's, 1984 and Lemarchand's, 1989 criticism of this). Peasant ruses, indirect tactics, pilfering, dissimulations, flights and recourse to rumour figure among the myriad forms of 'evasive strategies' (Olivier de Sardan, 1984: 186) and 'defensive strategies' (Spittler, 1979: 31) that peasants resorted to under French African colonial rule, but they are not necessarily related to a nostalgic longing after a former 'moral economy', or to rural resistance to commodification, and are not incompatible with a progressive integration into the world economy. Are not many of these reactions encountered in the heart of the informal urban economy, or even in the behaviour of numerous entrepreneurs and merchants?

In his latest work, Scott lapses into what we might call a 'resistance obsession', in his efforts to provide a systematic method of decoding, in space and time, the myriad forms of resistance 'from below' in the face of power and of the state. His efforts are oblivious to context and pay no attention to counter-examples (Scott, 1990).

It is undoubtedly unrealistic to see the peasant as a rebel, even if the term is used as praise rather than derision. Insertion into the monetary economy, commodification, integration into modern clientele systems rather than traditional ones, the interlacing of forms of production and of urban and rural revenues, not only appear obvious, but are also interiorized by most peasants, whether they approve or not.

The relative truth of stereotypes: the example of 'culture'

Obviously, this brief overview is by no means exhaustive. The scholarly conceptions that fuel the stereotypes developers have about developees are not restricted to these five categories though, in my opinion, they are the most prevalent. Moreover, these stereotypes, divergent as they may appear, enter into combination with each other in variable proportions. We have seen the extent to which various models fuel each other, *a contrario*. It is through opposition to a related stereotype that one develops one's own stereotype, and one occasionally encounters an outrageous combination of two elements diametrically opposed to each other! This is why the criticism of a given stereotype, be it scholarly or otherwise, does not necessarily mean that the opposite point of view should be systematically preferred.

By the same token, the grain of truth that a credible stereotype often contains should not be ignored. In fact, each of these stereotypes can call upon examples that support them: peasants are sometimes in consensus, they are sometimes entrepreneurs, sometimes traditionalists, sometimes submissive, sometimes rebellious … It is overgeneralization or one-sided explanation that transforms incomplete observations into unacceptable stereotypes.

At any rate, it is hardly reasonable to aim at defining the economic essence of peasantries in terms of just one principle. Let us take the case of the 'safety first' principle, which is often evoked, and not only by supporters of the moral economy, in order to justify a rebellious and/or traditionalist and/or community-centred image of rural societies, but which others invoke as the driving force of strategies that are individual, rational and calculating (see Popkin, 1979). Who could deny that the search for security regulates certain agro-pastoral choices? But is this sufficient grounds on which to claim that this is the key factor required in order to understand peasant specificity? The peasantry also has its adventurers, its gamblers and its inveterate hedonists. It is characterized by a cohabitation of various social and economic strategies. The search for a founding truth on which society or the peasant economy is constructed is clearly a search for an illusion. This remains true regardless of the scientific discipline in which this search is conducted, despite the obvious analogies between peasant societies the world over.[10] This calls to mind G. Foster and his excessively cultural model of a peasantry organized in terms of an 'image' of limited goods. This world vision is supposed to be a paradigm of peasant societies, organized in a systematically egalitarian manner, based on symbolic values that condemn all forms of individual promotion, in keeping with the principle that one can rise up in society only at other people's expense. The village is considered to be a world of 'friendly' games, played without stakes in mind. This in turn regulates peasant conceptions of wealth: allegedly, one can rise only by putting another person down (Foster, 1965). Critics of Foster's thesis point to numerous counter-examples which refute this excessive generalization.[11]

The notion of 'culture' is often used, as in Foster, to fuel the above-mentioned stereotypes. Indeed, these theses or clichés are rarely ever defended without making reference to 'culture'. It is to be noted, moreover, that outside the subject of development, among renowned sociologists – the authors of stimulating analyses – one can mark the use of 'culture' as a filter or as a mask. Thus Crozier, after providing a novel analysis of the French bureaucracy, attempts, finally, to account for its specificities and other of its characteristics that resist his attempts to account for them by invoking a 'French culture' (see Crozier, 1963: 257–323; Crozier and Friedberg, 1977: 167–91).[12]

Does this mean that we can no longer speak in terms of a traditional or of a common 'culture'? Are there no links with the past or with other people that need to be understood? Are we supposed to ban the word 'culture'? Don't people who live in the same village, speak the same language, and belong to the same rural civilization share a certain number of conceptions about the body, life, society? Don't they behave in keeping with these norms and common values, originating in the past, over and beyond variability and internal contradictions?

We are obliged to answer yes. There is an obvious stock of shared conceptions, based on a certain cultural heritage, of which language is the vector and foundation. But how can we distinguish the levels at which they appear: the village, the region, the 'ethnic group', or the 'cultural' zone? Such a definition is all the more complex as it varies according to the conceptions considered, and according to the context in question. But it is obvious that we are constantly in the presence of common conceptions, shared by groups of actors. This is precisely what the term 'culture' refers to; it is as simple as that.[13] But these stocks of shared conceptions

(a) are subject to evolution and change;

(b) do not afford equal coverage to all types of referents ;

(c) are not homogeneous;

(d) are not necessarily integrated into 'world views' and are not necessarily generated by fundamental 'values'.

These four elements, which I consider to be of particular importance, are often overshadowed by culturalist positions, explained and theorized as in the case of certain ethnologists, or implied and latent as in the case of many development operators, who believe that the shared conceptions peculiar to a given social milieu, or even more so to a given African village, are stable and ancient, exist at all levels, are homogeneous and reflect a world view cemented by common values. Conversely, the use of the word *culture* should not lead us to forget that it entails permanent dynamics of transformation of norms and concepts (that is, of everything that gives a concrete meaning to the word *culture*). These dynamics vary in form, contents and tempo, depending on the conceptions and referents in question and on the social bearers of these concepts.[14]

It is essential to distinguish between various levels of concepts. Those who overuse the word *culture* fail to do this, or do it only to a small degree.

The first, basic, level of differentiation makes sense only as an ideal-type. It compares, on one hand, the 'learned' concepts (in the 'hard' sense: sciences or theologies) peculiar to the intelligentsia, based on scientific references, inextricably linked to the debates surrounding a given orthodoxy which tends to function as a system, and, on the other hand, 'popular' concepts (broader, more diffuse, vaguer and less stabilized) which tend to organize themselves in 'configurations'.[15] But these popular concepts, which are all too frequently lumped together, can also be subdivided into several levels namely, common popular concepts, specialized popular concepts, popular sectoral concepts.

(a) There is, first, the commonsense level, the normal (socially constructed) perception of everyday reality, of 'the obvious' (Geertz, 1986; Giddens, 1987), which varies from latent and implicit codes to more conscious norms. These are largely shared by members of a given culture and differ from one culture to another. We could take the (very caricatural) example of the attitude of embarrassment in the presence of one's parents-in-law, or the joking relationship between crossed cousins or between certain ethnic groups which constitute standard customs in Africa. Europeans often refer to the subconscious while Africans refer to the 'double'. The former blame 'germs' where the latter incriminate 'bad luck', which can be either sorcery or black magic. These are examples of what we could define as 'shared popular concepts or representations'.

(b) However, these banal, everyday conceptions are not all used in the same way: certain relatively sophisticated and elaborate popular concepts are only called on, when needed, to provide a type of ready-made sense which is not required in ordinary interactions. Hence, everyone in Europe knows about the existence of 'social classes' or has some idea of what a heart attack is. Similarly, in the Sahel, everyone knows that there are various groups of spirits, and that sorcerers turn into headless donkeys ... However, these notions usually remain rather vague for most people (so long as they are not directly concerned), while certain individuals are more conversant with such notions and are therefore more competent than others in this respect. Though just about everyone roughly understands, these individuals are more skilful in furnishing definitions and in manipulating these terms than most. This is an example of what could be defined as 'specialized popular concepts': as in the case of healers, for example.

(c) Finally, we might mention a third level, comprising relatively sectoralized knowledge, in which certain conceptions are shared only by specific groups. In fact, the term 'culture' invariably conceals the fact that more or less distinguishable, independent 'sub-cultures' do exist: the most obvious example in Africa is that of 'women's cultures'; in each society, women's shared conceptual systems and the behavioural norms of women are in part different from men's, while still remaining a part of a broader, common culture. In the context of the Sahel, the sub-culture of slave descendants, the sub-cultures of professional castes (blacksmiths, griots ...) and the more unstable, fluctuating urban lower-middle-class sub-culture could be mentioned. We can perhaps speak here of 'popular sectoral concepts'.

Be that as it may, as a rule, these reservoirs of more or less common conceptions are not updated, mobilized or implemented by just anybody, any time, anywhere, anyhow or in the same way. In other words, they can be used in various ways.

The propensity for stereotypes: the example of 'needs'

To ignore these different levels, to ignore 'the dynamics of concepts' and the 'syncretisms on the move' that are manifested in them, opens the door to stereotypes. Most stereotypes are not deliberately constructed for the purpose. Notions or concepts like 'culture' become stereotypes only in consequence of the excessive use that is made of them. Conversely, certain words, of widespread use in development, have an almost irresistible tendency to turn into stereotypes. 'Need' is a very good example.

In fact, this terms aims at being 'objective' and almost scientific: 'needs' exist, of which some are readily defined as more indispensable, more inevitable than others. It is therefore necessary to 'identify' them. Isn't this an appeal for field enquiry? Moreover, the term 'needs' has the tremendous advantage of combining 'moral' and 'sociological' connotations: development must be achieved in order to satisfy the 'needs' of populations, that is, in order to serve their best interests. We could add a third (equally moral) dimension: the people concerned are the ones to state their own needs. One thus encounters a number of development ideologists who, on the strength of these three truths, go from seminar to conference boasting the merits of the type of development based on the expressed needs of the populations themselves ...

The hitch is that, as any serious ethnologist or sociologist will tell you, there is nothing vaguer, more uncertain, more imprecise or more utterly unusable than the notion of 'needs'. What is really a need, who is to define the needs of whom, how is a 'need' expressed, and to whom? Which reader of these lines is capable of giving a clear answer when caught off-guard, and even after mature reflection, to the question: 'what do you need?' And who would refrain from adjusting his answer according to his idea of the kind of 'need' the questioner might be willing to satisfy? In other words, the idea that objective needs exist, that these needs are common to an entire population, that its representatives are capable of making a spontaneous statement about these needs or of identifying them based on a consensus arrived at during village meetings, that it would then suffice to 'collect' or to give an attentive ear to these 'needs' is a misguided conception, whose shortcomings can be demonstrated by serious sociological analysis.[16] This is a example of the 'supply' producing the 'demand'. Villagers, when questioned by 'experts', civil servants and other consultants who arrive in their village to do 'rapid field studies', express 'needs' and 'demands' that are mainly determined by what they think the experts, civil servants or consultants in question are prepared to offer them. Hence, the identification of needs is merely a method of justifying, with the help of 'what the peasants say' and of hasty surveys, projects that the development operators had already, more or less, been carrying all along in their briefcases under the guise of 'offers'.[17]

So many 'rapid field studies' have been botched, so many hasty impressions have been transformed into truths 'resulting from fieldwork', so many interviews with a single individual have been dubbed 'knowledge of a culture', so many village meetings have been turned into 'needs analysis'!

Upon sound reflection, does an all-purpose expression like 'the populations themselves took charge of ...', so often pronounced by those involved in peasant self-development or self-promotion, mean anything except in ideological terms? For what is a 'population'? Who speaks in its name, or claims to represent it? What is meant by a 'collective decision'? And so on. It is by asking such questions that the anthropology of social change and development defines its space of investigation and stands apart from developmentalist ideologies.

Of course, the anthropologist cannot afford to change into a corrector of semantic errors or into a political commissioner of the discourses used in development milieus. He has empirical studies to do, positive research to get on with. But, understandably, he is liable to be irritated by the recurrent stereotypes, originating, in part, in social science vocabulary, legitimated on occasion by certain fellow scientists.

Notes

1 This shock was remarked on a long time ago and has even became the object, in psychology, of a certainly exaggerated theorization in the shape of a psychopathological syndrome (*culture shock*, according to K. Oberg) peculiar to technicians working abroad in a cultural context radically different from their own (quoted by Foster, 1962: 187–8).

2 A few revealing examples of 'erroneous' popular conceptions can be found in Berche (1998).

3 Daane and Mongbo have attempted an interesting comparison concerning the asymmetrical character of the perceptions of technical assistants, on one hand, and of certain local actors, on the other, about a given 'project': 'It is probable that some of the local actors, especially the association leaders, the bureaucrats, the merchants and the rich peasants, learn much more quickly than the technical assistants. First this is because the resources of the technical assistants are more visible and their intentions can in part be traced to official project objectives and, therefore, are more accessible than the myriad of partly hidden intentions of the local actors with their often

invisible (to the technical assistants) resources and complex history of conflicts and shifting alliances. And second, this is because it is often in the interest of the local actors partly to hide their intentions both from the technical assistants and from other local actors' (Daane and Mongbo, 1991: 69). Such particular local actors can therefore benefit from the knowledge they have of the conceptions of technical assistants: 'they will continue to pursue their own objectives, but they will do this by trying to play the game by the rules and codes of the technical assistants. They will champion their hidden parochial causes and particularistic interests using arguments based on the social justice philosophy of integrated rural development.'

4 However, it has also been regularly denounced (see, for example, Augé, 1973).

5 Here again, I am merely going over, in my own terms, ideas that have long since been expressed by others, but which have also been forgotten by many: 'Most of today's induced change is based on the assumption that groups of people will participate … This often means that if the members of one faction show interest in a new programme, the members of another faction will immediately declare against it' (Foster, 1962: 101–2).

6 See Labazée's demonstration (1994) of such a compatibility in the case of merchant–producer relationships in the north of Côte d'Ivoire (other examples are to be found in Grégoire and Labazée, 1993).

7 The 'neo-patrimonialism' described by Médart (1981), like the confusion between public property and personal wealth, is by no means specific to Africa or to 'underdevelopment' (many excellent examples of this have recently been observed in Europe), but it assumes an increased importance in Africa, where it takes on a particular hue. My analysis on this point coincides with that of Brown, who explains the specific traits of 'African bureaucracies' in relation to specific political constraints: their non-conformity to the Weberian ideal of rational bureaucracy, which happens to be more normative than descriptive, does not relegate them, for all that, to the world of 'tradition' (Brown, 1989).

8 See Chauveau and Dozon's demonstration (1985) on the subject of the development of coffee and cocoa in Côte d'Ivoire.

9 Hyden has been criticized in many other ways. Like a number of the theses discussed here (and which are in fact stereotypes), Hyden's are guilty of excessive generalization and generality. The identification of a few cases of peasant 'refusal' of the commercial agricultural sector and of peasant attachment to subsistence farming does not justify the creation of a concept like that of the 'uncaptured peasantry' or its application to the entire African continent. In the same way, the existence of networks of kinship solidarity and of permanent mechanisms of redistribution does not justify the concept of the '*economy of affection*', which recalls the consensual and traditional visions of African rural societies criticized above.

10 Dalton (1971, 1972) is one of the rare researchers to have achieved a broad-based comparison of peasant societies with hunter–gatherer societies, or with industrial societies, while avoiding many of the simplistic or monist errors inherent in such an enterprise. The characteristics that Mendras attributes to 'ideal' peasant societies (relative autonomy within a global society, the function of mediation of notables in relation to the former, the importance of the domestic group, face-to-face relationships, relative economic independence) also avoid the pitfall involved in searching for a 'peasant essence' (Mendras, 1976: 12).

11 On the debate arising from Foster's model, see Bennett, 1966; Kaplan and Saler, 1966; Piker, 1966; Gregory, 1975; Hutton and Robin, 1975.

12 Friedberg finally rejects the explanatory value of the notion of 'national culture' (1993:17), but he retains the term 'culture' in a sense that remains vague and general, at times to designate behavioural traits unrelated to rationality (Crozier and Friedberg, 1977: 54, 237), at times to evoke the way in which the framework in which actors evolve influences their actions: 'leur rationalité et leur capacité de choix sont pré-structurées par leur appartenance à des cultures (nationales, professionnelles, organisationnelles' (ibid.: 16).

13 It is clearly impossible to cite the abundant literature dealing with the numerous meanings of 'culture' in anthropological tradition: Kloeber and Kluckhohn (1952) have long since noted several hundred definitions. While keeping away from the centre of this debate and deliberately taking up a position on its periphery, I will content myself, for the fun of it, to a reference to Pascal Boyer's subtle and provoking paper 'Pourquoi les pygmées n'ont pas de culture' (Boyer, 1989).

14 In the area of concepts of health , a number of works have attempted to study the dynamics of transformation of popular concepts (Bonnet, 1988; Fassin, 1989, 1992a, 1992b; Jaffré, 1991, 1993, Olivier de Sardan, 1994; Jaffré and Olivier de Sardan, 1995, 1999).

15 Reciprocal influences and interactions do of course exist between these two broad types of culture. Moreover, learned people are also part of popular culture.

16 Criticism of the term 'needs' has long since been made. See, for example, Barnett: 'There are certain objections to the indiscriminate use of the term "need" as an explanatory concept ..., it is a much abused term ... . A group of people that we call society needs nothing because it is not an organism. It has no desires because it is an abstraction ... . It is a normative, an evaluative term with projections of arbitrary standards' (Barnett, 1953: 98).

17 For a few examples, see, among others, Bonnassieux, 1991 (on post-literacy campaign activities in Niger); Mathieu, 1994 (on NGO projects in Mali). The following quote from Foster, noted after these lines had been written but published a long time before, shows that the subject of 'felt needs' is not as novel as some would claim it to be, and simply lends legitimacy to ready-made development projects: 'Community development programs in newly developed areas pay lip service to the slogan of American community development – it becomes almost a religion – but "felt needs" usually turn out to be rather standard programs in environmental sanitation, medical services, agricultural extension and education, which are recognized – correctly, I think – by national planners as the major needs of rural areas' (Foster, 1962: 185).

6
Is an anthropology of innovation possible?

This question is already, in itself, an acknowledgement that an anthropology of innovation does not yet exist, or at least not in an obvious way, notwithstanding a few latent signs or an isolated trailblazer. The question amounts to asking whether or not there is a new anthropological 'discipline' in the making. Following on medical anthropology and industrial anthropology, can we announce the advent of innovations anthropology? Like it or not, the common anthropological connotations seem to imply that the answer is no: for isn't anthropology a science that shows more interest in traditional societies than in new worlds in the making? Doesn't it devote more time to decoding structures and invariants than in analysing innovations and emerging realities? Yet this type of response does not satisfy those who are appalled by the stereotypes that continue to be applied to anthropology, despite the fact that these are partially inscribed in its history. In Balandier's wake (see his reference to 'dynamic anthropology': Balandier, 1971: 6) many anthropologists, myself included, are persuaded that there is no reason why anthropology should not take innovation as an object: in fact, as I have often repeated above, we have long since been calling for an anthropology that accords as much importance to change as it does to permanence, that is equally interested in ruptures and in patrimonies. This is not a recent concern: before the Second World War, Malinowski already noted 'the fiction of the "non contaminated" native must be left on the outside of field research and study. It is an irrefutable fact that the "non contaminated" native does not exist' (Malinowski, 1970: 19).

The real problem probably resides less in the word *anthropology* than in the word *innovation*: is innovation an appropriate social science object, that is, does it define a field of research liable to generate new knowledge and/or to reorganize existing knowledge? This question must in fact be asked at the social science level: if we admit the profound unity of the social sciences, and if we declare with Passeron (1991) that, from an epistemological point of view, history, sociology and anthropology are inseparable, it then follows that if innovation is an appropriate object for one of these disciplines, it is appropriate for all.

But to provide a statement of the question, in the form of an overview of the relationship between social science and innovation, is a gigantic task and one which is beyond my ability. I will therefore concentrate on a more modest objective, namely the exploration of a few 'points of view' related to innovation in sociology and anthropology. In the present case, the term 'point of view' seems more appropriate than 'paradigm', which is either too 'rigid' or overused. Hence, I will restrict the subject even more by limiting myself to agro-pastoral innovation in particular. Of course, we could make profitable mention of other types of innovation, such as religious innovation or political innovation, while considering the way in which the same 'points of view' have possibly been used concerning objects as dissimilar as the emergence of a new type of chiefdom or the appearance of a new cult: but this would take us too far afield. As far as a definition, if only temporary, of innovation is concerned, Schumpeter's classic definition may suffice: any new combination of means of production (Schumpeter, 1934). We could also enter into the definitions game and propose our own: I readily accept as innovations any grafting of technique, knowledge or hitherto unused mode of organization (usually in the form of local adaptation, borrowing or importation) onto previously existing techniques, knowledge and modes of organization.[1] But this hardly matters: what is important is to avoid restricting the sense of the word *innovation* to mean invention, and especially technical invention, and to avoid restricting oneself to the misguided indigenous/exogenous or innovation/borrowing debate (see Balandier, 1971). It would be better to consider innovation as a social process (innovation could, for example, be analysed as an 'elementary' form of change).

Be that as it may, I would like to sketch a clear framework of discussion: not only do I intend to sidestep the risks inherent in establishing a statement of the question, I will further confess a number of omissions, for purely practical reasons, especially as regards entire sections of the social sciences to which innovation is of great importance. Thus, I will not attempt to lay the foundation for a general history of social science ideas on innovation, from Tarde to the present: this task is beyond my capacity. Nor will I refer to Leroi-Gourhan (1964), however interesting his comparative macro-anthropological study of the evolution of technologies or his micro-ethnological studies of the modification of an operational chain may be. Nor, among other reasons because of the complexity of the theoretical problems it entails, will I expound on the new sociology of science and technologies, which, with Latour and Callon, analyses the process of the social, political and semantic construction of innovation, in the laboratory and in the environment alike (Callon, 1988; Latour, 1989). Finally, I will not make any excursions into certain related social sciences, sometimes referred to as 'applied' – 'educaional science', 'communications science', marketing, and 'extension science' (a kind of combination of all of the preceding, directly related to agro-pastoral innovation) – despite the fact that they could teach us a lot on the subject.

A panorama in four points of view

Before proposing a few general ideas on the possibility of an innovations problematic in anthropology, I would like to mention four 'points of view' on agro-pastoral innovation, which, I think, define the contours of most of the statements that anthropology produces on the subject of agro-pastoral innovation: the latter has been considered sometimes as a process of social diffusion, sometimes as a phenomenon of social indexing, sometimes as the end product of popular creativity, and sometimes as the result of reinterpretations.

Innovation as a process of diffusion

This point of view has the strength of evidence in its favour: innovation is, as it were, naturally diffused, regardless of its point of origin: from North to South, from one region to another, from research centres to peasants, from one civilization to another, history and archaeology, in particular, have, since the outset, been associated with a 'diffusionist' perspective, incorporated into a kind of comparativism related to the processes of diffusion of techniques, the processes of diffusion of knowledge and even to the processes of diffusion of structures.

In sociology as in anthropology, the diffusionist viewpoint can be broken down into three components: two successive and somewhat dated anthropological 'points of view' and a more recent sociological paradigm (that is, diffusion studies, a research programme that is sufficiently coherent to justify the use of this term).

The first anthropological point of view: classic diffusionism at the beginning of the twentieth century

I will ignore European diffusionism, especially that emanating from Germany, around Grabner and his theory of cultural circles, which was often general and speculative, and thus of little interest for our purpose, in favour of its American counterpart, which was a lot more involved in empirical data collection, and paid attention to the diffusion of innovations or packages of innovations among North American Indians. Its output included studies of the 'maize complex' and the 'horse complex' (and, in a similar vein, but on the subject of ritual innovations, which I have refrained from analysing here, the diffusion of the 'sun dance').

The interest of this kind of diffusionism is that it falls in line with what we could call a 'diachronic comparativism of neighbouring phenomena', in other words it operates at a regional level (rather than at the planetary or continental level), by taking into consideration connected chains of societies associated through historically attested exchanges. Counter to the evolutionist paradigm of the beginning of the twentieth century, diffusionism makes equal room for field comparativism and for the establishment of an empirically founded diachronic perspective.

Unfortunately for anthropology, this point of view has been over-shadowed by the rise of American culturalism and of British structural–functionalism, which, as we all know, gave priority to internal coherence and to the reproduction of a social or cultural system, to the detriment of dynamic processes, exchanges, and modes of change. The culturalist and stucturalist–functionalist reaction against evolutionism has dragged moderate/empirical diffusionism into the storm.

The second anthropological point of view: the acculturation problematic

However, in the period following the Second World War, and not unrelated to an awareness of the colonial context, there was, within the culturalist tendency itself (that is, in particular especially in North American cultural anthropology) an attempt at redynamization 'from the inside', at a reintroduction into the cultural thematic (including all its substantialist deviations which transform culture into an essence) both of the taking into account of *intercultural interactions* (a culture also exists in relation to other cultures) and of the analysis of *intercultural hybridization* (a culture is also the result of borrowing and syncretisms).[2]

This second point of view differs from classic diffusionism in several regards. Three of these could be mentioned. The circulation of well-identified technical or ritual elements is no longer the crux of the matter, but rather the wider and more nebulous notion of the embeddedness of extremely variable cultural traits. The focus is no longer on chains of neighbouring societies, but rather on the confrontation of two cultures, usually placed in a relationship based on domination. The analysis is no longer diachronic, but focuses instead on ongoing interactions.

Nonetheless, as in the case of classic diffusionism, the acculturation problematic puts the emphasis on phenomena of *compatibility* linked to the process of diffusion of the two cultures in relation. Two major registers of compatibility, accounting for the rejection or the adoption of a 'cultural trait' or of an innovation have been pinpointed: compatibility in meaning (meaningful fit), that is, compatibility between the symbolic perception of an innovation by local actors and the value system of these actors; and functional compatibility (functional fit), that is, compatibility between the effects of the innovation and the social and technical system into which it is adopted (Katz, Levin and Hamilton, 1971: 250). These more or less extensive compatibilities are allegedly expressed through phenomena of selective borrowing, with the local culture acting as a 'filter'.

The acculturation problematic has a few advantages as well as a few disadvantages. Among the advantages is the fact that it provides a good description of situations of rural development prevailing in countries of the South, which are characterized by the interaction of two cultures which not only stand in stark contrast to each other but are also placed in a relationship of domination. Hence, the acculturation problematic places proper emphasis on phenomena of syncretism: new configurations are constructed out of the materials obtained from the two cultures in relation, and are not simply a matter of borrowing or of assembling pre-existing elements. Also, this problematic does not simply isolate technological features; it integrates them as an aspect of contact, of borrowing and, in broader terms, of everything we mean by the word 'culture'.

However, the acculturation problematic does not avoid the risk of diluting technical innovation in a much vaguer analysis of 'social change', nor that of homogenizing the two cultures entering into contact with each other. The result is that it fails to consider sub-cultures and the rifts and divergences existing within each of the cultures in question. Similarly, cross-cutting mediations and networks are scarcely taken into account. There is also the danger of an inaccurate understanding of the context and contents of the cultures involved. One might perceive a face-to-face between 'Western culture' and, let's say, Fulani culture (or Wolof culture, or Bambara culture, etcetera) while, in fact, what exists is a face-to-face between a technico-scientific culture (of Western origin) and a local peasant culture (see Chapter 10).

But the main drawback of the acculturation problematic resides undoubtedly in the fact that it leaves no opening for real research programmes: in other words, its fundamental assertions contribute little to the collection and treatment of new empirical material.

A sociological paradigm: 'diffusion studies'

On this topic Mendras and Forsé (1983: 75–80) make relevant reference to an 'epidemiological paradigm', to the extent that this sociology of innovation studies diffusion in the way in which epidemiologists study the diffusion of a disease. E.M. Rogers's frequently revised (1983) work provides a summary of the innumerable studies arising from this paradigm (he makes an inventory of

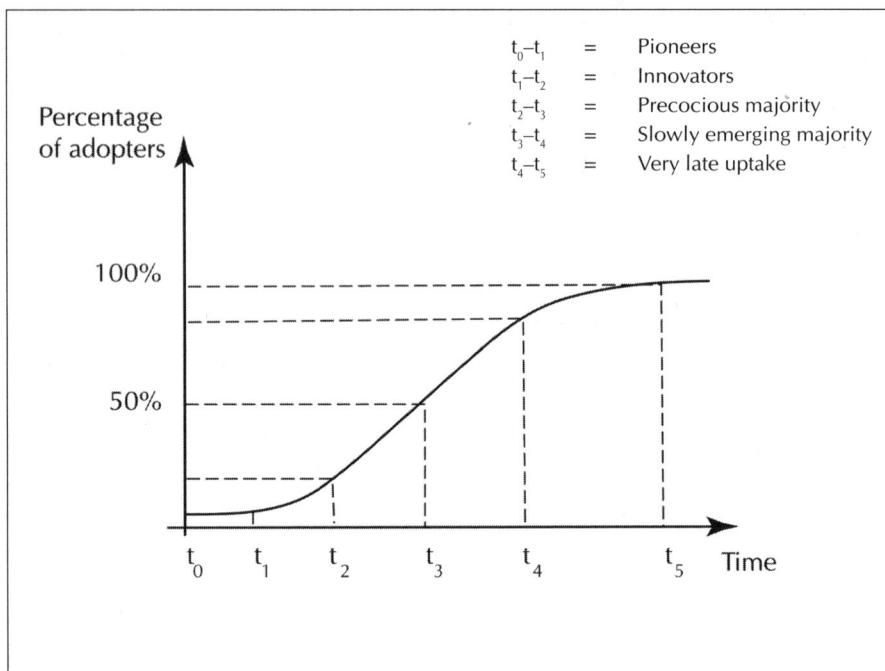

more than 1,500 research studies) and analyses their components.[3] Diffusion studies probably began with Ryan and Gross in 1943, on the diffusion of hybrid corn in Iowa. Originating in American rural sociology, where it was destined to prosper, the epidemiological paradigm later spread – if we may be allowed to apply its own analytical framework to diffusionism itself – to the sociology of education and, of course, to the sociology of health.

The foundation of the epidemiological paradigm is the exploitation of an S curve (year, number of persons adopting an innovation) already perceived by Tarde, and which remains valid regardless of the innovation being studied, while allowing us to differentiate between five types of adopters: pioneers, innovators, the advanced minority, the tardy majority and latecomers.

Research thus has a tendency to concentrate on the variables that identify pioneers or innovators, whether it be the case of a particular innovation, or of a cross-combination of several types of innovation. One therefore notices – and this is hardly surprising – that pioneers and innovators usually have a more elevated social status, are more learned and are more involved in associations than the adopters who follow them.

This paradigm gives rise to an analytical and programmatic definition of innovation, which could be put like this: 'Acceptance over time of specific items by individuals, groups, or other adopting units, linked to specific channels of communication, to a social structure, and to a given system of value, or culture' (Katz, Levin and Hamilton, 1971).[4] A simple commentary on the terms of this definition supplies the framework of the research programme resulting from this paradigm:

- *acceptance* ...: to try out is not to adopt, and it is the adoption of an innovation that counts; besides, to accept an innovation is, in a sense, to take it as one's own, to 'appropriate' it, that is, to set in motion a process of identification, interiorization and interpretation.

- ... *over time* ...: the time factor is essential; a diachronic perspective is needed to draw time as an abscissa, to draw the base curve of the paradigm.

We could open a parenthesis here concerning the first two points: the danger of tracing time as an abscissa, and the use of a single criterion for judging acceptance, which are the prerequisites for tracing a curve by flattening out qualitative differences between one moment and another, one acceptance and another. In fact, once diffused, an innovation takes on new meaning. The difference between early adoption and massive or late adoption is clouded by the effects induced by diffusion (see Lavigne Delville's demonstration, 1994: 389, on the subject of irrigation in the valley of the Senegal River).

- ... *of specific items* ...: the question here concerns the specificity of each innovation, and, in a way, the intrinsic qualities of each innovation, which in turn influence its diffusion. Some scientists refer to five factors which allow us to evaluate what we could call the intrinsic usability of innovations (Rogers, 1983: 221–36, re-used by Mendras and Forsé, 1983: 80):
  - the relative advantage of the innovation compared to what it replaces
  - its compatibility with the existing technical system
  - its more or less apparent complexity
  - its 'tryability'
  - the fact that it exists elsewhere.

Other scientists (Katz, Levin and Hamilton, 1971: 244) advance three factors:
  - the communicability of an innovation
  - the risks involved
  - its capacity of inciting acceptance (its pervasiveness).

- ... *by individuals, groups or other adopting units*...: the question here concerns the problem of the adopting units under consideration, be they 'real' units or units constructed through research; be they individuals (small farmers, consumers), as in the case of most agricultural innovations (or consumer goods innovations), or groups, which can either be corporate groups and institutions (like a hospital or a co-operative) – which poses the problem of the person representing the group or acting in its name – or aggregates and sociological artefacts (an 'endangered population', a socio-professional category, a culture), in other words, abstract sets of notional constructs.

- … *linked to specific channels of communication* …: in contrast to the exaggerations and simplifications of sociology as diffused by the media and of marketing techniques, the major contributions made by diffusion studies, with Katz and Lazarsfeld (1955), is probably the highlighting of the importance of interpersonal communication networks. The 'two steps flows' theory underlines the existence of two levels of communication. The anonymous messages delivered by the media are decoded and evaluated in the light of individual relationships (neighbourhood, kinship, affinities, professional group), of which network sociology attempts to sketch the contours, by emphasizing either the 'strength of weak ties' (Granovetter, 1973) or the 'strength of strong ties' (Rogers, 1983: 229).

- … *to a social structure* …: diffusion studies are therefore grounded, in theory, in the two principal sociological traditions, the first interested in the qualities of the social context into which the innovation is introduced (studies of social structure), and the second reflecting on the sociological characteristics of the individuals who adopt them (epidemiological-type studies).

- … *and to a given system of value, or culture:* this takes us into a domain often reserved for anthropology, in which 'world views', 'life-worlds', norms and 'customs' are invoked. As is the case above, analysis can begin from the context (culture) or from the individual (cultural traits).

The last two points are obviously complementary (with their respective 'society and culture' and 'society and social characteristics' poles); they constitute the weak points of empirical studies related to diffusion studies. The statements they make remain rhetorical, invoking social structure or group culture, usually resulting in an 'explanation' of the unexplained by the inexplicable.[5]

It is within the context of this 'shortcoming' that the following point of view, which considers innovation as a form of social indexing, has a place.

Innovation as social indexing

The basic postulate here is simple: innovations (borrowings) occur within a structured social system – they do not occur among an aggregate of individuals motivated only by need or interest. Obviously, there is nothing new about this insight. Thus the following remark can be found in the work of the historian M. Bloch, based on the observation that in social evolution, phases of innovation cannot simply be explained by pressing economic needs (thus, long in advance, he contested the arguments that would found Boserup's celebrity: 'I wonder whether these explanations are not oversimplifications, whether there are not other reasons, observable in the social environment itself, which would explain the periodic development and decline of the spirit of invention (…) It is appropriate, I believe, to look to the internal structure of the society and to the way the various groups that make it up impact upon one another' (Bloch, 1948: 112).

This remark ushers in the French rural sociological tradition of the period 1960–1980. In fact, the studies carried out under the direction of Mendras and Jollivet tended systematically to inscribe innovations and change within the context of local social systems, which alone can explain both the shape assumed by change and the existence of resistance to these changes. One thinks here of the classic study of the diffusion of maize hybridization in the South West of France, that is, of the battle of the 'great red' against the 'American' during the 1950s (see Mendras, 1976). Compared to the local variety of maize, which was adapted to self-subsistence and, in particular, to poultry rearing, American hybrid maize was capital-intensive, and presupposed a turn to commercial agriculture. However, this functional cleavage coincided, roughly, with an economic and political cleavage within the local society. The farmers capable of the necessary investments in hybrid maize happened to be rich peasants. Those who wanted to 'modernize' the countryside were young farmers belonging to the JAC (Jeunesse agricole chrétienne) and, consequently, had close relations to priests. The 'leftist population', of anti-clerical tradition, was nevertheless relatively powerful in the region and, at the time, mostly comprised poor farmers. Denunciation of American imperialism was also in vogue at the time (with demonstrations against US General Ridgway). All in all, the defenders of the local variety of maize (the 'great red') seemed to be 'leftist' (though remaining conservative in the face of change), while those introducing the hybrid maize appeared to be 'right-wing' (rich, clerical, and pro-American).

So, we can see that to understand the phenomenon of the acceptance/ refusal of an innovation, we need to situate the innovation within the framework of society. This means that an analysis of the local society is necessary, along with its political, economic and symbolic conflicts, which turns the innovation into a gamble.[6] It is this local society which was omitted, *de facto*, from the epidemiological paradigm.

Two major consequences – its main contribution – proceed from this 'point of view'.

1   Each proposal for innovation, each diffusion of innovation, invariably transits via *social bearers*, who occupy an important position in the local social structure. These social bearers vary from one society to another.[7]

They possess a greater or lesser degree of 'social credibility' or even of 'social credit'.[8] The social structures into which they are integrated are usually traversed by antagonisms and contradictions. The various social groups that can be identified within the local society do not possess identical resources, are not equally constrained, and sometimes have different values. The introduction of an innovation is very likely to serve the interests of some people while damaging the interests of others.

2 Adopted innovations produce, at least, indirect effects which are transferred onto the local social structure. Thus, the analysis of innovations should not be restricted to the phenomenon of adoption but should also take into account its ultimate effects on the local population: does an adopted innovation help to reproduce the existing social structure along with its system of 'traditional' inequality (in agreement with the famous statement of the Prince of Salina in the film *The Leopard*: 'Things must change so that everything can remain the same')? Or, on the contrary, does it allow for a reshuffling of the cards, either in the form of a reduction of inequality or in terms of the emergence of new 'elites'?

Differential bearers, differential effects: Marty demonstrates clearly that in Sahelian societies during the drought-engendered crisis of the past few years, technical agro-pastoral innovation was the doing of the poorest of the poor (survival adventurers, Marty, 1986: 45), or of those who had contacts with the outside world (migrants or traders). He shows how 'innovation, like drought, represents an element of differentiation between groups and between individuals' (Marty, 1986: 46).

The heuristic interest and the relative advantages procured by the 'social indexing point of view' are self-evident. As opposed to certain idealizations of peasant society, it reminds us that local agro-pastoral societies are neither homogeneous nor consensual, that their members do not share identical interests and do not develop identical strategies. We know that this holds true for Africa and Europe alike, because the majority of African rural societies are 'peasant' societies (see Olivier de Sardan, 1991), and because these so-called lineage societies are not without internal cleavages.

Notwithstanding, this point of view also has its pitfalls and exaggerations. The 'society as a whole' rhetoric, the fetishization of the 'social system' and of 'systems' in general (the local system included), as well as the marginalization of actors' strategies, figure among its deficiencies. We could also mention the stereotypes and ready-made images of internal cleavages (of the 'feudal lords/poor peasants' order) which flourish here and there. In this regard, the analysis of local modes of production carried out by French rural sociology and by Africanist economic anthropology alike (the later showed scant interest in innovation but shared the same point of view), during the 1960s and 1970s, nowadays seems ambivalent. It remains positive when it provides an empirical identification of systems of constraints and of social relations at the local level, which paves the way for an indexing of innovations, at least to a certain extent. It seems negative when it defends a ready-made theory of modes of production and of their articulation, or when it classifies all types of local cleavages as class relations. This approach is doubly simplistic: innovation problematics are boiled down to social indexing, while social indexing of innovation is reduced to class indexing.

However, indexing can also be perceived in a more open-ended and indeterminate manner.

Innovation as popular experimentation

This point of view could be summed up in a slogan like 'barefoot innovators'. The reference to Maoist China is not fortuitous. Maoist populism has influenced many Marxist intellectuals, including a number of sociologists and anthropologists. But populism as an intellectual tendency goes back even further into the past, and has not failed to influence tropical agronomy, a field in which it has long since drawn attention to the fact that peasants can adapt, as P. Richards reminds us on the subject of Lord Lugard (Richards, 1985). Richards's work provides, moreover, an excellent illustration of this point of view. His argument starts by demonstrating that African cultures are indeed adapted to their environments, and by underlining the internal coherence or relevance of extensive farming, farming on burnt land or intercropping. In other words, he rehabilitates peasants' logics or so-called 'traditional' systems of production, which are too hastily condemned as primitive or irrational by agronomists. But to leave the matter at that would limit research to a retrospective analysis, which credits popular know-how with only a long-term potential for adaptation, in an almost Darwinian perspective, in the light of which innovation is only a reaction, and a past reaction to be precise. The populist point of view allows us to go further, since it perceives innovation as a popular experiment, in progress here and now. It attaches importance to the multitude of micro-innovations effected by contemporary peasants, innovations that are indeed discreet by virtue of their dilution into the everyday undertakings of a host of actors and into countless micro-unities of production, but which remain innovations nonetheless. Richards thus proposes a very detailed analysis of the modes of selection and testing of local varieties of rice by peasants in Sierra Leone (Richards, 1986), and makes a convincing demonstration of the way in which they exploit the agricultural or nutritional qualities of the seeds that they attempt to develop, in keeping with the micro-ecological contexts in which the seeds are to be used.

Innovation is thus seen as an endogenous, 'local-level' phenomenon. We could go as far as to evoke an informal, peasant 'research and development', whose existence depends neither on the world of science nor on the world of the written word (contrary to Goody's suggestion). There is an 'internal dynamics of change among small scale farmers' (Richards, 1986: 2) on which one hopes to found an alternative model of development: 'Inventive self-reliance is one of Africa's most precious resources' (Richards, 1985: 17).

We see clearly here the coexistence of the two forms of populism distinguished above (see chapters 1 and 7). Seen from a certain angle, methodological populism appears to be a good research strategy, one that assumes that peasants (like all other 'local-level actors') have cognitive and pragmatic resources. The ethno-sciences were developed on the basis of such a postulate. The introduction of the innovation problematic brings new dynamism to this perspective. Beginning with the existence of popular resources in experimentation or with the demonstration of 'popular knowledge', we arrive at an analysis of the popular capacity to mobilize such resources and knowledge in an innovative manner, in agronomy as in religion or politics, whether in technical forms (through the transformation of operational chains or the creation of new ones), in ritual forms (by the transformation of rituals or the creation of new ones) or organizational forms (by the transformation of modes of collective organization or the creation of new ones). Yet, on the other hand, ideological populism has a persistent tendency to bias the analysis, by projecting a romantic image of these resources and by overestimating the potential for innovation of local-level social actors. Peasants undeniably deploy innovative strategies. But the fact that these are often underestimated should not lead us to forget the extent to which these strategies are liable to be combined with aid-seeking strategies, which exploit the 'development income' (see Chapter 11) or the 'migrant income' (see Quiminal, 1991; Lavigne Delville, 1994), nor the fact that, occasionally, innovativeness may even be eclipsed by these aid-seeking strategies.

In this respect, the fourth point of view has, for its part, the merit of including peasant strategies which 'use' external intervention and exogenous resources.

Innovation as reinterpretation

This last point of view is certainly the least homogeneous of all, in that it covers a relatively wide variety of positions. But these all have three fundamental, intersecting propositions in common:

- 'Reception' entails a complex process of construction of meaning by the receiver. Whether we limit ourselves to the 'message' proposing an innovation, or whether, in a more metaphorical light, we consider all innovations as 'messages', the conclusion remains the same: each innovation 'message' is recomposed by its addressee and final user. This obviously runs counter to linear conceptions of communication (which hold that the quality of reception of a message depends on its conveyer and on the distortions to which it is subjected before reaching its receptor).

• When restated in terms less of communication and more of strategy, this becomes a proposition on the subject of the agency of actors, that is, on actors' ability to act and to react. Local-level actors (in the present case, peasants and cattle breeders) are of course exposed to constraints (economic, political and cultural), but nevertheless they still retain some margin for manoeuvre. In the framework of 'development', which constantly generates innovation proposals, often originating from the outside, producers' agency is essentially reactive: producers transform to their own liking the proposals that are made to them.

• Actors are not isolated in the use of their room for manoeuvre: they do not recompose on an individual level the meaning of messages from the outside. Their transformation of innovation proposals is neither individual nor haphazard. Reinterpretation 'from the bottom up' involves processes of social interaction, and these reciprocal interactions are even more important when they occur in the context of 'face-to-face societies'. These interactions produce rather unpredictable repercussions.

I will refer to three works, each based, according to differing modalities, on this point of view.

The production of norms by the 'local professional group' of peasants

J. P. Darré was the first French scientist to develop this kind of analysis on the subject of innovation. This led him to study the discourse of cattle breeders in the Ternois (France) concerning cattle feeding and techniques of nutritional supplement. He demonstrated that the discourse developed by cattle breeders differed profoundly from that of agricultural experts. The new knowledge diffused by extension services was reinterpreted by peasants in accordance with norms of evaluation arising, for the most part, from their own interactions, at the level of local networks of discussion and mutual assistance. Familiarity, not only according to the traditional mode of the 'village community', but also, increasingly, according to the modern mode of exchange between professionals engaged in the same activity (peasants having become agriculturists) generates shared conceptions, evaluative judgements made using the same criteria, especially concerning technical proposals emanating from agricultural advisers.

If, in the French case studied by Darré (1985), in which technicians and breeders belong to the same linguistic community and share basically the same type of schooling, one observes this type of discrepancy between the discourse of the first and the reinterpretations of the second, the difference is, *a fortiori*, even greater in Africa, where the linguistic and educational disparities separating development agents and peasants are much more dramatic: in the latter instance, the gulf between the 'messages' diffused by technical services and the meaning reconstructed by the producers to whom these messages are addressed attains its maximum depth.

Development situations as interfaces

Norman Long's postulates follow basically the same lines as Darré's: development agents and peasant societies constitute two distinct 'epistemic communities' which development projects place in relationship with each other (Long, 1992c). However, while Darré places the emphasis on the technical discourse developed in each community, on the way in which agriculturists produce norms, and on their local networks of interconnection, Long insists on actors' strategies and on the more 'political' aspects of interaction processes. Originating, as we will recall, in the 'Manchester School' to which Balandier's research owes a great deal, Long sees 'development projects' as 'case study analyses' (see Mitchell, 1983; van Velsen, 1978), in which agents, who not only have different resources but also play the games according to different rules, confront each other. Development situations are situations of intercultural confrontation, of 'encounters at the interface' (Long, 1989) and may even be 'battlefields of knowledge' (Long and Long, 1992).

Developees' logics versus developers' logics

On the basis of a reflection proposed by J.P. Dozon in his analysis of the case studies conducted in Côte d'Ivoire (Dozon, 1978; Dozon, 1985), I have attempted, for my part, an identification of what we may call the 'invariants' of the interactions between the two sets confronting each other, and which can be subsumed respectively under the labels of 'developers' and 'developees', while taking the necessary semantic precautions required by an awareness of the fact that we are not dealing with homogeneous sets (see note 3 on page 39). Hence, the prevalence of two 'principles' has been advanced: the 'principle' of sidetracking and the 'principle' of selection (see Chapter 9), which subsume the basic reactions that populations have towards the packages of innovations with which they are presented. Indeed, innovations are rarely proposed in isolated unities but rather as an aggregate,[9] which those to whom they are addressed often pull apart.

These varying approaches share what I call the 'reinterpretive' point of view. This obviously can be described otherwise, depending on whether we prefer to place the emphasis on meaning or on pragmatic processes (the two being indissociable), that is 'reformulation', 'reinvention', 'refraction' or 'hybridization'.

Is an innovations problematic possible in anthropology?

The points of view reviewed above all have to do with innovation, in keeping with the broad definition previously proposed. Nonetheless, they reach beyond the scope of innovation and have to do with social change in general. On close examination, these points of view do not outline a specifically empirical anthropological 'research programme' centred on innovation. But is such a research programme possible?

Combining points of view

First, we should begin by resisting the temptation to restrict ourselves to choosing just one of the preceding points of view. It is true that they arose partly in opposition to each other. The analysis of innovation as social index-ing is allegedly in contradiction with the presumptions of diffusion studies, and especially with methodological individualism and hyper-empirical American sociology. The populist point of view ran counter to the above, which respectively transform the peasant into a consumer and into a victim. Putting the priority on reinterpretation corrected populism by giving prece-dence to reaction over creation.

This is in keeping with a kind of law of the history of ideas, in which each new point of view in social science can be established only in contradiction to a pre-existing point of view, or by 'hardening' the difference between itself and its predecessor or its affiliate. Nevertheless, the dogmatic and rhetorical deviations that come to bear on the social sciences have also contributed to a 'hardening' of the cleavages between points of view by transforming one or the other into an orthodoxy. Diffusion studies has been converted into a machine for making curves and for producing endless discussions about the sociological differences peculiar to innovators and to other early adapters. On several occasions, the social system has been construed to be an implacable sociological determinism reproducing the inexorable law of a structure of domination. Populism is constantly in danger of moving from methodology to ideology, and of taking its wishes for reality. Calling on the processes of reinterpretation does not annul the danger of falling into the snares of semiological rhetoric.

I am inclined to favour a relatively eclectic epistemological attitude, though this incurs the risk of being accused of 'lukewarm centrism'. Nothing, it seems to me, prevents a combination of points of view: in fact, everything seems to point in that direction. Innovations are diffused, but they are also embedded into a local social system that is exposed to pressure; local-level actors make experiments, development actions are both reinterpreted and sidetracked.

Let us take the example of the diffusion paradigm (point of view 1). The curves of diffusion over time, the identification of the sociological traits of 'first adapters', all this does not necessarily imply that one is lapsing into the *homo sociologicus* ideology, constructed, more or less, on the *homo economicus* model, nor does it indicate that one ignores the pressure of village social structures.[10]

To insist on a systematic analysis of these local social structures (point of view 2) entails neither an inevitable fetishization of 'society' and of the 'system' nor a denial that even the slightest room for manoeuvre may be available to individuals.

To identify the various forms of endogenous peasant innovations (point of view 3) does not necessarily oblige us to hypostasize them, or to underestimate the role of the transfer of knowledge from the outside.

Proposing an analysis of modes of reinterpretation and of sidetracking (point of view 4), does not necessarily reduce us to the last resort, which consists of playing word games, nor does it imply that we are forced to over-estimate the value of technological tinkering.

We may also note that there are a great number of spontaneous 'connections' between these four points of view. Let us take two examples. The importance attached to local networks within the framework of the processes of reinterpretation (point of view 4) is closely related to the theory of 'two levels of communication' which underpin a large number of diffusions studies (point of view 1). The social contextualization of the innovation within a local arena (points of view 2) is related to the structure of the interactions engendering the process of reinterpretation (point of view 4).

But can we be contented with a vague appeal for theoretical tinkering, in the hope that the dynamics inherent in empirical research will invariably point to the best possible combination of these points of view? Doesn't this imply a complete abandonment of comparativist ambitions? Can the latter be content with pleading the eclectic characteristics of these points of view? Let's take the example of two comparative studies, which, quite a while back, attempted a transcultural analysis of innovations and technical change: Barnett's work (1953) and that of Foster (1962). Each, indeed, had his own major orientation: Barnett announces, as a pioneer, the field of cognitive anthropology and gives priority to innovation as a socially regulated mental process, while Foster confirms his strongly culturalist orientation. But both make use of anything and everything at their disposal, while accumulating the most varied field references possible, based on the principles of cross-cultural studies.[11] Obviously, I do not agree with this unbridled and decontextualized conception of comparativism. However, as debatable as their method may be, they are both related, in a latent and disorganised fashion, at the level of interpretation, often owing to plain common sense, to the points of view that I have attempted to identify above. Both insist on the fact that innovation is a process of hybridization, of reinterpretation and of reorganization. Both underline the cultural and social factors that influence the speed or the intensity with which an innovation is adopted. Both make mention of the social pressures and conflicting interests that come to bear on a proposed innovation. And both appreciate the creativity of the populations in terms of innovation. Nevertheless, this miscellaneous accumulation of the various types of elements in which innovations are embedded, of everything that promotes or hinders innovations, and of all of the cognitive, social, and cultural processes they propel is bewildering: what is to be done with all of this?

One has a similar impression when reading Bailey's book (1973c, which is based entirely on European examples), which is as just as eclectic as Foster's. In the elaboration of this theme, Bailey, of course, uses some of the material included in his previous texts (see Bailey, 1969). He proposes a 'political' view of innovation, seen as a locus of confrontation between groups and factions (another variant of the social indexing point of view). But he also insists on the fact that, in each situation, existing 'cultural models' are more or less permeable to innovation (the cultural-diffusionist point of view). He places particular emphasis on the reorganization of values resulting from the adoption of innovations, on the debates surrounding legitimization and classification that accompany them, and on the interpretive leeway left open to each individual (the reinterpretive point of view). But the reader is, once again, left with a feeling of dissatisfaction:[12] what are we supposed to discover at such a general level, via this tepid comparativism?

It might just be that innovation in itself is not an adequate object for comparativist studies. We will get back to this point later on. However, beforehand, I might perhaps take the added risk of proposing a kind of synthesis, while attempting to steer clear of 'spineless eclectism' by resorting instead to a 'reasoned eclectism' capable of organizing the comparative convergence of points of view based on a minimum of theory. I will therefore propose the SCP (smallest common problematic) formula, which will assume the (definitely inelegant) shape of an accumulation of metaphors, taken from different registers, but whose sum is likely to make sense.

Indeed, it's a matter of considering innovation as 'an original graft, occurring between two vague sets, within an arena, via intermediaries' …

(a) An original graft …
Innovation invariably entails mixture, hybridization and syncretism. Pure innovations and faithful borrowings do not exist. Modifications of knowledge

or techniques, voluntary or involuntary, formal or informal, give rise to un-expected forms and unpredictable effects. The transformation of rituals and the emergence of sects or changes in established religions exemplify the appar-ently baroque occurrences at work in the rural economy. The end product of a graft does not resemble any of its initial elements, and the graft itself is unique and surprising.[13]

(b) ... between two vague sets ...
Regardless of the terms we use to designate them (developers/developees, technicians/peasants, technical and scientific knowledge/local peasant cultures, etcetera), the two worlds confronting each other are configurations whose contours are ill-defined, and whose differences alone are obvious and irrefutable. There is an interface between two sets of heterogeneous conceptions, but each set is a partially unstable and essentially composite reality. By the same token, strategies and logics of action differ greatly from one set to another, without it being possible to identify one and only one strategy within each 'camp': rather, what we find are partly convergent and partly divergent clusters. The norms of these interconnected worlds belong to very different registers, which does not preclude the existence of substantial differences internal to each. To evoke the confrontation between two cultures amounts to exaggerating the degree of coherence that really exists.

(c) ...in an arena ...
A proposed innovation, along with its 'social bearers' and 'brokers', takes place within a local arena comprising various 'strategic groups' in confrontation. These do not exist *a priori,* once and for all, but rather come together according to the stakes of the game. Social classes, defined in terms of relations of production, are simply one of the many possible shapes that strategic groups may assume, or, as is more often the case, they merely constitute two of the types of constraints and resources, among many others, that influence the formation of these groups. Distinguishing the strategic groups that crystallize around a proposed innovation merely amounts to identifying the groups of actors who adopt the same position when confronted with this innovation (an identification carried out either through an inventory of the conceptions of these actors, or through practice indicators), based on the knowledge that their mutual positions are interrelated at the level of the local arena (see chapter 12).

(d) ... via intermediaries
The *social bearers* of an innovation, through whose agency innovations penetrate into a local society or into a professional network, are always more or less situated at the interface of the two sets confronting each other. They sometimes belong to the world of development institutions, of which they

constitute the lowest rung: this applies to development agents, agricultural advisers and other supervisors and co-ordinators, who, nonetheless, have certain types of affinities and connections with the local culture which they do not share with the higher echelons of the development institution's pyramid. Sometimes they belong instead to the local society, of which they constitute the outer fringe, those who have the closest relationships with the outside world and who learn its language: 'elite' or 'contact' peasants, former migrants or those who went to school, local 'entrepreneurs', association die-hards, brokers specialized in the dialogue with NGOs or with public authorities, there is a long and diversified list of those who play the role of intermediaries between two 'worlds'. They are part of the local 'world' in which their interests are situated, but they have sufficient mastery of the 'world' of development to be able to use it to their own benefit. They are the transmitters of innovation (see Chapter 11).

Innovation as a way in

Finally, let us take a look at the way in which social science relates to innovation. There are two arguments against the elaboration of an 'anthropology of innovation' properly speaking.

1   Agro-pastoral innovation, which has been our main point of reference here, implicitly or explicitly, for reasons of simplification or of accuracy, cannot be as easily isolated methodologically as appeared. First of all, a technical innovation, particularly one that has been proposed in the voluntarist forms characteristic of the world of development, is often coupled with an organizational innovation in which it could be considered to be 'embedded'. We are aware of the degree to which the transformation of techniques of agricultural production are indissociably linked to the transformation of the forms of work, management and commercialization. 'Integrated' projects, which attempt, at a stroke, the introduction of 'packages' of techniques and of co-operative structures or other peasant organizations, bear witness to this within the development world. Technical and organizational innovations are themselves related to social, ritual or ideological innovations, which can hardly be identified by means of an analysis based on the single criterion of a 'system of production'. Hence, the role played by the prophets of certain sects must be taken into consideration as far as the various processes of agricultural innovation are concerned (see Peel, 1968, to take an example from Nigeria). When we take innovation as an object, in an attempt to avoid the pitfalls of the excessively polymorphic and 'feeble' perspective of 'social change' in

general, we nevertheless find ourselves confronted with the global social context which must be taken into consideration, in order to gain a proper understanding of innovation.

2   The collection and analysis of points of view and of the strategies of the producers and of those targeted by 'innovation messages' seem to be on the agenda of anthropology, which is particularly concerned with a restitution of the conceptions and practices of people belonging to the 'grassroots' level. However, to date, anthropology has produced more data on indigenous popular discourses in cosmology, divination and power than on technical innovation. Notwithstanding, it is clear that actors' conceptions on the subject of such-and-such a technical innovation are not restricted to technical and economic considerations, and are liable to go in very different directions. Once more, we are confronted with innovation as a starting point rather than a distinctly circumscribed field of study.

Hence, innovation appears to be a possible way in to the phenomenon of social change and of development rather than an object in itself. It is not easy to see how an anthropology of innovation could become an autonomous area within the field of the anthropology of development. But the interest of using it as a way in can also be considered in terms of its scientific productiveness. This type of perspective could be fruitful if it allows us to progress in the direction of comparativist studies. The type of comparativism I have in mind is an intensive rather than extensive comparativism, based on proximity and analysing the differential impact a given innovation (or 'innovation proposal') has on different local societies, or studying the way similar local societies react to innovations. It is undoubtedly at this level that the syncretism of 'points of view' that I advocated above can be effected, and it is clearly at this level that such a syncretism is likely to be most productive.

Notes

1   As will be recalled, Schumpeter clarified his own definition by listing five possible forms of innovation: a new product, a new method of production, a new market, a new stock and a new organization of production. As examples among many others, we may note that definitions of innovation vary from the very broad ('any thought, behaviour or thing that is new' for Barnett, 1953: 7) to the more narrow ('the production of new technical knowledge' for Elster, 1983: 93, who even places innovation in opposition to diffusion, contrary to most authors).

2   This tendency was in fact present from the beginning, to the extent that the founding father of culturalism, Malinowski, called for an 'applied anthropology', concerned with the process of change and with 'contact situations' (see among others, his articles, collected in a posthumous work significantly titled *The Dynamics of Cultural*

Change – see Malinowski, 1970 – which announces and revises the themes of all the studies on acculturation). Moreover, Malinowski criticizes diffusionism on the basis of two strong arguments: change is a by-product of the game of social forces and institutions rather than a circulation of 'cultural traits'; its end result is the formation of new sets rather than an assembly of odd elements (Malinowski, 1970: 42, 48). However, Balandier has pinpointed the shortcomings of Malinowski's analysis, the way in which it underestimates phenomena of domination, owing to a currently undefendable theory of culture (Balandier, 1963: 24–7).

3 It is worth noting the differences between the various editions: the 1962 edition, that of 1971 (which appeared under a new title, *Communication of innovation*, with Floyd and Shoemaker as co-authors), and the 1983 edition, which I am using as my source.

4 The same type of definition is to be found in Rogers, 1983: 10.

5 What is to be made of general functionalist definitions of this type: 'A social system is defined as a set of interrelated units that are engaged in joint problem solving to accomplish common goals' (Rogers, 1983: 24)?

6 See the articles collected in Barlett, 1980b.

7 This historical 'incorporation', in the strict sense of the word (*embodiement*: see Elster, 1983: 127) is doubtless at the heart of Schumpeter's great intuition: we know that he saw entrepreneurs as 'social bearers' (even though he does not use the term) of modern innovation and, consequently, as the source of capitalist dynamism.

8 'If the new item is being introduced by someone (a person or a group) it may be judged not (or not only) on its own merit, but (also) by the reputation and credit of those sponsoring it' (Bailey, 1973: 313).

9 'Technological clusters' is sometimes the phrase used (Rogers, 1983: 226).

10 Rogers must be credited with having developed an increasing awareness of the limits of the epidemiological paradigm and of having called for a widening of this point of view: 'to date, diffusion research has concentrated too much (1) on investigating the characteristics of adopters' categories and (2) in studying a rather limited range of such characteristic variables. Do we need a 276th study on the relationship of education to innovativeness? I think not. A much wiser use of research resources would be to explore other independent variables in their relationship with innovativeness, especially network variables and system-level variables that could help us escape the overwhelming 'individualism' of past research on innovativeness, in which most of the independent variables of study were individual characteristics that did not encompass the interpersonal relationships' (Rogers, 1983: 267).

11 Barnett makes a comparison, from the perspective of innovation, between three North American Indian societies, a Polynesian society, and modern American society. Foster, for his part, takes his examples from all the peasant societies on the planet.

12 For a critique of this work, see Silverman, 1974.

13 Unsurprisingly, the graft metaphor has been used before, by other scientists. Marty (1990: 125) attributes its paternity to Desroches.

7
Developmentalist populism and social science populism
Ideology, action, knowledge

'Anthropology thus unearthed information on a number of micro-facts and micro-processes that are ignored, glossed over or assembled into larger abstract categories by other disciplines. Yet it is precisely the working out of such micro-facts in the behaviour of "indigenous peoples" that influence, change, redirect or divert the course of development, projected only in general terms by social theorists or planners.' (Wolf, 1988: 104, cited in Arnould, 1989: 143)

In a way, this book is entirely devoted to the various aspects of the vocation that anthropology has of studying practices 'from below', looking at actors' behaviour and popular conceptions. Thanks to these specific competences, anthropology is capable of understanding how development actions are transformed, reworked, diverted and reinterpreted by targeted beneficiaries.

This entails a relationship between anthropologists and the 'people', which, as mentioned above, makes an inevitable allusion to populism. By the same token, populism, albeit of a different type, is also to be found in the behaviour of the stalwarts and activists of development, whose profession consists in seeking the welfare of the 'people'. We could, at this point, clarify this question, whose outlines have already been sketched above.

Populism is an endemic social science attitude: a relatively enthusiastic discovery of the 'people' by intellectuals has resulted in the production of a significant amount of knowledge in anthropology, history and sociology.[1] This, in turn, has had far-reaching, positive repercussions. However, the populism observed in social science is usually implicit, does not identify itself as such, and is not analysed as such. Nevertheless, a recent work focuses explicitly on this question, in the particular field of the sociology of popular cultures (Grignon and Passeron, 1989), through an association of populism and anthropology, while raising fundamental epistemological questions, to which I will return in a moment. In recent years, other works have attended to the questions raised by the populist thematic, and have also underscored the relationship between populism and anthropology. An interesting point to note is that these works are all devoted to the same field, quite removed from Passeron's: development, considered from the angle of the anthropology of peasant knowledge (Richards, 1985), development sociology (Kitching, 1982), or the anthropology of planned change (Robertson, 1984). The field of development has a particular advantage: whereas the populism peculiar to the social sciences, and the analyses that interest them, are generally restricted to the question of knowledge production, development also involves populism in action. And it would appear that the interface of social science and development practice is a privileged space for the emergence of populist attitudes. The recent French translation of a work (Chambers, 1983) – with a very revealing sub-title: 'Putting the last first' – which rapidly became a classic 'populist' reference on matters of development, will serve as a good starting point. Chambers centres his discussion on what he refers to as 'the poor', namely those overlooked by rural development, and proposes the reversal of a number of attitudes, research programmes and policies: these reversals allegedly allow us to place poor people at the centre of rural development. This type of rehabilitation is obviously inspired by the populist thematic; and Chambers' book is revealing in regard to the advantages and disadvantages of intellectual populism as seen either in the world of development – Chambers's world – or in that of the social sciences, to which it relates continuously. But gradually I will go beyond Chambers, with the intent of broadening the subject, in order to propose a series of differences between moral populism, 'miserabilism', methodological populism and ideological populism.

Intellectuals and their ambiguous populism

A preliminary definition is required. By 'populism' I mean to evoke neither 'popular' movements (American peasant populism at the turn of the twentieth century or populist parties of central Europe between the First and Second World Wars ...), nor the attitude of a charismatic political leader (Perón or Walesa ...). Several meanings are instilled in the word 'populism' (Ionescu and Gellner, 1969). It is, moreover, strongly connoted, usually in a pejorative and stigmatizing light. In this case, I will concentrate on just one of these meanings, which sees populism as a form of social relationship (ideological, moral, scientific, political) which intellectuals engage in with the 'people', if only on a symbolic level. This relationship can generate knowledge as well as action among intellectuals, and sometimes both, simultaneously or successively. Hence, it is primarily a question of the friendly attitude that intellectuals have towards the people, and which can be expressed politically (Russian *narodnicki* of the nineteenth century or French Maoists of the 1960s), in the field of research (Chayanov and the analysis of the Russian peasantry, or Labov and the study of black American language: Chayanov, 1966; Labov, 1976), in literature (the populist novel) and, of course, in many other domains. In the face of a system that scorns, disregards and exploits the people (regardless of how the system is defined, in terms of culture, politics, economics – or of all three simultaneously), certain intellectuals (who generally originate from within this system and remain linked to it), discover the 'people' and transform this discovery into a social, moral, intellectual or scientific 'cause' …. This is no doubt a procedure with which many readers are familiar. This is what comprises, to my mind, the *core* of populism, according to the restricted definition proposed in this chapter, in which we inscribe both the value and the ambivalence of populism, not to mention the endless questions it generates. Is it possible to rehabilitate the people without idealizing them? How can we bring to the fore those who are (and are placed) last? Why and how can intellectuals, who by definition and culture are not a part of the people, speak of the former, or even act on their behalf or in collaboration with them?

Populism thus defined is not only political, social or moral activism. It is situated at the centre of a number of intellectual and scientific enterprises and at the centre of a number of development practices, into which it imports its ambivalence. For ambivalence is indeed at the heart of the populist enterprise. In social science, scientific populism permits the discovery of cognitive resources disregarded by the dominant culture, but this usually leads to a colouring of popular knowledge in keeping with the aspirations of researchers. In the development world, developmental populism provides an opportunity for criticism of dominant models and appeals for respect of the populations involved, but its exaltation of peasant 'participation' is often combined with naive stereotypes. How can we embrace the 'cause of the people' while avoiding clichés and activists' illusions? To the extent that Chambers's work cuts across these ambiguities, I will use his work as a background for my analysis of the contours of developmental populism and the description of its modalities.[2]

The poor according to Chambers

First, it must be clearly understood that for Chambers 'the poor' and 'the people' are one and the same. In his opinion, the 'poor' constitute a variable category: his intent is neither to define the poverty line, nor to propose a definition of poverty. In his estimation, the 'rural poor' (Chambers limits his analysis to the rural milieu) includes women, villagers who live at a distance from main roads, simple peasants and old people ... The poor are thus, in his particularly broad and imprecise definition of the word, all those who are excluded, marginalized and ignored by development, that is to say, the vast majority of the rural populations. When Chambers uses the word 'poor' he is not referring to some 'fourth world' of the Third World, or to any specific downtrodden class of people belonging to rural areas of the South. What he refers to as the 'poor' is precisely what others refer to as the 'people'. The 'poor' are 'those who are invisible and unknown' (Chambers, 1990: 48), those who 'do not speak' (ibid.: 40), 'the last in line', those who are 'forgotten' (ibid.: 40). These characteristics are all negative, but herein resides their strength: the observation they make is irrefutable. They situate the poor (the people) at the other extreme of the pole of celebrity, the pole to which developers and researchers belong, namely the world of decision makers and of professors. How can we deny that the cosmopolitan–urban–privileged world in which developers live mis-understands and ignores the vast majority of Third World rural populations? It is the latter, victims of this misunderstanding and ignorance, who constitute the world of the poor as seen by Chambers. In fact, he attempts to propose an impossible definition of poverty, seen as a combination of 'five prejudices' (ibid.: 172), as a fibre woven out of a combination of elements: insufficient reserves of cash and food, physical debility and illness, isolation, vulnerability in the face of the unexpected, and a lack of influence (ibid.: 46). As can be easily demonstrated, this all-inclusive definition does not stand to reason nor does it make allowances for a reasonably relevant classification of 'poverty' as a category. But, ultimately, this is of little importance: Chambers's definition of the 'poor' is just as unconvincing as the usual definitions of the 'people',[3] and yet this word, vague as it is, has no substitute, to the extent that it defines a vacuum: those who dwell in the dungeons of history and are completely absent from the public scene. They are invisible to those in power and to those who have power (political, economic, academic). The populist project, and this is its great strength, puts this invisible category on the stage, makes them visible, unavoidable, demonstrates their existence and their concrete reality in the very spaces in which they are usually condemned to move as phantoms – in intellectual, cultural, political or economic space. The populist project, seen from this angle, is incontestably relevant. Practically every anthropologist is more or less a populist ...

The developmentalist populist complex

Inverting the way one looks at things, reversing perspectives, are leitmotivs of the populist approach. Numerous examples, taken from different periods and from various fields, can be found. But the developmentalist configuration, at least in the shape assumed by its modern phase, after the Second World War, was and remains a favoured contemporary space for the exercise of populist practices. The expression 'Third World', which has become somewhat pejorative, designated a certain ideological configuration which was not unrelated (though at another level and in another context) to this particular brand of populism. For isn't it true that intellectuals from rich countries wanted to rehabilitate the oppressed and to fight for their rights? The current situation is not quite the same. Development has become a profession, the development world a 'market'. However, within this profession and in this market, the populist ideology is far from marginal. It is currently institutionalized. Populism has indeed succeeded in selling a certain type of product on this market. It has produced a body of arguments, practices and institutions which could be called the 'populist developmentalist complex' (a sub-set of the developmentalist configuration), whose main particularity resides in the fact that it counters, not without success, and in the view of a certain audience, the theses of the 1950s and 1960s (a period marked by so-called theories of modernization): small projects versus big projects, adequate technologies versus heavy technologies, subsistence crops versus commercial crops, peasant logics and knowledge versus scientific knowledge, country versus towns, small producers versus rural entrepreneurs, 'women too' versus 'men only', peasant organizations versus agricultural supervisors, NGOs versus big projects, etcetera ... Chambers was not a trailblazer in this domain but more of an amplifier: he wrote at a period when this stream of thinking was in its prime (moreover, he refers to Schumacher and to Freire as the authorities, pioneers and beacons of developmentalist populism: Schumacher, 1978, Freire, 1980) and – this is a detail that he apparently overlooks – when leading development institutions had already begun to draw inspiration, in part, from populism.[4]

Herein lies another characteristic of populism, namely its tendency continually to re-invent itself. Populism might be said to take as a model now Sisyphus, now Marco Polo, now Bernard-Henri Lévy.[5] The people, having once more been forgotten, and never having been taken seriously, must be perpetually reannounced and reproclaimed. That's for Sisyphus. But this continuous rehabilitation regularly generates new and authentic discoveries: the exploration of these eternally renewable resources represented by the knowledge and life-worlds of the people makes room for endless discoveries of new facets of popular cultures. That's where Marco Polo comes in. However, concomitantly, the converts to populism, paying scant attention to the cumulative character of knowledge – on which topic the social sciences fall short – are constantly in the process of rediscovering America, and of taking the clichés they unearth for intellectual novelties. That's the Bernard-Henri

Lévy side of the matter. Yet populist exploration can be as fruitful as populist cant is annoying. And this is exacerbated by the fact that the bards of populism are not the only ones talking about the people. Even those who are pinpointed as the enemies of the people and condemned for neglecting them join in the song of praise for the people ... Official, 'Western', 'dominant' culture makes constant reference to the people. This is a commonplace cliché of political rhetoric. Populist rhetoric, which claims to be an alternative, sometimes has a lot of trouble distinguishing itself from official rhetoric: nothing looks more like a cliché than another cliché. Development politicians and populist developmentalists sometimes use the same words.

An author like Chambers, who vigorously takes development politicians to task, is not in fact impervious to clichés. Nevertheless, his reflections are not to be confused with political cant. He employs a moral and ideological register, combined with abundant scientific references. His audience is also different. He addresses himself to external interveners, to those he refers to as 'outsiders': experts, consultants and development supervisors. He demands that they change their ways, that they listen to peasants, to women, to those who are neglected, and that, regardless of their capacity, they use the room for manoeuvre at their disposal to the advantage of the poor ... Several aspects of intellectual populism can be observed in his arguments – since various types of populism exist. Over and beyond hard core populism (the discovery of the people by intellectuals), which constitutes a kind of invariant, or at any rate the point of origin, various forms and levels of populism need to be highlighted. Hence the need, at this point, to subdivide populism into its numerous components. Developmentalist populism, which displays some of these elements, is a appropriate field in which to carry out this exercise, and Chambers's book is a good guide in this particular.

Moral populism

The first dimension of Chambers's populism is moral populism. Those intervening in development must invert their approach and thus start from the 'bottom up' (with the 'people') instead of starting from the 'top down' (with institutions, bureaucracies, science ...). I am not sure whether this type of exhortation is effective in itself (especially if it remains on a moral level); however, we cannot but agree with its praiseworthy intention. But the real centre of interest is to be found elsewhere. Moral populism, in fact, has two facets – that is, it also has a polemical dimension: to affirm that the poor (the people) exist and that little attention is paid to them implies a condemnation of those who are guilty of this refusal and of this disregard, or of those who uphold it. Affirmative moral populism (it is good to discover the people) is usually associated with denunciative moral populism (it is bad to ignore the people). Chambers is particularly well inspired when he plays in this key, to the extent that his polemical onslaught draws on an acute sense of observation of the everyday practices of his colleagues. In other words, his denunciative moral populism, far from being just a matter of imprecations, happens to be highly relevant. The acerbic and poignant pages in which he describes the everyday practices of consultants ('tourists in rural development', Chambers, 1990: 26–30), or in which he describes researchers in mid-career (ibid.: 22) and demolishes development civil servants (ibid.: 23–4), are right on target and provide a good description of the gulf separating developers and developees.

Cognitive populism and methodological populism

The need to 'discover' the people rapidly gives way to the question, What are we to discover about the people? The moral motivation results in a thirst for knowledge. Moral populism becomes exploratory, cognitive populism. The populism displayed by researchers and scientists represents its most sophisticated form. It corresponds to an identification of systems of conceptions, logics, symbolic productions, and of knowledge peculiar to the 'people', in other words, to 'neglected' or 'dominated' cultures. Berger thus evokes the cognitive respect due to the 'people' (Berger, 1978), and anthropology is, in one sense, entirely founded on this type of rehabilitation of indigenous cultures. Someone like Chambers, who exhorts us to 'go to the school of the poor' and to learn from them, is fascinated by this ethnological 'immersion' and strives to benefit from it. Moral populism, by generating an appeal for cognitive populism, inevitably encounters anthropology. It is to ethnoscience that Chambers turns in his search for scientific references. In his opinion, anthropologists, unlike experts, make an effort to gain inside knowledge about cultures which differ from their own. This is why anthropologists are able to recognize the complexity, the variety and the value of indigenous sense systems ... (Chambers, 1990: 41); in contrast, experts from the outside and local bureaucrats limit themselves to acquisition of pseudo-knowledge, which instead of bringing them closer to the poor draws them even further away. He cites two typical examples of a certain 'culture' common to experts: on one hand, guided tours of villages close to the main road; hard surveys on the other. Chambers thus launches a particularly devastating attack on quantitative surveys, which he refers to as 'the pathology of rural surveys', while painting a picture that is dismal yet true: enquiry is the armoured tank driven by servile researchers; the distortions that abound are eliminated from final reports (ibid.: 93-94). Such proceedings obviously hinder the 'recognition of the knowledge of rural populations' (ibid.: 41). If Chambers's polemical verve happens to strike the right key on this topic, it is because the absurdities he denounces masks a number of fundamental methodological problems, which could be stated thus: in the context of a yawning cultural and cognitive gulf between the surveyors and the surveyed, the developers and those they develop, the enquirers and the enquirees, hard quantitative research tends to produce knowledge that estranges experts, developers and surveyors from the life-worlds and concepts peculiar to those being experted, developed or surveyed, while ethnological research, on the contrary, tends to produce knowledge that brings us closer to them. But, in the context of rural development, how can we overlook the notional systems peculiar to the populations involved (Chapter 3)? Hence, qualitative enquiry seems to be a preliminary step: in the event that quantitative survey is feasible, it can only be conducted on the basis of an in-depth, detailed knowledge of 'indigenous' categories of thoughts and behavioural norms.

This is the aspect of scientific populism that I refer to as methodological populism: it opens the way, *under methodological monitoring*, to new fields of knowledge. It is a heuristic postulate: social science should observe the conceptions and practices of the 'poor' with the keenest attention. They need to apply themselves to a collection of these conceptions and to a description of these practices, and must, to this end, elaborate appropriate methodological procedures, many of which appertain to the anthropological professional culture. Anthropology and populism share a common destiny, and this is not a recent phenomenon.

Ideological populism

Nevertheless, social science populism also incorporates certain elements that are less in line with methodology than with ideology proper. These extend far beyond the universe of research and are prevalent among the intelligentsia. Over and beyond the discovery of popular values, behaviour and resources, there is an idealization that taints the discovery itself, since the scientists making the discoveries have a tendency to portray the people in keeping with their own desires and fantasies. This exaltation of the cognitive, political, moral, cultural virtues of the people is what I refer to as ideological populism.

Chambers unwittingly provides us with numerous examples of this. Some of these are mere caricatures: 'Rural populations are generally long-suffering, hard working, ingenious and very resistant ...' (Chambers, 1990: 173).[6] The people (whether 'near to home', namely the 'popular classes' in Western societies, or 'far away', namely Third World peoples and more particularly their popular classes) represent a privileged space for the projection of stereotypes on the part of intellectuals or dominant groups (Rancière, 1983). These conceptions appertain to various ideological configurations and are sometimes disdainful, sometimes exotic, sometimes pessimistic, sometimes populist. Populist stereotypes stand out because they appreciate and defend the people. They have a certain flavour of nostalgia – they tend to prefer the people who lived in the past. While those of the present still show generosity and other philanthropic qualities, those of the past were the real champions of reciprocity and solidarity (Chambers, 1990: 173). The problem with populist stereotypes, and with stereotypes in general, is that their value is liable to be rapidly inverted. Similar stereotypes that reflect on 'traditional peasant societies' (solidarity, self-reliance, consensus, tradition: as we will remember, Belloncle provides a large sample of similar stereotypes; see Belloncle, 1982) can result either in condemnation (cultural obstacles that hinder development) or in praise (the foundation of 'another' kind of development). The works of Hyden provide a remarkable illustration: in his first book, Hyden congratulates the 'uncaptured' peasantry, regulated by an 'economy of the affection', for resisting 'capitalism'. But this resistance is subsequently denounced as a hindrance to modernization in Hyden's second work (Hyden, 1980, 1983). But other unexpected reversals are possible, and the following in particular: a populist ideology fascinated by the resources of the people easily coincides with pessimistic statements about the deprivations suffered by the people, these wants being identified as so many signs of exploitation. We are once more confronted with various facets of the fundamentally ambivalent character of populism.

Populism and miserabilism

Let us dwell for a moment on the ambiguous relationship that exists between populism and miserabilism, as postulated by Passeron in particular (Grignon and Passeron, 1989). Chambers sometimes insists on the 'resources' of the people, on their potential for creativity and adaptation: regardless of the conditions in which they live or are forced to live, the 'poor' are able to manage the situation with a remarkable savoir-faire. Invoking the talent with which Indonesian mothers raise five children on half a dollar a day, Chambers invites us to consider the poor as 'experts' (Chambers, 1990: 332). Though he does not look down on anecdotes, he also attempts to provide a more general interpretation, via the identification of four domains (why these four in particular?) in which rural populations have, in his opinion, demonstrated their outstanding competence (ibid.: 146–56): agricultural practices (Chambers mentions the current rehabilitation of diversified intercropping formerly decried by agronomists), environmental knowledge (a Bushman, he says, recognizes no less than 300 plants), powers of observation (a Bihari is supposedly capable of instinctively predicting certain meteorological conditions, such as good weather, cloudiness, humidity, temperature and the weather according to the behaviour of animals), and experimental capacities (the Hanunoo, he says, are very curious about unfamiliar plants which they observe by sowing them in small experimental plots).

We thus encounter a complex combination comprising, on one hand, a distinct methodological populism (the people as a reservoir of sense, accessible either through popular 'traditional' knowledge or through the survival strategies deployed within what O. Lewis calls a 'culture of poverty': Lewis, 1969) and, on the other, an approach that falls under ideological populism (the romantic ideas intellectuals have about the people). But then again, at times, Chambers becomes pessimistic: the people live in constant fear of the future (he declares that survival is their major concern – procuring food, avoiding illness and accidents, Chambers, 1990: 233); they have neither independence nor room for manoeuvre (limited power and freedom, ibid.: 314). The very choice of the word 'poor' is revealing. This is undoubtedly a 'miserabilist' or 'dominocentric' attitude (that is, focusing only on the processes of domination), which Passeron contrasts with the populist attitude: populism overestimates the autonomy of the people, while miserabilism underestimates it. Miserabilism is only interested in the mechanisms of domination or in its consequences; it sees the people as victims, and it characterizes their cultures in terms only of an absence or a deficiency (Passeron takes Bourdieu as an example of this second attitude). Passeron demonstrates, extremely convincingly, that these are the two poles between which researchers and writers often oscillate. Chambers's work provides an illustration of this point in the field of development.

However, the problem with this continuous back-and-forth movement between 'populism' and 'miserabilism' can probably be solved by dividing populism into various expressions. In this particular instance, moral populism appears to be the common ideological denominator between these two complementary/contradictory ideologies: the 'populist' ideology and the 'miserabilist' ideology. Understanding the gulf separating intellectuals and the people and aversion to the disdain and ignorance with which the 'dominant' (or the 'privileged') treat the 'dominated' (or the 'outcasts') constitute the common ground on which the exaltation of the virtues and potentials of the people, the denunciation of the oppression they endure, and the observation of their powerlessness are established. Moreover, the populist and miserabilist ideologies not only arise from the same indignation (moral populism), they are both situated in the same semantic register, namely the stereotype. We therefore understand why it is so easy to go from one to the other. The exaltation of the merits and resources of the people is readily converted into a denunciation of the privation they undergo and the powerless condition to which they are confined. Besides, these two statements are not necessarily viewed as incompatible.

Where action becomes compromise

But what happens when the 'soft' ideological register is abandoned, when ideology is incorporated into an institutional system? And, in particular, what happens when the matter is taken into the field of action or into the field of knowledge? Ideology is then subjected to professional constraints, either those specific to 'development', in the case of action, or those of the social sciences, in the case of knowledge. Let us dispel two potential causes of misunderstanding. The contradiction outlined here between knowledge and action is of an institutional character: the rules of the game that govern researchers and those that govern development operators are obviously not the same. However, there is nothing to prevent the same individual from occupying, successively, or even simultaneously, a position in both systems, difficult as this is bound to be. Additionally, so-called applied research, expertise, or evaluation are not necessarily situated in the field of action, irrespective of the fact that the rules that govern them are different from those that govern academic research. Even in the event that the former are legitimated as 'aids to decision making', such undertakings belong solely to a register of knowledge acquisition and are subject to specific pressures (agendas, terms of reference dictated by donors).[7]

Whether we place ourselves in the register of action or in the register of knowledge, populist and miserabilist ideologies do not disappear, far from it, but their mutual relationships assume new dimensions. The contradiction that unites/opposes them raises very different problems seen from one register or from the other.

Let us begin with the example of action, that is, with development practices. Populist ideology gives rise to a policy that promotes characteristic popular resources and supports the dynamics of local societies, while miserabilist ideology generates an educational policy providing for a vulgarization of knowledge coming from the outside, aimed at populations who are incapable of managing on their own. This contradiction is in fact inherent in the developmentalist system: on one hand, development situations imply that the local populations are self-reliant and inevitably rely on an endogenous dynamic, but, on the other, they just as inevitably involve external interveners and assume that transfers of knowledge and resources will naturally take place. There is a constant shift in the balance between these two imperatives. Development practices differ and tend to insist on one pole to the detriment of the other. They cannot abandon one in favour of the other. Indeed, the rhetorics associated with practices sometimes focus on a privileged pole which they use as a means of legitimating their 'commercial talk'. Nonetheless, at one point or another, they will have to take the opposite pole into consideration: those who position themselves in the camp of ideological populism will still have to make allowances for external interveners, while those on the miserabilist side of the fence will still have to make allowances for internal dynamics; this is precisely the dilemma that Chambers finds himself in, and this explains why he oscillates between populist and miserabilist statements. His populist position implies that 'rural populations are actors and not subjects under observation or sources of data' (Chambers, 1990: 126): participatory research is therefore necessary, so that the poor might 'have access to the control of their own destinies' (ibid.) and might rely on their own knowledge and competence. But this is only possible, as he explains with reference to Freire (1980), 'through a pedagogy of the oppressed', which allows the poor to develop a critical outlook on their society and thus escape their 'culture of silence' (ibid.). The intellectual and the populist developmentalist will thus open the eyes and the mouths of the poor, and provide them with the necessary tools for criticism. The now-classic theme of 'raising consciousness' oscillates continually between 'spontaneism', or 'basism', on one hand, and the 'missionary complex' or the 'avant-garde complex', on the other. Basism (we must rely on the creative potentials of the people at the grassroots level) now appears as the expression of the populist ideology in action, in the same way that the avant-garde complex (the people must be enlightened and educated) appears as the expression of the miserabilist ideology in action. This invariably brings to mind another debate, which takes place in another register of action, namely political action. It also reminds us of Lenin's theory of the avant-garde, expressed in *What is to be done?* (Lenin, 1968). Developed in opposition to Russian populists, it insists on the need to import class-consciousness into the proletariat.[8] We could also mention the way in which Mao Zedong attempted to combine this Leninist 'avant-garde' perspective with a remarkably 'populist' perspective, in which the people become the source of all good ideas and moral values, an ideology couched in terms similar to those encountered in the 'populist developmentalist complex' (the barefoot doctors of the Chinese Cultural Revolution have also left their mark on the World Health Organization). In fact, on the subject of action towards social change, the question of the relationship between 'intellectuals' and the 'people' was raised in similar terms by revolutionary action and development action: how will intellectuals, initially motivated by a moral reaction, professionalize this motivation in order to help the people to change their own living conditions? In fact Chambers's vision of the 'new man' – who could be defined as an 'expert of the third order' (doesn't this smack of Lenin's professional revolutionary, or of Mao's communist civil servant, dedicated to the people's cause?) – belongs to this type of perspective. Chambers calls for a 'third culture' which is neither the culture of classic experts nor that of classic researchers (unfortunately, he provides only an overview comprising a somewhat depressing catalogue of pious intentions and philanthropic sentiments). But he does in fact recognize that 'even though there is a lot of talk about "participation", and "research-participation", when all is said and done, it is always an external intervener who tries to change things' (Chambers, 1990: 231). This is precisely at the point of intersection between grassroots populism and avant-garde pessimism, a crossroads that is common to developmentalism and to revolutionary politics: how should 'the strong desirous of changing the conditions of the weak' proceed (ibid.: 231)?

... and where knowledge can become opposition ...

Conversely, when observed from the angle of knowledge, and more precisely of knowledge production in the social sciences, the professionalization of moral populism obeys another set of rules. The tension between miserabilism and populism increases: miserabilism tends to present itself as logically incompatible with populism. Once they have discovered the people, anthropologists

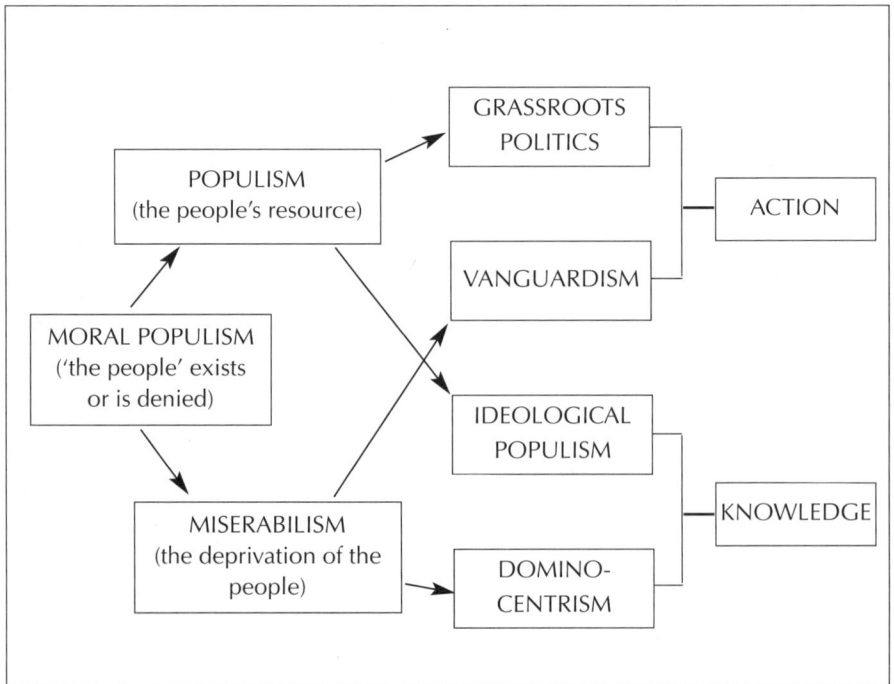

and sociologists either describe the hidden resources at the disposal of the people or analyse the deprivation under which they labour. They rarely attempt to do both. Passeron (Grignon and Passeron, 1989) makes a very subtle analysis of this dialectic of opposition between populism and miserabilism within the social sciences. The problem is that we find ourselves face to face with an apparently inextricable combination of scientific ideologies and heuristic points of view. Two couples confront each other: on one side the points of view concerning the resources peculiar to the people (methodological populism) and the idealization of these resources (ideological populism); and, on the other, the point of view concerning mechanisms of domination (analysis of modes of domination) and the point of view in which the people are defined by the exploitation they endure (which we call, following in Passeron's wake, by the barbaric name of dominocentrism). Thus, miserabilism in the social sciences is also a combination of a cognitive bent (analysis of modes of domination, highlighting structural and systemic constraints, of a sociological type) and of an ideological bent (dominocentrism, that is, the projection of stereotypes of deprivation). Conversely, populism in the social sciences combines both a heuristic tendency ('methodological populism' exploring the resources of dominated people, which is of a more anthropological order) and an ideological tendency, which overlooks the effects induced by the internalization of domination (it operates in accordance with ideological populism and projects romantic stereotypes).

Let us compare the situation as observed in the social sciences (register of knowledge) and in development (register of action). The constraints of development force grassroots and avant-garde activists to make mutual concessions, while the freedom they enjoy as researchers (or their symbolic constraints) allow the miserabilists and populists in social science to present themselves as belonging to two competing, parallel and incompatible standpoints.[9] Opposition between populism and miserabilism tends to be more radical and more persistent in the social sciences than in development because these terms have been established as scientific ideologies competing for an intellectual clientele. Yet their rhetoric has no effect whatsoever on the social practices of the people they evoke. Consequently, social science researchers, free from the constraints of action, unlike development operators, are able to focus exclusively on one pole without having to make allowances for the other. A sociologist studying domination can spend his entire research career ignoring popular conceptions, in the same way that an anthropologist can turn out one publication after another without ever taking political constraints into consideration. As we have seen, this is a kind of luxury that neither the most populist nor the most miserabilist of developers can afford: they are obliged, for their part, to compromise with the other position.

... yet methodology should combine!

'Ideologically' founded due to the constraints (or the lack of constraints) inherent in the world of social science research, the antinomy between these two poles has no 'methodological' foundation. The paradox is that, seen from the perspective of the heuristic (or methodological) requirements, that are the bases of the legitimacy of the social sciences, nothing gainsays a combination of methodological populism with domination analyses. Indeed, combining these two heuristic points of view on one hand, and a popular resources approach with a global structural approach on the other, seems to be a matter of plain common sense.

An epistemological rift between methodological populism and ideological populism and between the analyses of domination and dominocentrism (as a form of the miserabilist ideology within the social sciences) would then be obligatory. This is the price that has to be paid in order to arrive at a scientifically valid combination of the discovery of popular conceptions and popular logics while highlighting the constraints that regulate them.

However, this entry fee is not paid once and for all. It has to be paid over and over again. This is why the critical activity inherent in research is irreplaceable, in the fields of action (political or developmentalist) and knowledge (anthropology) alike. How else can we avoid the ideological rhetoric that proliferates as soon as intellectuals raise the inevitable question of the 'people', in regard to which the field of development represents a major contemporary site?

Notes

1 For a general analysis of the complex relations between populism, anthropology and social sciences, see Olivier de Sardan, 2001a.

2 Brown (1994), on the basis of the analysis proposed below, develops various aspects of Chambers's populism, in which he discerns the foundation of 'managerial consultancy', which is increasingly dominant within the developmentalist configuration.

3 The Marxist-Leninist-Maoist tradition had, indeed, attempted a positive definition of the people as an alliance of the oppressed classes. But there is nothing sociological about such a definition, which constitutes a political argument (rhetoric on the relation between the avant-garde and the masses) or a political strategy (the determination of a 'primary contradiction' defining an enemy and allies).

4 As of 1970, the World Bank underwent a change of policy with McNamara and directed its efforts towards the 'rural poor'. In 1975, USAID demanded a 'social soundness analysis' of all projects, and made a massive appeal to anthropologists who introduced a certain view of development 'from below' (Hoben, 1982). At the same

period, a work with the evocative title *Development from Below* called for a recourse to anthropology in order to promote an alternative development founded on consideration of the grassroots level (Pitt, 1976). The populism/anthropology/development process was already in place prior to Chambers, and was to continue after him (see Cernea, 1991b. Author, anthropologist and World Bank expert, Cernea chose the following title for his work: *Putting People First*, a new populist variation on the theme which had already inspired the titles chosen by Pitt and Chambers).

5 A fashionable French intellectual.

6 Indeed, from time to time Chambers expresses his reservations on ideological populism, since he takes the precaution of declaring that we should not go from disregard to an overestimation of the knowledge possessed by rural populations (p. 144). But this type of rhetorical caution is too general to be of use.

7 The problem related to Rapid Rural Appraisal (RRA) and Methode accélérée de recherche et planification participative (MARP) (see Chapter 13) is therefore crucial whether or not they are satisfactory in terms of knowledge, that is, whether they provide those who order them with trustworthy and relevant data (and not just rapidly collected data). This is indeed a methodological debate.

8 This does not take the Marxism/populism debate into consideration, despite the fact that this debate has a lot to do with the peasantry and with development. Not only is this debate extremely dense, complex and partially outdated, but it also implies an excessively narrow definition of populism, linked to its polemic with Marxism. This brand of populism is indeed theoretical, and extends from Herzen to Chayanov, for the 'classic' period, and is redeployed by contemporary authors sometimes dubbed 'neo-populists' (e.g. Lipton, 1977; see Byres, 1979). The populism referred to here obviously goes far beyond the theories defined as populist theories in the strict sense of the word (either by their authors or by their Marxist detractors). It moreover includes a number of these Marxist authors themselves.

9 I now realize that Bailey had already underlined, for his part, this contrast between the 'debate' (which accentuates differences and antagonisms) and the 'compromise' (produced by the negotiations inherent in all types of action): Bailey, 1973a.

8
Relations of production
and modes of economic action

We could begin with the following question: how can an analysis of relations of production help us to understand social change or popular practices and attitudes in reaction to development actions? In other words, what are the shortcomings of economic anthropology, influenced more or less by Marxism, when it comes to accounting for peasant reactions to rural development?

This is a question that has occurred to many scientists who have spent time looking into the articulation of modes of production: what has become of these paradigms since the outmoding of the intellectual trend that produced them? What is the practical value of the social morphology models, produced by French Marxist anthropology of the 1960s and 1970s, which describe the organization of fundamental socio-economic relations in terms of relations of production?

The answers to these questions must, at least at the outset, be specific, circumscribed and contextualized. Recourse to 'field research' is therefore inevitable. Caution is also advisable. I will take as a point of departure the 'model' I used a few years ago to describe the socio-economic structure of Songhay-Zarma societies (Niger, Mali) under colonial rule (see Olivier de Sardan, 1984). After a brief recall of this model, I will attempt to understand the extent to which it was able to explain peasant practices. I will then proceed to question this model in the light of contemporary reality. Is this approach still valid today? Is it capable of shedding light on the way cultivators behave towards development operations?

Songhay-Zarma societies under colonization: peasant mode of production and relations of production

In many respects, the colonial period brought about a profound transformation of relations of production in western Niger and eastern Mali. It led to an erosion of various pre-colonial relations linked to 'slavery' in the Songhay-Zarma milieu ('familial' or domestic 'captivity', slave trading, slave domains belonging to chiefdoms), and to a dilution of tributary relations related to subjection, war or razzia. The patriarchal domestic system of production gave way to the family households while junior/senior, master/captive relationships (seen here as relations of production internal to the production unit) were eroded. Unequal access to land emerged. These elements, indicating a rupture of 'traditional' social structures, were already visible before the Second World War. A new mode of production was already in place, which I defined at the time as a 'peasant mode of production' (an expression that can be replaced by any other suitable term that designates the combination of commodity production and subsistence production). It was characterized by a nuclear family as the basic unit of production and reproduction, by a reproduction strategy based on a combination of self-subsistence and the sale of surplus produce on the market ('market subsistence'), and the levying of taxes by the state, upstream or downstream of the process of production, as a means of 'capturing surplus' ('despotic exploitation', that is, forced labour, taxation).[1] Moreover, temporary migration was already playing a central role in the total reproduction due to the episodic entry of migrants into 'urban' relations of production (paid labour, the 'informal' economy, leasing, apprenticeship).

This model, which was created in order to account for the empirical data on Songhay-Zarma societies, which are encountered in much of the Sahel, avoided making any kind of reference to the theory of the 'articulation of modes of production', for two reasons. The first is a personal misgiving about the mechanical and formalist pitfalls entailed in 'structuralist' marxism,[2] exacerbated by the strong reservations that I already entertained at the time concerning anthropological structuralism properly speaking (Lévi-Strauss). Second, pre-colonial relations of production having disappeared for the most part (or existing only as marginal phenomena) in western Niger, it is difficult to conceive of any kind of 'articulation' with the capitalist mode of producion. Indeed, the theory of 'the articulation of modes of production' entails a hint of dualism (the coexistence of a 'traditional sector' and a 'capitalist sector') which was hardly compatible with the empirical data at my disposal. In this respect, the very different concept of a 'combination of relations of production' would have been more feasible, because it meshes better with an empirical register, because it admits the coexistence of a variety of relations of production, and because it does not necessarily imply the permanence of a previous mode of production. The system of economic production and reproduction in western Niger at the end of the colonial period and during early independence was in fact defined by a non-binary combination of 'new' and heterogeneous relations of production. Relations of production based on gender (men/women) – characteristic of the 'peasant mode of production' –

occupying a central position, were in fact combined with a variety of rural relations of production that may be termed 'minor' or 'secondary' (in the sense that, present or not, they did not change the functioning of the peasant mode of product): métayage, temporary paid agricultural labours, residual customs linked to 'slavery'. This range of rural relations of production, revolving around peasant domestic production, was in turn combined with various 'urban' relations of production engaged in by migrants on a temporary basis. Finally, the whole was articulated with the demands of the larger society, namely the apparatus of the colonial and post-colonial state, through 'despotic exploitation' (manpower, produce and cash) or through the market (by fixing the price of agricultural produce in a manner enforcing 'unequal exchange'; see Emmanuel, 1972).

Subsistence logic during the colonial period

What light does this model shed on the subject of peasant behaviour under colonial rule? This is an obviously related field and gives rise to an analysis in terms of actors and action: it is a question of the multiple conflicts which placed the colonial administration in opposition to cultivators on the subject of taxes, requisitioning, forced labour, etcetera. I had suggested that the reactions of the Songhay-Zarma people to state levying should be considered as varied expressions of a 'strategy of evasion'. As mentioned earlier (Chapter 5) similar modes of behaviour had been described as characteristic of peasant communities (everyday peasant reaction, evasive reactions, defensive strategies). In the case of Niger, the pressure of tax levying that the state brought to bear on rural domestic units led to clashes which I have attempted to describe from the angle of social or anthropological history, considered from the 'grassroots' level.

This kind of analysis is indebted to a certain extent to the Marxist heritage, which associates class struggle with the structure of relations of production, seen as the main or even the sole form of the relation between social morphology and actors' strategies. However, 'peasant resistance' in Niger (and elsewhere, it appears) did not assume the classic forms of collective action, duly classified by the labour movement. Nor did the 'confrontations' between Songhay-Zarma cultivators and the colonial state apparatus coincide with the usual mediations referred to by classic Marxist theoreticians in their description of the transition from class affiliation to class behaviour: 'raising consciousness', organization, role of an avant-garde ... The isolation experienced by each agricultural unit in face of the process of production and of the modes of extortion at both ends of the production continuum reflected the isolated nature of the resistance to exactions: they were individual, diffuse and non-organized. Their aim was neither to change nor to reform the system, but simply to minimize exactions, at the lowest possible cost: that is, by reducing the risks of possible repression. Hence the recourse to guile, dissimulation, lying, evasion and inertia.

Certain 'development operations' – though the term 'development' did not exist at the time, the reality as defined at the outset of the present work was already in motion – carried out by the colonial state thus came up against resistance of this type, either because these operations were just another aspect of the system of despotic exploitation (the creation of infrastructure through forced labour) or because they resorted to similar methods (reserve granaries or cereal storehouses), or yet again because they were executed by the same administrative agents (see commercial crops, in some instances).

Nonetheless, peasant strategies were mostly individual in nature and conflicts were not expressed through collective actions. Peasant behaviour was not regulated by any kind of 'co-ordination' whatsoever. Nor was there any kind of 'village community' to dictate the modes of economic action of its members. But this does not mean that, on the basis of the constraints defined by modes or relations of production, individual strategies were 'free' or haphazard. The accumulation of individual strategies operated along obvious lines of force. Peasants did not consult with each other in order to conceal from the 'commandant' the number of domestic animals they possessed, but almost all of them did dissemble, each after his own fashion. Young men did not meet in general assemblies to decide to depart for coastal countries, but almost all of them went, each in his own way. How can we explain the convergence of such economic behaviour?

One might think that within a general economic space structured by a given combination of relations of production, the modes of economic action available to peasants would be limited, and would reflect a more or less common 'logic' of action. I described this as a 'logic of subsistence'. This could also be termed a 'logic of reproduction'. The term 'subsistence' might be confusing. I am referring here not to immediate needs in terms of food (the theory of 'basic needs'), but rather to social 'subsistence', in other words to the satisfaction of a family's social needs, to its cultural reproduction.[3] It is not a matter of self-reliance in the area of agricultural production: to my mind, the 'logic of subsistence' did not imply opposing subsistence farming to the sale of surplus (millet, rice) or to the introduction of commercial crops (peanuts). This dichotomy, which tends to present self-reliance as a virtue of authentic peasant production, and commercial crops as the sign of 'capture' by capitalism, coincides neither with pre-colonial realities (goods were often traded) nor with colonial realities (in western Niger, the increase in trade during colonisation involved both subsistence and commercial crops).[4] In fact, in the case of western Niger, the sale of surplus crops, subsistence or commercial, on the market, was essentially a subsistence strategy (used in order to acquire the cash indispensable to social reproduction) and was in this respect distinct from strategies of speculation (merchants) or 'capitalist' strategies (accumulation for investment).

Incapable of influencing market rates, unconcerned by speculative or plantation farming, and deprived, at the time, of any reliable means of improving an output essentially dependent on rainfall, the vast majority of Songhay-Zarma peasants had no other mode of economic action at their disposal, so far as agriculture was concerned, than a combination of subsistence production and small-scale commodity production. This was even combined with two other, 'non-agricultural' modes of action: evasive strategies, on one hand (in the face of exactions), and migration, on the other. We need to recall that the temporary migration of young men to Ghana was a massive phenomenon. These seasonal migrations were perfectly integrated into the subsistence logic, by extending its application to the urban milieu; that is, by going outside the universe of farming in search of complementary resources.

Hence, *the logic of subsistence cut across different relations of production in which the peasants (who were not only peasants) were engaged.* The terms 'merchant subsistence' (sale of agricultural produce) or 'wage subsistence' (sale of one's labour power) or 'self-sufficient subsistence' could have been used to define the different forms assumed by the logic of subsistence, depending on the type of relation of production through which it was expressed. These three forms were characteristic of the major sectors in which family reproduction was an objective. A given actor sought to achieve subsistence through a combination of strategies. Hence, the subsistence logic was put into action within relations of production that were various and multiple.

In this perspective, an analysis of relations of production becomes an analysis of the constraints brought to bear on the logic of subsistence, the obstacles in its path. In a way, such an analysis provides a list of possible solutions, and sketches the subsistence network available to a given social group, within a given society, at a given time. It also indicates inevitable and probable points of transit. Finally, it indicates possible points of conflict, the sensitive areas liable to provoke confrontations between peasants engaged in their subsistence logic and other social groups with logics of a different kind (colonial civil servants, indigenous agents of the administration, entrepreneurs, etcetera …): the price of produce, levels of exaction, the level of salaries …

The concept of 'subsistence logic', as I then understood the term, on the basis of Songhay-Zarma material, coincided with the way in which certain sociologists used the term 'logic'. However, my use of the term was not totally identical to theirs. Indeed, using 'logic' to mean a logic of action amounts to putting the emphasis on the social actor and the elements that support his system of action. It is an attempt at looking at structures in a more dynamic light, of going from structures to behaviour, and of linking the two. When the various actions under consideration are economic in nature, or express themselves economically, the underlying logics that propel them must be discovered in reference to the modes of economic action involved. The 'subsistence logic', read as the common denominator of the economic behaviour of a majority of peasant actors, allows us to break away from economic structuralism and from classic Marxism.

But, for those authors who are more or less affiliated with the 'moral economy', the word 'logic' remains linked to the term 'relations of production'. A given mode of production is said to correspond to a specific type of actors' logic, and to be related to a system of norms, itself associated with the mode of production in question. Hence, the logic of subsistence or of food security would be inherent in the mode of peasant production, according to Hyden, or to the 'feudal' (or 'patron/client') mode of production, according to Scott (1976; see Chapter 5).[5] This brings us back to the risk of taking a given logic as the only explanatory principle behind the peasant or 'traditional' economy.

It appeared to me that, on the contrary, the 'subsistence logic' had to be disconnected from a given mode of production, or relation of production. I saw it as transversal, at work at the heart of a variety of relations of production. In fact, the 'subsistence logic' can be viewed as a kind of link between the various modes of economic action covering the range of individual peasant practices, on one hand, and the system of constraints to which they are all subjected, on the other. The 'subsistence logic' represented, in a way, the ultimate point of coherence of the various strategies deployed in the playing of an economic game whose rules were defined by the relations of production and the local normative system (so-called 'cultural constraints') and, at the same time, by social power struggles (what we could call 'political' constraints). Indeed, we could suppose that the fact that information circulates in a village and that networks of interconnection exist implies that modes of individual economic action are canalized within limits that are compatible with norms of group affiliation, with the list of possible relations of production, and with the power struggles linked to these relations of production. This defines the possibilities that exist in a given space–time.

Relations of production and contemporary transformations

Is it feasible to hold that analysis of the relations of production and the subsistence logic conducted with reference to colonization is rendered obsolete when one considers contemporary society? This is far from the case. The 'peasant mode of production' is still the major regulator of Songhay-Zarma agricultural production. We are as yet far away from the 'extinction of the peasantry' diagnosed in Europe. A few changes have of course occurred in 'secondary' rural relations of production: the erosion of the final vestiges of tributary relations and the marginal development of a capitalist type of agriculture. The forces of production have been developed in certain sectors (hydro-agricultural infrastructure). But these have not resulted in a disruption of rural relations of production. Migration has chosen new destinations, but the phenomenon remains as important as ever.

Notwithstanding, there is one area of significant change: despotic exploitation has essentially come to an end. Its cessation did not coincide with independence. A first stage in its cessation occurred in 1945, with the end of the 'colonial golden age' and the suppression of forced labour. A second break with the past occurred in the 1970s with the coming on stream of uranium income and the years of drought, the joint effects of which led to a spectacular reduction in taxation. The plundering of the countryside came to an end.

But there are other types of change that cannot be analysed in terms of relations of production, to the extent that they occur at another level and are played out 'within' the relations of production already in place. This applies to most of the innovations resulting from the various development operations, either directly (infrastructure) or indirectly (diffusion of techniques and material), often by the market rules of 'free competition', or by means of an imperceptible change in 'individual' behaviour ... Indeed, both heavy interventions (dykes and irrigation) and light incentives (diffusion of animal traction, post-harvest vegetable gardening) have managed to integrate the pre-existing relations of production, without causing change (as far as the time scale we are using is concerned).

Hydro-agricultural schemes installed along the Niger river (mostly oriented towards rice farming) were the major development operations in the west of the country. After modest beginnings, they turned out to be an unquestionable success, thanks to massive investments, and led to a marked improvement in the lives of the peasants concerned. However, the installation of these 'co-operative' structures has not affected the predominance of the peasant mode of production. These developments are based on the principle of the attribution of one lot to each family living along the river, in a context in which the pre-existing rice fields were already a rare commodity which could be rented or ceded, a context in which strategies of land accumulation were already under way. It is true that corruption and influence led to certain families and civil servants acquiring more than one lot. Nonetheless, the developments served to consolidate the mode of peasant production (extended families were no longer units of production at the time: see Olivier de Sardan, 1969) and the developments furnished nuclear families with an additional and secure base of reproduction (commodity subsistence, since the rice was for sale). This was a direct result of the increase in the number of rice fields (owing to equipment) and of the increase in productivity (owing to irrigation).

It is possible that these innovations affected 'secondary' relations of production most of all, with the development, on a temporary basis, of the use of paid labour in the rice fields (most of whom came from the 'interior' of the country) and with the shift in the gender division of labour (rice paddy being sold directly to the factory for industrial hulling and no longer to women who formerly husked the rice by hand). But this did not result in any significant changes in the social structure. Moreover, and for separate reasons, permanent migration to urban areas (a definitive 'exit' from rural relations of production) took the place of temporary migration.

The development of vegetable farming, the possibility of obtaining a second harvest of rice, the use of inputs and of more sophisticated equipment (animal traction) do not stand in contradiction with the 'subsistence logic', which apparently continues to regulate the majority of peasant economic action. As the situation now stands, one can hardly mainstain that rural 'entrepreneurs' or capitalist agricultural exploitation have become a dominant reality. What is noticeable, at the most, is an increase in strategies of accumulation. However, this usually takes the form of proceeds from non-agricultural activities (trade, migration, the civil service) reinvested in rice production. The question is whether this tendency will gain momentum and ultimately become a threat to the small-scale production of cash crops that is the order of the day. That is possible, but it is far from being a present-day reality.

However, the constant flux of migrants from zones equipped with infrastructure raises a number of questions surrounding the subsistence logic. Why is the drift from the land still going on, largely undisturbed, despite the relative increase in agricultural resources?

1 First, we could propose a series of answers that does not put the prevalent subsistence logic in doubt. Indeed, this logic works so long as work on the local scene is compatible with urban migration, and providing that, even by increasing one's input in one area, both activities can still be combined. So long as the workforce available on site is sufficient (taking extra paid hands into account), those surplus to requirements can continue the outflow to other areas. We could advance the hypothesis that the diversification of means of subsistence is a characteristic element of the subsistence logic. Last, one could argue that the revenue gained on account of migration far exceeds the revenues available locally (work on the hydro-agricultural schemes).

2 To answer this question on another level we need to include other kinds of parameters. In the past, migration was attributed solely to 'cultural' reasons

(see Rouch, 1956). Conversely, one should avoid the other extreme: interpreting the phenomenon as a result of economic mechanisms alone (see Painter, 1987). Complex social phenomena are generated by complex factors ... Migration is the combined result of a search for ready cash, the emancipation of juniors and the search for prestige. The effort to provide for the needs of one's family, or for one's own need, plus the means of gaining social recognition or admission to new social networks all play a role in this phenomenon, though they are not always easy to discern. At any rate, migrations cannot be analysed on the basis of a single cause.

The interesting thing about migration is that it constitutes a spontaneous economic behaviour, independent of external interventions. On the contrary, successive governments have all attempted to stall migration by reverting to policies based on a voluntarist approach. Be that as it may, these connections with far-off countries, through migrants (like those connections made through the 'war veterans' and the 'tirailleurs sénégalais' of another age, who survived the wars in Europe or in the colonies), have often led to the introduction of various ('informal') innovations in the rural milieu, separate and apart from any type of development action.

Thus, when producers 'decide' to adopt innovations from the outside, whether introduced by migrants or by development intervention, the processes involved cannot, in themselves, throw any direct light on the analysis of relations of production, nor are they liable to pinpoint the transversal logics that regulate these relations of production. Hence, in western Niger, attempts to promote the use of ploughs and carts remained ineffectual for a long time; then, all of a sudden, word got round and has led to a rapid increase in their use. It is clear that phenomena of this type cannot be understood by means of references to small-scale commodity production or subsistence logic.

Conclusion

Concepts should not be expected to do the impossible. As mentioned above, the concept 'relations of production' is related to social morphology; it cannot explain the everyday practices that development comprises. 'Relations of production' constitute a 'macro'-type indicator, which is relevant for long- or medium-term analysis (as stated in Braudel's well-known typology). Its potentials have long since been explored. The basic forms of the organization of production or the extraction of surplus labour within the process of production, or in its preparatory stages are limited in number. Those that apply to western Niger can be observed elsewhere, and many scientists have reached similar conclusions in other fields, though with differences in vocabulary and in details of analysis. The total number of structures of fundamental relations of production under which contemporary African producers can be classified are quite limited, amounting to ten or so. This can be taken as a given fact, once and for all, thus sparing the pains of reinventing the wheel.

The concept of a 'subsistence logic' or a 'logic of reproduction', is, for its part, a lot more dynamic than the concept of 'relations of production', to the extent that it underlines the rationality on which a whole range of modes of economic action are grounded (regardless of the relations of production involved). The 'subsistence logic', however, is not a kind of 'master key', capable of explaining everything. It is itself relatively abstract, since its aim is to indicate the basic economic coherence of a variety of concrete modes of behaviour. But there is another difficulty involved: the 'subsistence logic' is not the only specifically economic logic at the base of most peasant reactions to development initiatives. Logics of 'speculation' and 'capitalist' logics, though they start by affecting particular social groups, can of course gain a broader influence, if only over short periods of time. Though it is true that the small farmer is, as a rule, mainly involved in a logic of reproduction, this can also coincide with a logic of accumulation; thus, the logic of accumulation is not monopolized by 'great families', comprising civil servants–aristocrats–landowners, though these great families provide the most outstanding and effective examples of accumulation strategies in action. This fact has already been underscored by Yung and Zaslavsky (1992). In their analysis of the productive behaviour of cultivators and cattle breeders in the Sahel, the behaviour of this group is defined as a combination of 'defensive strategies' (aimed at warding off risks, minimizing risk and 'by-passing' risk factors) and of 'offensive strategies' (corresponding to goals of growth and accumulation). The defensive strategies in question correspond to what I call 'subsistence logic'. Defensive strategies that are mainly deployed by small-scale producers are not incompatible with the putting into practice of 'offensive' strategies appropriate to the 'investment logic'; it all depends on the climate and the economic context.

Hence, the 'subsistence logic' can exist in combination with other logics of economic action, and with logics of non-economic action, in a wide variety of relationships. Obviously, this is far removed from the kinds of equation that rule that 'a mode of production = a mode of economic action'.

Notes

1 The term 'peasant mode of production' as used here does not coincide with Hyden's definition; first, because the system in question here is an economic system resulting from the disintegration of 'traditional' forms of production, and second, because this

system is also based in part on small-scale commercial production, linked to the global capitalist economy.

2 The 'Maoist' movement, in which many researchers of my generation were involved (I was), has resulted in a tendency to place a higher priority on 'the resources of the masses' than on economic determinisms (a kind of populist voluntarism which Trotskyists often qualified as 'spontaneism').

3 Despite their often ostentatious character, the spending linked to social exchanges (like marriages) is therefore included: in fact, this is compatible with Marx's definition of 'historically determined needs' regarding the 'use value' of the workforce.

4 As has already been noted, the rising importance of commercial crops in forest and coastal plantations zones (coffee, cocoa), during the colonial period, was not the direct result of a ruling by the colonial masters. In part, it sometimes ran counter to their prescriptions or was not quite in keeping with their expectations (see Chauveau and Dozon, 1985). Nonetheless, the surplus that could be generated here and there by commercial crops was obviously one of the factors in the emergence of strategies of accumulation in agriculture.

5 Inversely, the defenders of so-called methodological individualism (in fact ideological individualism), tend to take for granted the existence of a general and practically universal actors' logic.

9

Development projects and social logic

A development enterprise is always an arena in which various logics and strategies come into confrontation: those of the initiators of the development enterprise confront those of the so-called target population. Here I will take as the ideal type of development enterprise the development 'project', which is undoubtedly currently the most widespread and the most conspicuous type of development structure. But there are other institutional forms designed for improving development. Separate and apart from the classic project and its methods, there are different ways of organizing development: the 'game' public technical services usually play, the circulation of agricultural advisers or commercial agents, rural training, extension activities or the action of the social services, the creation of public or private infrastructure, the piloting of communication campaigns, the establishment of a banking network. These are all means of organizing development. However, regardless of the type of organization or the mode of intervention, a development action inevitably gives rise to interaction between social actors belonging to different worlds (developers/developees, for example) and whose behaviour patterns are regulated by a variety of logics. To this extent, our comments on projects also apply to other types of development enterprises, so long as we acknowledge that each development enterprise obviously has its own particular modes of organization and labours under specific constraints. At any rate, in the face of the resources, opportunities and constraints of which a particular development undertaking is composed, in interaction with the milieu (a 'project organization', in this instance), the social actors involved behave in various contrasting, sometimes contradictory ways. This is not only a matter of distinct personal choices; it is also a reflection of dissimilar interests, different norms of evaluation, a divergence in 'objective' positions occupied by individuals.

I will continue to use the term 'logic', while extending its field of application. It will be a question of pinpointing certain levels of coherence, surrounding the interaction between a project and a population, which allow us to explain similar types of behaviour (and their internal differences). In reality, despite the existence of an infinite variety of individual actions and reactions, the number of behaviour patterns is limited. I will attempt to define these in terms of 'logics' or 'strategies'. It would be a waste of time to propose formal definitions with the aim of distinguishing 'strategies' and 'logics': these two terms are usually employed as synonyms. For example, what Yung and Zaslavsky call a 'strategy' corresponds to what I will define here as a 'logic': 'By the strategy of agricultural producers, we mean the understanding put into practice by those for whose way of life agricultural and pastoral processes of production are central, and who bring agricultural means to bear as one element in achieving the maintenance, reproduction and growth of the family unit, in a context ever increasingly affected by uncertainty' (Yung and Zaslavsky, 1992: 24). This point of view even allows us to coin the expression 'strategic logics' in order to typologize the various 'arts' that actors deploy, as opposed to their 'notional logics', which is a category defining various ways of perceiving reality.

In fact, reference is sometimes made to a subsistence logic or to a strategy of reproduction as a mean of homogenizing a vast range of behaviour patterns by reducing them to the ulterior economic objectives actors set for themselves. Sometimes, too, reference is made to a security logic or a strategy aimed at minimizing risks as the means of enveloping another collection of modes of economic behaviour, which can be defined, more or less, as subsets of the former: the management of risk and security is one way of ensuring reproduction and subsistence. Sometimes, one speaks of an aid logic or of an aid-seeking strategy in order to designate another set of behaviour patterns (see also below), which intersects with the preceding: they may promote security but not exclusively. This variability in the use of the terms 'logic' or 'strategy' should not disturb us overmuch. If they cannot be stabilized at a single level of application this is simply because the behaviour patterns of the actors themselves occupy a variety of levels of overlapping coherence. Reference to actors' logics in general or to strategy per se is fruitless and even absurd.[1] A logic or strategy must always be specifically defined in order to make sense from a sociological point of view. On condition that one respects this imperative of clear definition, which is the only way of clarifying the level of coherence of the practices being investigated, the highlighting of overlapping or interfacing logics and strategies is merely a reflection of the complexity and diversity of social practices.

The context of interaction

Let us get back to the question of the interactions between a method of intervention and the population involved, seen from the angle of the impact of a development project. From the very outset, we need to bear in mind the fact that 'project/milieu' interactions take place in a particular context (whether ecological, economic, institutional or political) which deeply affects the outcome of this intervention. Developers and developees enter into relationship in the context of an environment that does not depend on them and that exerts a significant pressure on their relationship. Hence, a rural development project is faced with a variety of factors beyond its control, on which it is partially dependent: unpredictable climate, pricing systems, structures of securing and commercializing stocks, other interventions occurring in the same milieu (concurrent projects, taxation, administrative measures), opportunities existing outside the local system of production (migrations, schooling ...). The way peasants react to a project depends to a great degree on external factors. This is one element that analysis must take into account.

Moreover, current projects all take place in a milieu that has already experienced previous interventions which have left their mark,[2] despite the fact that 'the natural tendency of any project is to assume that history begins with the project, to underestimate everything that came before and to overestimate its own impact' (translated from Gentil et Dufumier, 1984: 25). Peasant societies all have an economic history of trade (pre-colonial), of 'mise en valeur' (colonial) and of 'development'. They also have a history of rural training, of agricultural popularization, of co-operatives, of the one-party system, of projects small and large, of producers' associations, of the coming of NGOs, of the creation of village–member associations, etcetera. This history is also interlaced with tales of corruption, patron–client relationships, bureaucratic tyranny and incompetence – four fundamental themes which are factors in all long-term relationships between the African peasantry and the outside world of the state or of parastatal institutions. In this respect, 'projects' which strive to break away from the modes of state intervention and to substitute themselves, in part, for state interventions (or to short-circuit them), reproduce, often unwittingly, the state's methods of functioning, while contributing a few perverse effects of their own (see Daane and Mongbo, 1991: 65; Tidjani Alou, 1994).

Be that as it may, it is possible, everywhere, to bring to light a particular local history, which we could call a local history of contact with politico-economic interventionism, which necessarily structures current behaviour patterns, at least in part.

Consequently, the synchronic and the diachronic contexts should in no event be ignored or underestimated.

Levels of project coherence

A project always claims to have a specific coherence which justifies its existence, and which is often opposed to former or neighbouring projects, the development configuration being a world of fierce competition. However, this necessary declaration of coherence, which is one of the essential conditions of funding, and which is often expressed through a specific rhetoric (the 'project language': see Chapter 9), is always undermined not only by the interaction between the project and the target population (see below) but also by the various elements that participate in the project itself. Let us take the example of the classic rural development project, which is still relatively prevalent (though it does not enjoy the same hegemony as before and has undergone certain transformations), and which derives its coherence from a production model arising from agronomy research, founded on clearly stated technical rationality.[3] In this perspective, which draws its inspiration from the 'green revolution' in India and from European experiences, it is a matter of importing a model of intensive production into the African peasantry, which also implies, over and beyond popularization and training, an in-depth transformation of peasant 'technical culture'. We could note, for example, the criteria that presided over the elaboration of the model and which regulate research in tropical agronomy: the creation of species and techniques that allow a high yield per hectare, adapted to average climatic conditions. These techniques are supposedly easily adoptable, and classified as 'simple', in terms of the technical culture of the Western peasantry, taken as the reference.

However, this technical rationality is confronted, within the developmentalist configuration itself, and therefore prior to any kind of interaction with the local populations, with other registers of coherence.

In fact, the technical model derived from agronomic research invariably promotes production goals intimately connected with the strategic considerations of national policies (balance of payments, structural adjustment, etcetera) which determine the general orientation that projects adopt. Thus technical coherence is overshadowed, if only nominally, by another level of coherence – economic policy or national planning – which has no direct relation with agronomy and its techniques. Notwithstanding, this declared coherence is sometimes in contradiction with the 'real' modes of functioning of public administration. As a result, this type of project is almost always short of at least some of the means required for action (see the comments on context on the previous page). In some cases, the problem concerns a lack of control over commercialization, in others it concerns the disastrous situation of the co-operatives in question and, everywhere there is the problem of corruption. These are a few examples that illustrate the extent to which the logics of action of certain mechanisms of the state apparatus or of the national economy, which totally escape the project's control, are liable to jeopardize its policy.

A third level of coherence, also independent of the two mentioned above, concerns the role of financiers and donors. Their influence is manifested indirectly, in the choice of technical agricultural models, in the national economic policy and the projects it approves. Moreover, in the context of the rapid decline of local administrations, financiers and donors claim an increased right to examine the exactitude in finances and accountancy on which, to a great extent, their norms of evaluation are based.

The structure of the project proper – that is, the project as an institution, apparatus, organization – constitutes the final level of coherence, which is also independent. It is a well-known fact that a project has its 'organizational logics', its specific constraints, its dyfsunctions, its 'informal economy', which are quite different from the official flowchart. The hierarchical ladder, the collection and flow of information, the capacity of adaptation and self-correction are therefore parameters of primary importance. At this level, the 'professional culture' of development agents and the norms that regulate their training and career must be established as objects of anthropological investigation (see Koné, 1994). In more general terms, it is the project as an organization or as a system of interaction between employees and agents that inevitably leads to various types of sidetracking of the project as it exists 'on paper'. It will suffice to raise the example of the serious discrepancy that exists between the idea of a project, which is supposed to be temporary and whose intention is to the provide the populations it assists with the means of carrying on on their own and freeing themselves from the project as soon as possible, and the project as an organization and as a system of resources whose agents intend, on the contrary, to prolong its existence as far as possible (see Berche, 1994; Koné, 1994).

In other words, all development projects – projects aimed at health, institutional or rural development, or otherwise – are connected, over and beyond the single level of coherence they are obliged to exhibit (the project 'on paper'), to several partially contradictory levels of compatibility:

(a) the internal coherence of the technical model

(b) the compatibility of the project with the national economic policy

(c) the conformity of the project with donors' norms

(d) the internal dynamic of the project itself.[4]

Thus, even if the problem of its contacts with the population is put aside, a project is still a partially incoherent entity, since it comprises various types of coherence. The fine coherent, technical and argumentative rationality around which projects are generally elaborated comes up against serious difficulties even before the project work begins.

Peasant reactions

The way in which the various categories of producers react obviously enhances the 'dismembering' of a project. This is an example of the 'sidetracking' mentioned above: it is the inevitable outcome of contact with reality. The question is whether or not everyday sidetracking can help us to learn a few lessons, even if they only illustrate the fact that 'developers' and 'developees', of necessity, do not have the same logics.[5] We could make a test based on two examples.

1. Dominant agronomic logics (those of research institutes, for instance) pay only scant or incomplete attention, in the process of research, to the range of 'non-technical' systems of constraint to which producers are exposed. The reactions of peasants are often linked to economic rationalities properly speaking, which integrate data on the economic and ecological environment (which is not the case with 'pure' agronomic researchers in laboratories): producers tend to take as the point of reference a year of insufficient rainfall rather than a year of average rainfall; to minimize on inputs if cash is limited; to avoid farming methods that rely on a workforce that is unavailable at a time when numerous tasks need to be performed; to preserve or gain access to land and to increase patrimonial land. Such preferences are in keeping with an economic logic familiar to peasants around the world.

2. The point of view of national planners and economists, whose problem is to increase the gross national product (GNP), to reduce reliance on foreign aid, to increase the inflow of foreign exchange, to obtains loans from the World Bank (depending on the case in point, on the region, on the historical period), is obviously different from the point of view of the head of a peasant household (or that of his junior brother or of his wife) whose problem is to find means of subsistence and reproduction (and of extension, wherever possible …). The criteria on which peasants and experts base their professional activity and the risks they respectively face are completely different: when a project fails, the professional in charge usually suffers no professional consequences, but the peasant gambles his security on each harvest.

As concerns rural development in general, the way peasants react to the proposals a project puts forward is usually, despite the variety of local situations, linked to a limited number of constraints. The following logics or strategies, more or less updated depending on the context, local situation or social groups, are the most frequently encountered:

- Maximizing workforce productivity as opposed to productivity per hectare (the option prescribed by agronomic research).

- Attempts at capturing land or staking off lots of land when the process of improvement begins.

- Placing priority on extensive farming whenever possible (that is, when land is relatively available) to the detriment of the intensification preached by projects. This is linked essentially to the two preceding points.

- Minimizing climatic risks. Hence frequent mistrust of selected seeds, which perform better in average years, but are more fragile in bad years.

- Minimizing of risks due to the dysfunctioning of official circuits of maintenance, of commercialization, and of provision of inputs. Hence the recourse to 'traditional' or 'informal' networks (local merchants and local artisans …).

- Annual revision of the choice of crops, and, in particular, of the ratio of subsistence crops to cash crops. This is not only a strategy of self-reliance, but also concerns the comparative profitability of both types of crops as speculative investments (food crops being cultivated also for profit).

- Control of the recruitment of the labour force (kinship or 'ethnic' network strategies).

- Modes of accumulation and use of an eventual surplus based on norms of ostentation and patron–client strategies.

- Use of non-agricultural resources (migration …).

- Making investments outside agriculture (schooling of children …).

- Personal appropriation of collective resources.

- Using credits obtained for ends other than those declared officially.

This list is not exhaustive. But the problem of enumeration might be simplified if an attempt is made to define 'types' of behaviour, or a few major alternatives. We might note, for example, that contemporary African peasants are faced with a series of more or less conflicting alternatives: safety versus risk; intensification versus extensive farming; agro-pastoral production versus non-agricultural resources; consolidating inheritance versus investment; redistribution (patron–client investment) versus savings (productive investment). However, the decisions peasants make at each of these levels appear to be connected essentially to context-related variables, and not to standard solutions or to the solutions that technical services and development operators usually prescribe. We could attempt to identify a number of these context-related variables: the gravity of the ecological crisis, the degree of civil service corruption, the degree of reliability of circuits of commercialization, the availability of opportunities outside agriculture, the amount of tension surrounding issues related to land, etcetera.

Other typologies could be used – for instance that of Yung and Zaslavsky (1992), mentioned above, who propose a more dynamic method of distinguishing between 'offensive strategies' and 'defensive strategies', in an attempt at summarizing peasant reactions, based on a corpus of Sahelian development projects.

As we will recall, the recurrence of similar behaviour patterns, encountered in a variety of situations, is by no means the result of discussion between the people involved. Peasant logics are expressed through fragmented, individual economic behaviour. They do not constitute a 'collective' (that is, deliberate, concerted) reaction of the peasantry in question (which is not a collective agent and does not constitute a relevant level of decision making), but rather an aggregate or composite effects (the same causes – a given social logic – are likely to produce the same effects, at the level of a given set of relevant actors: women, seniors, juniors, leasers, etcetera). Convergent, atomized actor behaviour should not be seen as the doing of a collective actor; hence our reference to actors' logics. The problem could be shifted to another level of abstraction at which recurrent behaviour empirically observed could be defined as the working out of a number of basic principles. These go beyond the framework of rural development, since they appear to regulate various behaviour patterns in other domains.

Two principles

Two very general principles seem to be deducible from the infinite variety of concrete behaviour displayed by populations in the face of various types of development operations: the principle of selection and the principle of side-tracking.

The principle of selection
Technical messages, development projects and interventions are all 'packages' or sets of co-ordinated measures which claim to be coherent. The package proposed is never 'completely' adopted by the 'target' population: it is always picked apart, to a greater or lesser degree, by the selections that 'target' populations make among the elements proposed.

In this game the rule is neither 'take all' nor 'leave all'. The usual process is one of selective adoption. Certain themes 'work' while others do not. Thus the technical coherence presented by an agronomic project in the form of 'packages of techniques' is systematically disarticulated. This results in a number of 'perverse effects', which annul the effectiveness of the improvements proposed and might even induce outright negative results (see, for example, Yung, 1985). As for so-called 'integrated' development operations, which combine technical packages with other elements (training, management, literacy programmes, women's groups etcetera) with a view to achieving 'horizontal coherence', these are even more subject to selective adoption. This is all the more paradoxical considering their ideology (liable to be interpreted as a 'totalitarian' and ineffective vision of development) which advocates complementarity between modes of intervention as a necessary requirement.

This principle also applies in the field of public health: doctors in the North will not be surprised by selective strategies as they are well aware that their patients never observe their prescriptions rigorously, that they make their own selections (of drugs or dosages) in keeping with the dominant family traditions, sub-cultures and networks to which they are affiliated, in consequence of factors such as finances or the pace at which they live, etcetera.

The principle of sidetracking

The reasons that motivate the adoption of a given development measure by potential users is generally at odds with the reasons cited by the experts who propose them. In other words, peasants exploit the opportunities at their disposal in keeping with their own particular objectives.

Credits granted by a development project for the acquisition of oxen and the promotion of animal traction are diverted to produce milk or fatten cattle; a vegetable farming co-operative proposed by an NGO with a view to ensuring self-sufficiency uses the proceeds to buy a minibus to conduct regular tourist visits to the village; the managers of a village pharmacy distribute drugs primarily to acquaintances, parents, close relatives and important men: there are endless examples of sidetracking.

Selective adoption and sidetracking can both be considered as ways in which a target group 'appropriates' a project. The paradox is that this appropriation, which in theory is the end sought by development operations, assumes shapes that often run counter to the project's objectives and methods.

These two very general principles aside, one can attempt to draw out some more specific logics encountered in a variety of practical situations. I will mention only three of these. There are many others.

Three logics, among many others

Seeking safety

Minimizing risk is a fundamental peasant strategy. One example is the resistance to high-yield seeds distributed by agricultural services (these thrive under average rainfall conditions, but are very vulnerable when rainfall is insufficient). Another example is the refusal to introduce new crops which might not sell well, or the choice of increasing a herd rather than selling meat on the market ...

'Tried and proven methods' – the way local peasants practice agriculture is usually the result of a long history of adaptation to a given environment, an adaptation that has proven its worth in the long run[6] – are, logically, preferred to taking risks. And the proposals made by development agents usually entail a high degree of risk taking on the part of peasants (risks which in no wise affect the development agents themselves – they have their salaries), and the experience of recent decades has too often confirmed the dangers involved.[7]

One could go even further and estimate that routine behaviour generally ensures safety for the peasantry (given the dominant mode of production based on the use of kin as the labour force and on a combination of self-sufficiency and commodity exchange) and for the development agents (who generally belong to bureaucratic organizations) who are not very flexible, as a rule, and who often propose innovations – to other people – in a very routine manner!

So far as the problems related to health are concerned, the situation is even more complex, despite the fact that, in the final analysis, the problems remain the same: peasant experiences confirm the fact that 'traditional' therapeutic procedures are uncertain and precarious, significantly more so than agricultural practices. Despite the fact that their effectiveness is not at all guaranteed, they also function as systems of meaning (modes of interpreting illness), which, for their part, have stood the test of time, in the sense that they allow those who use them to account for forms of suffering, for the vicissitudes of the individual condition, for possible therapeutic failures. In other words, popular health conceptions serve both in the quest for therapeutic methods considered locally to be 'effective' (seen from a strictly pragmatic angle) and in the construction of arguments that explain failure or success (seen from an essentially semiological point of view). This helps us to understand the paradoxical situation that Western medicine faces in rural Africa: in great demand as a therapeutic course (which is, nonetheless, often beyond the means of rural populations), it has not yet become an alternative to 'traditional' meaning systems (which partially belong to the register of 'magico-religious' beliefs, a universe peopled with spirits and sorcerers, but which also integrate the more prosaic universe of naming: see Olivier de Sardan, 1994). Time and again, rural populations have witnessed the relatively higher therapeutic effectiveness of Western medicine (even though of course it is not without uncertainties or risks). It also benefits from the prestige of Western knowledge and techniques. But it is not adopted as a credible system of interpretation, at least not in the popular classes, and it does not take the place of the dominant modes of interpretation of local cultures (despite the fact that these do evolve, but at their own pace). This is not specific to Africa: in Western countries as well, the awareness and widespread use of experimental medicine has not been enough to ensure the construction of a coherent system of meaning, and 'magico-religious' attitudes, in the broad sense of the term, to medical practices – official or otherwise – are still common: we are well aware of the role 'rumour' plays in touting the effectiveness of a given therapy or of a particular practitioner.

In the final analysis, it would appear that the superposition of 'magico-religious' meaning systems and the strong demand for Western medicine observed in Africa, far from being a sign of cultural 'backwardness' or of 'ignorance', corresponds to a perfectly rational pursuit of security: it is a matter of combining the empirical search for therapeutic security all round (in Western and in more or less 'traditional' local practices) with the need for symbolic security (essentially guaranteed by the meaning systems associated with local therapeutic practices).

Aid seeking

The notion of self-sufficiency, or of 'self-reliance' (relying on one's own resources) has often been a key-factor of recent development projects (we may observe, in passing, that such a notion is not as novel as it appears: certain local economic programmes dating back to the beginning of the colonial era were based on this principle, though couched in other terms[8]). The assumption is made, a priori, that the populations share this point of view and that it coincides with their best interests (but this is merely an ideological or moral point of view, which is praiseworthy in itself, but which cannot be attributed to or imposed on other people with impunity).

In fact, the opposite strategy, which we could qualify as aid seeking, since it aims at making the most of external aid, is extremely prevalent. There is nothing surprising about people attempting to gain as much as possible from the financial and material benefits that a project provides, while giving as little as possible in return. The development agent does exactly the same thing when he lays personal claim to the bike provided by the project that employs him. The expert with his *per diem*, the foreign technical assistant with his financial perks act in the same way. And what can we say about our own case? As specialists in sociological research don't we spend our time searching around for external subventions?

It could of course be argued that these examples do not all fit in the same category. For some people (experts, foreign technical assistants, researchers), seeking subventions or obtaining *per diems* are legitimate procedures, in keeping with the rules of the game (regardless of what we might think about the morality of the game in question). One could say that others (peasants, project agents), do not respect the rules; their practices are therefore illegitimate. This objection needs to be taken into account: it is true that the peasants give their official consent to reimburse the loans they contract and that project agents know that they ought to distinguish between material belonging to the project and their personal belongings. The problem is that in the case in point the game is being played according to two sets of rules: legitimate rules, laid down by institutions (in this case development institutions); and pragmatic rules, which dictate the way in which actors behave. Legitimate and illegitimate rules sometimes coincide, as in the case of researchers and foreign technical assistants. Sometimes they don't, as in the case of peasants and project agents who play the game according to pragmatic rules, at variance with those they apparently accepted, but which they consider to be illegitimate and imposed from the outside. Thus, anthropology of social change and development, which takes into account practices as well as legitimacy, ends up classifying in the same category (the principle of aid seeking) behaviour patterns related to similar practices, which nonetheless have varying degrees of legitimacy, when compared to official rules.[9]

The health agent is not unfamiliar with aid-seeking strategies: the demands made on him or her usually translate as 'take care of me', rather than 'help me to take care of myself' ... The attempts made to help rural populations to become 'responsible' in the face of health problems, to ensure 'sanitary self-reliance', as it were, at the village level, do not necessarily coincide with what the people concerned really want, that is – utterly understandably – to get 'help'. The paradox here is that the Western health system was essentially constructed, for its part, on a socialization of risks which ultimately resulted in a 'welfarism', at the other extreme from the 'responsibilization' strategy mentioned above. It therefore appears paradoxical that such a strategy is promoted as appropriate for those, in Africa, who are deprived of any form of social security whatsoever (this being reserved for a minority of urban wage earners).

Monopolizing aid opportunities

Development operations are sometimes 'appropriated' in ways their directors do not condone: specific groups within the 'target' population use development aid for their own ends (they appropriate it), in order to increase their privileges or simply to obtain privilege. This means that development actions can be seen as putting facilities, advantages and opportunities at the disposal of a population divided into groups, factions and networks. Development aid is also a stake in face of which certain persons or certain groups are better prepared or better armed than others when it comes to taking advantage.

There are countless examples of the ways in which the more fortunate or more influential among targeted peasants take advantage of a project established in their vicinity in order to extend or improve patrimonial land, to enhance their political influence, or to accumulate capital, revenues, resources or prestige. Given the inequalities inherent in African rural societies (even if these inequalities are more pronounced than in other parts of the Third World), it will come as no surprise to us to observe that development is a game which favours those who have the best cards in hand at the outset. We must, however, acknowledge that the converse is sometimes true; a low-status group (women or youth, for example) can monopolize to its own advantage a project that was not specifically designed in its interests, in order to improve its position in relation to other groups. Many projects are specifically tailored for low-status groups with the aim of empowering them, through a strengthening of their resources and of their influence in negotiation and decision making. The unfortunate and paradoxical truth is that such projects are subjected to 'side-tracking' as frequently as any other type of project, and are often monopolized either by one particular 'low-status' group or by 'high-status' actors.

Development in the field of health does not escape monopolization: co-operative chiefs, rural development supervisors, or village health assistants who use their responsibility for the local distribution of medicine as a useful resource in their clientelist relationships, groups of 'traditional birth attendants' who use the health training they receive to put down other 'traditional birth attendants' in competition with them, building permits for a dispensary given on the basis of political criteria, veterinary health care monopolized by certain owners of cattle herds ...

Strategic logics and notional logics

Many logics could be highlighted to demonstrate how the practices displayed by developees differ from the intentions, objectives and preconceptions of those who initiate and supervise development projects. This is the case when peasants opt in part for economic strategies outside agriculture (the schooling of children, migration) at variance with the aim of developers, which is to keep the rural population on the land. This is the case when village strategies for draining off the labour force or constituting landed heritage conflict head on with the policies of collectivization or of levelling up of means of production, which certain projects promote. This is the case when the mobilization of 'networks' based on various modes of social relationships (kinship, patron–client, neighbourhood, affinity ...) comes into conflict with the 'egalitarian–individualist' viewpoint of many development operators. This is the case when myriad popular forms of accumulation, investment, saving and consumption depart from standard economic behaviour as defined by experts.

These diverse logics are all 'strategic' in the sense that they form the grounds on which explicit peasant action systems, at the interface between politics and economics, are based. It is precisely for this reason that the meanings of words like 'logics' and 'strategies' are practically identical. Nonetheless, strategic agendas are not the only kinds of logics that enter into confrontation, as far as development logics are concerned. Relatively implicit logics of a more or less symbolic or cognitive nature also come into play. Misunderstandings and discrepancies between development institutions and the populations are connected in part with the register of 'latent conceptions' or 'implied conceptions'. This is not a question of 'global world views' confronting each other, but of 'specific cultural blocks' or 'specific notional configurations' at variance with each other. The perspective defended here has nothing to do with culturalist viewpoints and their systematic conceptions of a specific culture, or their idea that dialogue between two cultures is impossible. To put this in simple and more prosaic terms, certain notions that developers consider obvious are not shared by developees. There are certain 'notional discrepancies' involved in the interactions between interveners and populations.

M.L. Mathieu gives a few examples of this kind of 'notional discrepancy' on the subject of development projects in Tuareg zones in Mali. She provides a good demonstration of the radical differences between the images that promoters and nomads respectively have of space. Promoters act on their own conceptions without even thinking about it because it seems so 'obvious' to them. Nevertheless, a certain mode of appropriation of space on the part of cattle herders can explain a variety of 'project failures'. The same also holds true for time, of course, and for other semiologic entities like 'wealth/ poverty', 'need', 'feeding', 'participation', 'recompense' or 'water' (M.L. Mathieu, 1994: 265–337). Deep divergencies arise as a result of the difference between the conceptions of project agents and those of populations, differences that go a long way towards explaining why projects are thrown off track. Notional logics thus take their place alongside strategic logics.

Three conclusions can be deduced from the above reflections.

1. Resistance to an innovation has its motivations and its coherence, whether strategic or notional; this does not amount to mythologizing popular behaviour or to claiming that such kinds of 'resistance' are always inevitable or that they invariably produce positive effects. Not at all. What it implies is that they are 'normal', that is to say that they are explainable, understandable. It is only by explaining them 'from the inside' (from the users' perspective) that we can acquire the means of overcoming 'resistance' if necessary. A good comprehension–explanation 'from the inside' is the kind that allows us to say: 'In their position, I myself would act in the same way, and here's why!'

Mastering this type of comprehension–explanation should figure among the central objectives of development institutions. However, comprehensions–explanations do not arise spontaneously. If this were the case, they would become mere stereotypes. They have to be sought out through enquiry, through appropriate enquiry: in other words, through field enquiry.

2. A successful (adopted) innovation is the product of 'invisible bargaining' and of a compromise between various groups of development actors and various groups of social actors. It does not imply that the technico-scientific and economic logics of its conceptors have prevailed.

3. Projects are subject to 'sidetracking'. What I mean by this is that there is a difference between what is expected and what really happens. Sidetracking is a sign that the actors involved have 'appropriated' the development project (see Chapter 13).

Notes

1 This is one of the reasons, among others, which explains the impasse in the dialogue between Bourdieu's sociology on one hand and the sociology of organizations on the other: both make abundant reference to logics and strategies, but only 'in general'. Bourdieu, for instance, never defines what he means by 'logic' or 'strategy': in fact, in his case, both terms are always combined, directly or indirectly, with the concept of 'habitus', which, by emphasizing the 'process of conditioning' (see Bourdieu, 1992: 105), refutes the various theories of rational choice or 'methodological rationalism' (Friedberg, 1993: 54). Hence, on one hand we have a sociology which insists on the immanent, unconscious, incorporated, inculcated, character of pragmatic logics, and on the other, a sociology which insists on the deliberate, explicit, calculated aspect of logics of action. It is not in my intention to engage in this debate: 'logics' will simply mean lines of coherence which the observer can deduce based on empirical observation of sets and of specific differential practices, without casting judgement on any particular sociological theory of the subject, of rationality, or of 'habitus'.

2 See the example provided by Crehan and von Hoppen (1988: 118–22).

3 For a general critical analysis of this dominant model, see, among others, Richards, 1985. For critical field analyses, carried out on specific cases in a perspective identical to the one we are using, see Yung, 1985; Pontié and Ruf, 1985. This model has also come in for criticism from agronomic research, and numerous attempts have been made to elaborate alternative research strategies connected with agro-pastoral development (see farming system research, development research) which make the most of peasant dynamics or place the priority on local varieties.

4 Other considerations, connected to more specifically political stakes and which are generally unspoken truths, also come into play. One of the reasons that explain why Niger authorities finally approved the 'Maradi project' after a long-standing disagreement with the World Bank, concerning the contents of the project, has to do with the military putsch and the new ruler it brought into power: 'they proved much more amenable to the World Bank's approach ... especially since they were turning

away from a development strategy focused on rural facilitation, which the new masters of the country viewed with suspicion because of its "political" connotations' (Raynaut, 1989: 31).

5 Sautter (1978: 242) had already made reference to the 'deviations' of 'programmed actions' in rural tropical Africa, which he saw as the result of the difference between the respective logics of suppliers of infrastructure – those of modern Western production-oriented agriculture – and of peasant users.

6 Hence the problems that arise when, as often occurs in Africa nowadays, a brutal (demographic and/or ecological) imbalance is provoked, which annuls the effect of 'traditional' solutions adapted to the milieu, such as cultivation on burnt ground or extensive rainfall cropping (see Raynaut, 1986, 1989).

7 The highlighting of safety logics is not a recent phenomenon. Scott's work *The Moral Economy of the Peasantry* (1976) emphasized the 'safety first principle'. We might even go as far back as 1924, and refer to Chayanov as the original source (see Chayanov, 1966). The theme of the risk factor has recently been rediscovered as an important data entry in empirical pluridisciplinary analyses (Eldin and Milleville, 1989). However, the limitation of risk factors, common to all peasant practices, should not be equated with a global refusal of all types of risk taking.

8 See Chauveau 1992, 1994.

9 Kintz (1987) proposes a beautiful empirical demonstration of the difference between official and pragmatic norms. It is true that she does not deal with questions of development, since she describes how adultery (reproved by official norms), is practised in the 'bush' Fulani milieu (here as elsewhere, and perhaps a bit more than elsewhere) while respecting certain pragmatic norms of decency.

10
Popular knowledge and scientific and technical knowledge

Development actions bring two worlds into relationship with each other. These could alternatively be referred to as two cultures, two meanings systems, or whatever ... Let's put it this way: two configurations of contrasting conceptions and notions come face to face. On one hand, there is the notional configuration of the 'target population' (to use the technocrat's vocabulary) or of the 'peasant community' (if we prefer the idealist vocabulary). On the other, there is the notional configuration of the development institutions and of their operators. The two sets of knowledge and meanings enter into relationship in the context of attempts at transferring skills: development in fact comprises attempts to transfer certain skills from the meanings systems of development operators to populations who have other kinds of meanings systems. The 'graft' metaphor has already been referred to above: a skill is not easily integrated into a foreign meanings system, and the mechanisms that determine the chances of rejection are not predictable a priori.

However, from the point of view of the development operator who wants to do his best to make the graft catch on (without rejection or trauma), it is not enough to sit back and observe that there is a conflict between two sets of knowledge and, in more general terms, between two meanings systems. These obviously involve symbolic spheres which have no direct relevance to a development problematic. This is why so many ethnological studies are disappointing to the (rare) development operators who consult them: these studies are particularly interested in the intricate details of magical–religious registers or of esoteric conceptions, but these are of very little help when it comes to understanding why peasants react in a certain way to the introduction of animal traction, for example.

Regardless of the numerous interactions that occur within a given culture, between various fields of knowledge and various norms of interpretation, and notwithstanding the productiveness of methodological holism and its reminder that a culture is a whole that cannot be divided into slices (see Chapter 4), we are still left with the task of establishing a 'workable' distinction between certain fields, and pinpointing sets of particular relevance to a given problem. Let us take the example of a specific 'culture', that of development operators, which should be familiar to some readers: it does not seem necessary to take the entire 'culture' into consideration in order to understand the logics of a given development project being executed by these professionals. It would appear that the artistic preferences or the metaphysical choices of agronomists from CIRAD[1] are of little interest when it comes to analysing the aims and results of the irrigation programme they propose (even if a study of such preferences and choices might be highly interesting to the sociologist, and despite the fact that such a study might uncover certain distant and indirect but very real links with the problem at hand). Besides, studies of the feudal system that regulates the world of research, of the processes of professional recognition in the field of agronomy, of corporate modes of legitimacy, of the material advantages linked to working abroad, etcetera, would be a lot more useful for those who wish to understand the culture and professional practice of CIRAD agents.

By the same token, if we want to find out why a vaccination campaign failed, it seems unrealistic to make, as a preliminary, an exhaustive study of the cultural heritage of the villages in question. A more reasonable approach would be to give priority to certain apparently relevant domains and to overlook others which seem less pertinent. Local therapeutic procedures, or the relationships between human beings and the spirit world, which are of primary relevance when it comes to vaccination, might be of little relevance in the case of difficulties faced by a co-operative involved in procuring agricultural material.

If action is to be carried out on the basis of understanding (and therefore of research), choices will have to be made concerning priority areas. But can we distinguish between priority and non-priority areas if we refuse the comfort of a 'holistic' ethnological position that considers culture as a whole (a position which is quite admissible seen exclusively in terms of pure research)?

As arbitrary and restrictive as this might seem, I will concentrate here on only one aspect of the confrontation between the meaning system of a development project and the meaning system of rural populations for which it is destined: the confrontation between technical knowledge (originating in a Western system of cosmopolitan technical and scientific knowledge) and 'popular knowledge' (technical and non-technical alike).

Popular technical knowledge

It is a matter of distinguishing from the popular culture, seen as a whole, certain areas that appear more relevant than others, a priori, so far as development, that is to say transfers of technical and scientific knowledge, is concerned. One way of solving the problem is to consider the local equivalent of what is seen in the culture of development professionals as the technical–scientific knowledge. In other words, it is a question of examining popular technical knowledge. In any given village, knowledge presents an infinite variety of overlapping facets, regardless of the type of knowledge in question, be it social, political, religious, etcetera. Nonetheless, it remains possible to define popular technical knowledge, applied to specific fields. Rural development calls upon three broad areas: popular technical knowledge in the field of agriculture, animal husbandry and environment; popular technical knowledge in the field of human and veterinary health; and popular technical knowledge in the field of management and economy. The notion labelled 'popular technical knowledge' is, of course, somewhat arbitrary, and corresponds in fact to the point of view of an external analyst: local African cultures do not necessarily draw a neat line between 'technical' and 'non-technical' knowledge, and when they do, the contents of these terms do not necessarily correspond to 'outside' definitions. Nevertheless, the notion remains helpful for two reasons. First, it has the merit of highlighting the fact that many fields of popular knowledge have an empirical foundation. Second, it allows us to differentiate between such practical-empirical knowledge and other more diffuse, broader and more speculative types of social knowledge (as long as we bear in mind the fact that this difference is both relative and fluctuating …).

In development terms, the initial postulate is simple, and irrefutable: the technical messages diffused by development agents and the skills they attempt to import into the peasantry do not intervene on virgin soil. It is not a matter of introducing knowledge into a space that was formerly ruled by ignorance, as development agents too often declare (among other reasons, because of the biases of their training). The peasants whom these messages address already have competence and skills in all the areas with which development is concerned. These competences and skills are based on complex fields of knowledge and meanings systems that evolve continuously. If we accept the hypothesis that the knowledge and skills that development agents are commissioned to introduce are preferable (to the extent that they are more effective, profitable, productive, etcetera) to the competences and skills that already exist,[2] common sense still dictates that we interest ourselves to some extent in the latter in order to discover the best way of making the transfer. It is hard to imagine how new agro-pastoral techniques can be introduced without first taking into consideration the agro-pastoral techniques already there – the peasants' knowledge of agronomy, botany and ecology, on which these techniques build – or the constraints under which they work. It is therefore all the more surprising to note the extent to which development operators in general, and development agents in the field in particular, overlook popular technical knowledge, and display a variety of attitudes which go from ignorance to contempt.

Yet taking popular knowledge into account is by no means a new phenomenon. Back in the 1970's, Paulo Freire was the reference point for all those who allegedly used popular knowledge as a basis for establishing an alternative type of development, development from below, of which numerous NGOs claimed to be the living embodiment.[3] It is possible to go back further in time, to the traces left by the era of colonial administrators, before the Second World War, or to the efforts to promote a 'mise en valeur' (the expression then used to describe what we know as development) based on local technologies and skills. So far as ethnologists are concerned, the study of popular knowledge has been on the agenda since the turn of the twentieth century, starting with the first field work, but it was not until the 1960s that a programme of systematic investigation was inaugurated in the United States, constructed around the notion of 'ethnoscience'. An international colloquium held in 1978 (already) has as its title: 'Indigenous Knowledge Systems and Development' (Brokensha, Warren and Werner, 1980).

This did not fail to produce changes in attitudes, especially on the part of certain NGOs and in the area of development research (the study of local systems of production), changes that are reflected by a contemporary tendency to rehabilitate popular knowledge. It might be helpful at this point to define some of the characteristics of popular knowledge.

A few properties of popular technical knowledge

1.   Popular technical knowledge constitutes a pool of pragmatic notions and skills, which rural producers put into practice, and which covers all areas of social life, from management to soil sciences, from climatology to health, etcetera. A development operation that aims at diffusing new knowledge will find no field in which popular technical knowledge does not already exist, and does not already regulate the practices in question. In some cases, this is almost obvious: we are all aware of the high degree of specialization of Fulani herdsmen (see Kintz, 1991). Yet despite the recognition of their technical competence, the world of development is often reserved on the subject of their economic competence. The countless works devoted to the 'anti-economic' attitudes of the Fulani herdsmen who refuse to sell their animals out of sentimentality, or who choose the wrong time to sell, is evidence enough. But here again anthropological analysis demonstrates that the behaviour of the Fulani people that is so often stigmatized is, to the contrary, based on an entirely economic rationale, seen from the herdsmen's point of view (see Bierschenk and Forster, 1991), and bears witness to an economic competence,

properly speaking. How can a project aimed at encouraging cattle rearing afford to ignore this type of data?

This type of postulate can be applied to almost any area, including areas in which we may not, at first sight, expect to find it relevant. This is how 'methodological populism' works. Hence, a birth control project which intervenes in the Muslim Sahelian milieu cannot assume that it is working on unbroken and even hostile soil, on the grounds that this is a cultural universe in which procreation is highly valued; in fact, unmarried young women have always resorted to 'hidden' practices of abortion and contraception, which are both dangerous, in the first case, and ineffective, in the second (charms and talismans aimed at 'tying the belly'), but which bear witness, nonetheless, to a culture (underground though it may be) that already exists in this particular area, despite the fact that public morality advocates virginity before marriage and procreation afterwards.

Popular technical knowledge is thus based on different types of thinking. Some are of a technical nature, while others are magic or religion. However, all are characterized by a *fundamental popular pragmatism*. In the field of agriculture, the 'technical' nature of peasant thinking has long since been underlined: many systems of local production have thus turned out to be models of adaptation to the constraints of the milieu (see ORSTOM, 1979).

2. Popular technical knowledge also comprises clusters of meaning, which make possible the interpretation of practices, which make them meaningful. It is largely owing to their mediation and in keeping with their norms that the external technical and scientific knowledges proposed are evaluated and interpreted by local populations. Peasant knowledge on the subject of millet germination, or about the classification of varieties of millet based on very precise taste criteria, constitute two systems of knowledge that serve as grounds for the evaluation of the seeds the agricultural services propose, and help peasants to 'get an idea' of what they are worth … This evaluative and normative aspect of popular knowledge, which is pointed out less often than its pragmatism, is nonetheless important.

3. Popular technical knowledge assumes variable, numerous, heterogeneous, and unequally distributed forms according to gender, age, status, surrounding milieu, or personal trajectory: a standard popular technical knowledge, held in common by everybody, would be a mere figment of the imagination. Prevalent types of common knowledge, available to all and sundry, do exist, alongside specialized knowledge monopolized by a few (see Dupré; 1991. For a detailed example of female knowledge among the Mossi people, see Maïzi, 1991, 1993). There exists a whole range of nuances between 'common sense' or routine knowledge mastered by just about everyone in the village, symbolic and technical knowledge specific to one gender, 'caste' or professional group, and individual knowledge acquired on the road. The

relationship between popular technical knowledge and money is also extremely variable: certain types of knowledge have market value and are highly 'commercialized', while others are 'free of cost' or inextricably linked to personal attributes. An itinerant drug peddler, a famous marabout-cum-healer, and a grandmother who is a member of a spirit possession cult represent three types of therapeutic knowledge which have different modes of 'retribution/ gratification' and different relationships with 'patients'.

Hence it is possible to propose at least a distinction between commonplace popular knowledge and specialized popular knowledge, as long as we bear in mind the inconveniences of this rough type of distinction. Indeed, some types of unspecialized popular knowledge do not belong to the category of common knowledge (knowledge about childbirth and infantile disease is the domain of elderly women). There is a wide gap between a particular inherited 'gift' for healing 'itches' and the sophisticated and essentially ritualized knowledge of a spirit priest. Not to mention the problem of how to classify those 'learned peasants' (Colonna, 1987), or those Islamic scholars who dot the countryside and who are called on to treat various disorders.

4. Popular technical knowledge undergoes change, evolves and hence is not merely 'traditional': it incorporates numerous accretions gained through former contacts with neighbouring producers and with technical and scientific knowledge. Far from being static, it has a permanent tendency towards syncretism. Contrary to the commonly held view that popular knowledge = tradition = routine, the innovativeness of popular knowledge, especially in the field of agronomy, in the form of borrowing or in the form of endogenous experimentation (Richards, 1985; see also Chapter 6 of this volume) has often been emphasized. However, the dynamism of popular knowledge is not restricted to the 'natural' environment, but concerns the social environment as well. A peasant does not only have skills related to nature, he also has skills in the areas of local politics, and has acquired, over the years, certain competencies in relation to development institutions and to the projects under way in his vicinity (he knows how to benefit from a system of credit, how to behave in a co-operative meeting, how to use cunning in dealing with a sociologist, etcetera).

5. However, popular technical knowledge does not necessarily occur as a 'system' and is not always based on an indigenous, harmonious founding 'theory'. Essentially founded on individual experience, it frequently takes the shape of a flexible agglomerate, which makes no pretence at providing explanations on a mid-term or long-term basis. Sometimes, peasants refuse, as it were, to increase their knowledge (see Last, 1981). Anthropological approaches in search of 'knowledge systems' thus tend to 'over-systematize' popular knowledge. Research in this field, however, should imply that one is also interested in what people do not know or do not classify (namely, most of

the things in which they are not interested), or in fragmented local knowledge.[4]

Popular technical knowledge and technical–scientific knowledge

But what is the difference between popular technical knowledge and technical–scientific knowledge? Could we make a rapid comparison, restricted to the problem at hand, considered from three different angles?

1. The various types of popular technical knowledge are localized, contextualized, empirical, while technical and scientific types of knowledge are uniform and formalized. A millet cultivator in the Sahel, for example, has a much finer knowledge of the local micro-ecosystem (and of that alone) than a university-educated agronomist; the latter, however, is able to make a 'rapid' interpretation of a variety of local situations, by classifying them under general 'types'. The peasant transmits knowledge through *in situ* practice, and in the context of personal relations, while the agronomist is capable of addressing an anonymous public in any school of African agriculture.

2. The relations between these two types of knowledge are not symmetrical. Popular technical knowledge is applied by the producers and social actors themselves, 'at the end of the line', while technical–scientific knowledge is diffused by agents who do not put it into practice themselves. Popular technical knowledge exists 'on the spot' and has to be modified, whilst technical–scientific knowledge is introduced from the outside and provides little scope for retro-action. Popular technical knowledge overlaps at the local level (a peasant's ecological knowledge is linked to his therapeutic knowledge) and occurs within the same meaning system (or culture), while technical–scientific knowledge comes in packages and 'messages', in the form of disjointed spare parts: its coherence is situated on the outside, (cosmopolitan technical–scientific culture), and those it addresses do not have ready access to the meaning system (the interpretive grid) that constitutes the 'natural' symbolic environment of the knowledge in question, namely the standard technical–scientific culture fostered by Europe in particular, during a century and a half of universal schooling, which is usually not the case in rural Africa. This is why a given type of technical–scientific knowledge, diffused in bits and pieces in the context of any kind of development operation, can only be adopted (in the event that it is) through a paradoxical process, due to which it invariably modifies the configuration of the popular technical knowledge on which it relies for its adoption ('integration', 'appropriation') as a constituent of the configuration itself (see Chapter 6).

3. The opposition between popular technical knowledge and technical–scientific knowledge is not tantamount to an opposition between 'Western

rationality' and 'traditional rationality'. In rural Africa and industrialized Europe alike there is a coexistence of several systems of knowledge, meaning and interpretation. Popular technical knowledge and technical–scientific knowledge are only two elements which figure among a variety of types of knowledge and logics of interpretation into which people delve according to circumstances. In both Africa and France, technical, empirical and scientific types of knowledge cohabit with social knowledge, magical knowledge, etcetera. It is true that the African peasant combines an empirically earned ecological knowledge (= popular technical knowledge) with his conceptions about the role that spirits and the ancestors play in matters concerning fertility (= magical–religious knowledge). But the Western technocrat who holds operational research (= technical–scientific knowledge) in high esteem also consults his horoscope or prays in a church (= magical–religious knowledge). Nonetheless, there exists an important difference. technical–scientific knowledge (originating in experimental science) does *not* incorporate magical–religious knowledge as such (if magical–religious elements find their way into western laboratories, and they do, they do so illegally, so to speak). The converse is true: technical–scientific knowledge is constructed (at least in theory) in opposition to the magical–religious approach (experimentation versus belief). This means that the technician trained in keeping with a technical–scientific culture is supposed to set aside his religious convictions or his magically oriented attitudes while operating in the time–space of technical action or thought, and to take them up again at other times and in other places (he is then free to go to mass or to consult his homeopath).[5] Popular technical knowledge, for its part, can be easily interwoven and imperceptibly combined, and legitimately so, with magical–religious knowledge, in the form of practices in which the two become indistinguishable. It suffices to call to mind the classic problem of magical acts to which social actors resort when faced with very down-to-earth problems. This often leads to the interpretation of such acts, for this and other reasons, as being more 'technical' than religious.

At this point, three clarifications might be useful. First, it may be noted that although technical–scientific knowledge runs counter to magical–religious knowledge and employs rather different methods, the former also gives rise to 'religious' attitudes to the extent that 'belief' (faith in a hospital doctor at the individual level, or scientism as an ideology, for examples) is involved. Second, there is the obvious fact that popular technical knowledge is not restricted to Africa alone and that countries of the North also have a large share of this in addition to technical–scientific knowledge. Moreover, the fact that actors carry out their actions within the framework of technical–scientific knowledge is not at all incompatible with the fact that they call upon other systems of reference (magic, religion, politics, kin, etcetera) for interpretation or legitimacy. Finally, there is the fact that popular technical knowledge and technical–scientific knowledge interact, thus producing hybrid phenomena.[6]

This explains why the comprehension and analysis of popular technical knowledge alone cannot account for the modalities of reinterpretation of technical–scientific messages by their peasant targets. As we have already observed, certain types of popular technical knowledge cannot be dissociated from non-technical conceptions: popular knowledge in the field of management is inextricably linked to the social norms which rule in favour of ostentation and redistribution in the same way that 'popular therapeutic knowledge' is inseparably connected to social conceptions of the ways in which spirits intervene in people's lives. It would be absurd to deny the existence of essentially 'technical–empirical' and 'prosaic' logics of interpretation in certain specific fields of popular knowledge (see for example and in general terms, peasant knowledge related to soils, plants, animals and to the human body) and to attribute all types of interpretation to ultimately religious values and founding cosmogonies. But it would be just as absurd to deny the profound interference of social or magical–religious logics in other specific fields of knowledge (see for example, the norms of decency and values of ostentation in the case of management, or cults of affliction, and the relationship with ancestors, in the case of therapy).

Besides, we need to bear in mind the fact that peasants do not have access to technical–scientific knowledge properly speaking (as knowledge which is taught in schools, over time). This knowledge comes to them in the form of 'deconstructed' bits and pieces, in the shape of the messages diffused by development agents, as opposed to the systematic character of the technical–scientific culture itself.

Seen from another angle, popular technical knowledge is obviously a part of the local culture. But to dissolve it into the broader notion of culture incurs the risk of erasing its 'operational', 'economic', 'modern' characteristics, or of reducing it to mere vestiges (sometimes 'impediments', sometimes 'folklore'), or of merely conceding that it has only cultural or traditional legitimacy, a concession made by the West or by national 'elites', caught up in their search for 'authenticity'. However, the term 'culture' can sometimes be used on the topic of popular knowledge with a very different meaning, and rightly so: this applies to Last, who, in order not to condone the supposition that a systematic traditional therapeutic knowledge exists, prefers the expression 'local medical culture', which is a fundamentally syncretic or even heteroclitic reality (Last, 1981).

Fields of popular knowledge and infrastructure

It is also necessary to make some distinctions between the various types of popular technical knowledge depending on the fields in which they are applied.

As has already been mentioned above, it is more or less difficult to establish a line of demarcation between a technical knowledge and a magical–religious knowledge when it is a matter of health or of agriculture, for example.

So far as animal rearing and agriculture are concerned, production practices are obviously accompanied by magical–religious acts aimed at ensuring a good harvest or providing protection against spoliation. Propitiatory rites, libations offered to ancestors, the invocation of spirits, prayers addressed to God the Father or to Allah, sacrifices, rogations or charms, the recourse to the supernatural world, to the beyond and the invisible, appear to constitute widespread responses to the precariousness of agro-pastoral production. But from an analytical point of view, ritual time and weeding time are separate and apart from each other. Magical–religious knowledge and popular soil-scientific, agronomic or climatological knowledges enter into combination with each other and complete each other, but despite their interlacing, each of these types of knowledge remains distinct.

In the field of health, ritual time and the time of health care are often indistinguishable. Any given therapeutic practice can also coincide with magical–religious elements which cannot be dissociated or separated from its 'technical' components. This does not imply that each and every indigenous therapeutic act necessarily calls upon the intervention of spirits, God Almighty, ancestors or sorcerers. Many popular practices in this domain rely on 'ordinary' knowledge, not so far as the external observer is concerned, seeing that the latter is hardly in a position to discern the difference between the magical, the religious and the 'ordinary', but rather in the minds of those involved. In fact, all cultures make distinctions between what is 'magical–religious' and what is not, but the criteria on which these distinctions are made obviously differ from one culture to another. To put this another way, there are indigenous 'emic' definitions of what is magical and what is not. Thus, in the field of health, entire chunks of popular technical knowledge are clearly related to phytotherapy, 'old wives' remedies', or specialized knowledge and do not incorporate magical–religious procedures (see Olivier de Sardan, 1994). However, other series of conceptions and therapeutic practices involving supernatural agents (or human agents with supernatural powers) do exist: in this case, it becomes impossible to distinguish between the technical and the magical–religious.

This is not the only difference between popular agro-pastoral knowledge and popular therapeutic knowledge. Many of these differences result from the fact that agro-pastoral knowledge is more easily verified: the effects of human practice can be deciphered with greater ease, and are therefore more easily stabilized, when it comes to monitoring plant growth than when it is a matter of monitoring healing in human beings. As far as therapy is concerned, it is particularly difficult to ascertain when there is improvement, whether the person involved is healed or is in a period of remission, or whether the apparent effectiveness of a given therapeutic act is a relief of symptoms or a treatment of the pathology itself. In more general terms, the fact that myriad, complex 'placebo' effects do exist, added to the 'natural' reaction of the body's immune system and to the 'normal' course of evolution of certain diseases, continually clouds the issue, thus depriving popular therapeutic conceptions of a significant degree of solid experimental grounding. Yet in this area, more than in others, there is a tendency to overestimate the effect of therapeutic acts and of all kinds of medication, crediting them with an effectiveness that can rarely stand the test of experimental research. In other words, patients systematically believe that the healing or improvement they experience is the result of 'treatment', although, from a bio-medical point of view, it could be a consequence of a natural defensive reaction of the body, or of the normal evolution of the disease, or of psychosomatic mechanisms.

Anxiety in the face of disease and death, the lack of control that rural African societies have over this kind of danger, the fact that there is insufficient knowledge about certain pathologies (which occurs even in the case of Western clinical medicine, and becomes even more dramatic in places where western methods of diagnosis are unavailable): all of this helps to create a situation that is very different from the context in which popular agro-pastoral knowledge operates. Soil and plants are not sensitive to placebo effects, and are immune from anxiety.

This probably explains why agro-pastoral knowledge is relatively standardized in a given ecological and cultural zone (cultivators from the same village have roughly the same knowledge about the soil, plants, cultivation, climate, over and beyond the inevitable variety of individual competence). This stands in stark contrast to the diffuse and heterogeneous character of popular therapeutic knowledge: despite a number of recurrences, 'grandmother's remedies', or 'common popular knowledge' are far from being the same in all families. The great variety of discourse and practices which characterize healers or holders of specialized popular knowledge about such-and-such a type of disease tends to be highly individualized (each personal competence is, at the same time, a specific knowledge).

In fact, various types of popular knowledge differ from each other, to a great extent, precisely because of the nature of their empirical referents. In other words, according to the fields in which they are applied, they are subjected to different systems of constraints, which in turn give rise to configurations of concepts whose logic, construction and content are not the same. In the field of illness, for example, there is an enormous difference between visible, simple, easily identifiable disorders (like eye diseases) and diffuse, complex, ambiguous complaints (like internal diseases; see Jaffré and Olivier de Sardan, 1999). The wealth of semantic conceptions involved and the more or less experimental nature of the types of popular knowledge to which they correspond are obviously affected by such 'objective' variables.[7]

Hence, it is possible to speak in terms of external mechanisms ('dispositifs'), which differ according to the field of social practice in question, and which influence the configuration of popular technical knowledges, and in particular their degree of independence in relation to magical or religious phenomena.

The term 'dispositif', which I borrow from Foucault, has already been used elsewhere (see Jaffré and Olivier de Sardan, 1999) to designate what Jaffré refers to as 'the material base' on which diseases are defined (the metaphor employed is an allusion to the infrastructure/superstructure relationship in Marxist analysis; see Jaffré, 1993). The term in fact refers to a range of more or less 'objective' factors, which do not depend on the conceptions of social actors, but which, on the contrary, influence them. These include: the prevalence of a given disease; whether or not effective treatments exist; the clinical signs of the pathology in question (visible symptoms). This analysis can be extended beyond the field of health. The production of millet during the rainy season, for example, like nomadic cattle breeding, depends on ecological, biological, climatological or other specific contingencies. They constitute constraints that come to bear on the respective popular technical knowledge required, and thus influence its internal configuration, as well as its degree of 'tryability', its empirical basis, the degree of its relative symbolic significance, or of its effectiveness, in the event that the latter can be evaluated.

Notes

1 CIRAD is a French public agency involved in agro-pastoral development in countries of the South.
2 The hypothesis is not always proven, but that is another question.
3 Nevertheless, Freire (1980) often disdains popular knowledge, which he holds is truncated, erroneous, mythified and reflects the severe conditions of domination to which the people are subjected: see Brown, 1994, who demonstrates, for example, the ambiguity of Chambers's quotations of Freire. Freire's attitude is more miserabilist than populist (see Chapter 7).
4 'Just as there is no theology in Dogon religion, there is no systemization of Dogon ethno-science' (Beek, 1993: 58).
5 I will therefore sidestep the problem of non-scientific attitudes which scientists themselves reintroduce surreptitiously into scientific procedures. This would lead to other general problems, such as the extent to which scientific statements are also and above all social or cultural constructions. Lloyd's work (1993) provides some interesting comments on the conditions of the emergence of science in Greece and the polemical and political context which facilitated this emergence.

6 Our insistence on the dynamics of popular conceptions and technical knowledge, which are both endogenous and reactive (due to the contact with technical–scientific knowledge) is in fact a response to Long's objections concerning the 'scientific knowledge' versus 'local or indigenous knowledge' dichotomy. He contends that this dichotomy plays down the creativity demonstrated by cultivators, their experimental capacities, the ease with which they absorb techniques and ideas from the outside (Long, 1992a: 270–2). In reality, there is nothing to prevent us from maintaining the nonetheless useful distinction between 'popular technical knowledge' and 'technical–scientific knowledge', without falling into this kind of trap, while still recognizing, with Long, that 'the encounter between different configurations of knowledge involves a transformation or translation of existing knowledges and a "fusion of horizons" (i.e. the joint creation of knowledge)' (Long, 1992a: 274).

7 For more analysis of popular conceptions about some 'internal' and 'external' diseases in various West African cultures, see Jaffré and Olivier de Sardan, 1999.

11
Mediations and brokerage

Interactions between the developmentalist configuration and African populations do not occur as dramatic global confrontations. They develop via discreet passageways, relays, extended or restricted networks of transmission, interfaces. This is, fundamentally, a process that relies on mediation, which proceeds through a wide range of multiple, embedded, overlapping, intertwined mediations. However, for mediation to occur, we must have mediators.

The central role played by certain intermediaries was already noted during the colonial epoch. Hampaté Bâ's beautiful novel, *L'étrange destin de Wangrin*, based on real-life events, makes allusion to the stratagems of a famous interpreter employed by the colonial administration.

Each epoch and each context generates specific types of mediators. In the current development era, two kinds of mediators seem to play a particularly central role: development agents and development brokers. They will be considered in turn.

Another way of viewing the problem, which will be explored at the end of this chapter, is to concentrate on a specific process of mediation: instead of focusing on actors, the emphasis is placed on the use of a specialized vocabulary, in certain ritualized contexts, comprising what we could call the 'development language'. It would appear that the use of this language has become a must for all those who intend to play a role on the mediation scene.

Development agents

Development, in its operational form (the everyday activities of a technical service or the project routine), invariably passes through the hands of development agents who constitute the inevitable interface between an intervention and those to whom it is destined. The names given to these development agents vary according to their field of intervention and their competence (and even, at times, according to trends or doctrines): primary healthcare agents, nurses, midwives, in the health sector; supervisors, extension workers, agricultural advisers, rural social workers, in the field of rural development. Literacy workers, social workers, educators, workers in animal husbandry and veterinary assistants could also be mentioned. Over and beyond their specific technical competences, these 'field' agents all have a number of characteristics in common. It is through their agency that the development institutions who employ them address themselves, at the end of the mediation chain, to the beneficiaries of development. They are the ones who are supposed to pass the 'technical message' on to the 'target populations' or who are responsible, in a vague and general kind of way, for sensitizing and building awareness in the 'village communities'. It is essentially at their level and due to their mediation that the world of the developees and the world of the developers enter into contact with each other. This holds true for both the 'heavy' development operations managed by public and/or international institutions and the 'micro' projects initiated by NGOs .

Little is known about these development agents, despite the fact that, in more ways than one, they occupy a central position (in fact, their position could be seen as both revealing many of the difficulties entailed in implementing development projects and as being a strategic site for remedying some of these difficulties). Silence on the subject of development agents represents a blank page in the abundant literature on development: serious investigations devoted to their 'real' practices, their 'real' difficulties, their 'real' degree of integration into the rural milieu are scarce. There is, of course, no lack of normative studies on this topic. Most are devoted to describing the mission of development agents, or touting the merits of a particular method of executing development projects. Their authors present themselves as the unconditional defenders and active practitioners of the method in question. However, the information contained in such works has more to do with their authors' ideologies or the self-promotion of the institutions they work for than with the way in which development agents put all this good advice into practice, or with the practical nature of the relationships between development agents and peasants. It is as if these development agents are supposed to be transparent, thus finally accomplishing the long-standing institutional dream of becoming 'transmission belts'. But everything points to the opposite. Many development actors are aware of this: it suffices to listen to their off-the-record discussions, their private conversations or 'pub talk' if we want to hear about the 'real' development agents, with their personal strategies, failures and the wide variety of contradictions to which they are exposed by virtue of their position. Nonetheless, this very significant portion of social reality is expunged from what one has the right to say in public (and from the scope of what it is legitimate to know, to investigate or to 'evaluate').

A parenthesis on corruption

The development world is filled with moral, symbolic or ideological taboos, as a result of which many other domains are relegated to the periphery of knowledge and to the zone of what it is forbidden to say in public, despite the impact that such knowledge is likely to have on the analysis of the success or failure of development projects. Corruption, which constitutes a very important mechanism of social regulation, is one example that comes to mind. Now, regardless of whether, and especially if, one's aim is to contribute to its abolition, the first step is to understand how it works. This means that we must begin by regarding corruption like any other research object, not as a theme of moral denunciation. Highlighting the basis on which the 'moral economy of corruption in contemporary Africa' is founded amounts to pinpointing the norms and practices, the values and justifications, which form the 'positive' ground, so to speak, on which the various forms of corruption are erected.[1] This brings to mind the constant symbolic struggle engaged in by social actors in their attempt to distinguish where legitimate corruption (generally the kind they benefit from) ends and where illegitimate corruption (usually the type to which they fall victim) begins. This also applies to the numerous mechanisms of compensation, remuneration, redistribution and solidarity into which corruption is so deeply embedded as to be indistinguishable.

But corruption is even more intricately involved in mediation processes. Intermediaries comprise the primary vectors of the moral economy of corruption. Power is, of course, the major centre of corruption, to the extent that it is regulated by a 'neo-patrimonial' vision which blurs the lines between public wealth and private wealth, crown property and the king's property (see Médard, 1981, 1991; Bayart, 1989). But it could also be argued that playing the role of an intermediary or monopolizing certain mediations is also a part of the functions of power. Be that as it may, corruption, mediation and brokerage belong to the same kind of practice and are components of common conceptions. How can we surmount the difficulty entailed in differentiating between a 'commission' (considered to be the just returns of brokerage) and a 'bribe' (considered as an illegitimate remuneration)?

Needless to say, development agents are also eminent actors in the moral economy of corruption (see Koné, 1994; Berche, 1994) by virtue of their functions, which are centred around mediation.

Development agents as mediators between types of knowledge

Development agents play various types of mediation roles. The one that concerns us here is the abstract role they play as mediators between types of knowledge. My main hypothesis is that the development agent assumes a double function: he or she is the spokesperson on behalf of technical–scientific knowledge and the mediator between technical–scientific knowledge and popular knowledge. This double role is a kind of double bind (see Bateson, 1980): on one hand, the development agent must promote technical–scientific knowledge and must present this as superior to popular knowledge; on the other hand, he is supposed to create a balance between both types of knowledge. This 'real' contradiction is obscured because the development institutions attribute only one of these two roles to the development agent. He is considered, first and foremost, as the spokesman of technical–scientific knowledge, and trained with this aim in mind. He is not trained to mediate between different types of knowledge; instead, it is expected that he will assume various pedagogical roles, in order to cast light on those who are still in the dark. According to the specific circumstances, he is expected to be an extension worker, a missionary, a propagandist, a supervisor, a technician or a relay agent, or sometimes all of these in one. Nevertheless, the role of 'mediator', which is either disregarded or overlooked, seems to be extremely relevant to his real functions, especially when we bear in mind that the development agent is the person responsible for 'grafting' the technical message (originating in a cosmopolitan, scientific terminology) onto a system of significations that is peculiar to the rural population in question. Let us make no mistake about it: development agents and their employers are not necessarily aware of this role of mediator, since the role of spokesman is invariably emphasized, even more so as this role is always defined and legitimated with reference to a 'technical competence' (within the field of technical–scientific knowledge). Moreover, their training, however unsatisfactory its contents may appear, is almost entirely devoted to the acquisition of this competence. Obviously, our intention is not to deny the importance of real technical competence; on the contrary. Competence is what legitimates, or should legitimate, the presence of the development agent in the field. However, real competence is not always demonstrated, and the populations are not unaware of this. But our contention is that there is another type of competence which is extremely necessary and which is not included in the training that development agents receive. In most cases, development agents are not taught to be mediators between two systems of knowledge, especially since their technical competence is constructed on the denial and rejection of popular knowledge. Yet their capacity to penetrate and to understand popular knowledge is central to the function of mediator that they in fact assume.

The fact that development agents are not trained to be mediators does not mean that this role does not exist, nor does it render the role inessential: it simply means that the role is not assumed, or only inadequately, notwithstanding its incorporation, its embeddedness into the concrete role played by the development agent in the field. Because development agents do not have the competence required to serve as mediators between various types of knowledge, they mediate inappropriately or unilaterally. Nonetheless, mediation must take place, whether in good or in adverse conditions, with its corollary of misunderstandings, slippages or distortions of meaning; the fragments of scientific and technical discourse that transit through the intermediary of the extension worker or of the nurse are invariably reinterpreted by the peasant in reference to his own particular° system of knowledge and of meaning.

Notwithstanding, many development agents have progressively acquired 'spontaneous' competence on the job, and have become skilful mediators. Yet, it must be admitted: (a) that this type of competence hardly receives any kind of recognition from the institutions to which they belong; (b) that such competence is far from being the order of the day; (c) that much would be gained from its incorporation into the initial or ongoing training development agents receive.

For a better understanding of what this role of mediator entails, we may turn to one of its simplest aspects, namely language. Development agents are mediators first because they are interpreters.

Language, literacy programmes and communication

Let us agree to place ourselves, for a moment, within the classic framework of the transmission of a technical message (however inappropriate this might be for the understanding of what 'grafting' implies): to transmit we must translate. Translation, or, in the most trivial sense, the passage from one natural language to another, is the initial stage of rural development in Africa. Developers speak in French and English while developees speak in Bambara, Fon, Hawsa … This apparently simple problem has not received the serious consideration it deserves on the part of the institutions of development. They are always willing to consider that the use of French as the official language (in the so-called francophone African countries) is sufficient grounds on which to ignore the so-called national languages spoken by the entire rural population, and to act as if development operations did not need to concern themselves with the real linguistic situation. The problem being disregarded, development agents are generally forced to improvise translations of messages and to manage, through their own devices, linguistic relations with the populations (in the event that they know how to speak the local language, which is not always the case!)

This problem has, in part, been raised by literacy campaigns in the national languages (or more precisely, in the mother tongues). But a literacy programme based on the national language is not a miracle solution. All too often, it adopts the framework of 'message communication', communicated from the top down, expressing technical–scientific knowledge in a peasant language vastly revised and corrected by urban intellectuals, whose terms are deplorably formal and schoolish. Other difficulties, for which the literacy services are not responsible, also hamper their work: rural populations often want training to be carried out in the official language and through the official school system (see Ouedraogo, 1998), and there is also the problem of the absence of a truly 'literate environment' (newspapers, books, signs and symbols) using the mother tongues.

Hence, over and above the specific literacy problem, the issue is about communication in the local languages, and this communication is first and foremost an oral phenomenon. Even in cases where the written word seems predominant, in the heart of industrial societies, we should remember the extent to which personal networks and interpersonal discussions (oral relations at close quarters) contribute, as much as the media and written material, to the structuring of popular attitudes in the face of innovation and technical change (see Katz and Lazarsfeld, 1955; Rogers, 1983). But, in any case, communication in the African rural milieu (using mother tongues) usually assumes an oral form (including on radio and television). The fact that certain 'integrated' development programmes make room for literacy training (for which they are to be congratulated) does not necessarily mean that communication in the mother tongues 'really' occurs: the written translation, in Baoule or Tamasheq, of a technical message originally emitted in French in no sense guarantees effective communication.

But above all it is important to go beyond a simplistic notion of what translation really is. It is not just a matter of finding the most appropriate Fulani or Wolof word for 'fertilizer', 'diarrhoea', or 'investment': translation in the full sense of the word is not merely an exercise that consists in finding the equivalent of a given word in another person's natural language, it also involves bringing two different semantic fields, two distinct ways of dissecting or of perceiving reality (see Jaffré, 1991; Bouju, 1991) into relationship with one another. Seen from this point of view, a lexical notion of translation makes very little sense, and the anthropological problematic in this domain has more in common with semiology than with linguistics. Regardless of the choice of media, and whether the developer speaks the developee's language or not, the problem surrounding the transmission of a 'technical message' still amounts to the inevitable confrontation between two systems of meaning. The development agent finds him/herself at the centre of this confrontation. Reference has already been made to Darré's works, which show how, in France, the terms used by agricultural advisers (the French version of the development agent) were reinterpreted by cattle breeders in keeping with a coherent logic, which was far removed, however, from technical–scientific knowledge (see Darré, 1985). Yet these cattle breeders not only spoke the same language as the development institutions, they were, moreover, literate and had all of them received several years of schooling.

The conclusion is clear: a development agent cannot play the role of spokesperson for technical–scientific knowledge (or more precisely fragments of this) without also assuming a role as a mediator. He or she cannot transmit without first translating, and the 'quality' of the 'translation' will depend on the degree of the development agent's mastery of both languages.

But there are other facets to the role of mediator.

Mediation and negotiation

Different types of knowledge are not the only elements entering into confrontation with each other in the context of a development operation. Other conflicting elements include modes of behaviour, practices, interests: in short, social actors in flesh and blood, with their respective multiple, diversified, ambiguous, fluctuating logics and strategies. Knowledge provides resources for action: which means that the technical and social competences of the partners involved (on the part of the development institutions and of the peasants alike) are executed by means of practices and modes of behaviour. These are not only of a technical nature, and do not simply entail an application of popular technical knowledge. Practices and modes of behaviour also involve social evaluations, various logics, tactics and strategies. The development agents themselves are situated at the interface between these tactics and strategies. In this case as well, the development agents are required to assume a mediatory function for which they received little or no preparation: they must understand the various logics of action of the people around them, recognize the various forces at work in a village, analyse the capacity of a particular group to take advantage of a project or to throw the project off track; they must appraise the local political, economic and symbolic stakes. All this requires a capacity for listening and a certain savoir-faire. The execution of a development project within a local milieu can be compared to an extensive process of 'informal negotiation', with the development agent caught up in its centre. It is the agent's responsibility to manage (efficiently or otherwise, consciously or not, with or without control) power struggles, underhand strategies and compromises.

In this respect, development agents must assume three functions; an almost impossible task that entails an accumulation of contradictions and ambiguity. They must:

- defend their own personal interests,
- defend the interests of their institution,
- mediate between various actors' interests and those of local factions …

Seen in the light of this 'mission impossible', the development agent seems to be a very special actor in the local arena (see Chapter 12).

Brokers

Any social process that brings localized low-level actors or groups into relationship with global structures (the town, the state or the market being the most obvious of these) requires the service of go-betweens or mediators who occupy a clearly strategic function. The social facts of development are not an exception to this rule. But there exists a specific form of intermediation which can be fruitfully analysed às a type of 'brokerage', to the extent that development aid flows can be interpreted as rent.[2]

The development rent

Among the countries of the South, African countries are the most dependent on external aid, as compared to the resources they generate on their own. This is a well-known economic fact, but one that also has some less perceptible sociological implications, linked to the modes of circulation and redistribution of the 'development rent'. Indeed, without going off on a normative or moralistic tangent, development aid can rightly be defined as a 'rent', despite the fact that this rent operates in a context of poverty and is based, as opposed to mining rent, on the mobilization of external resources. Defining the African state as an assisted state is just another way of saying that it is dependent on external rent. However, one aspect of the 'crisis of the African state' is related to the fact that African states are currently incapable of siphoning off or of controlling a significant percentage of the cash flowing in, from the North to the South, because of the fact that they fail to inspire confidence in the donors. Thus, the 'development rent' transits essentially through national intermediaries, who are separate and distinct from the classic public administrators and political systems. The growing importance of NGOs as development agents, as well as that of the 'project' system, in both bilateral and multilateral co-operation, provides ample evidence. The result is the increasing importance of local interlocutors.

Local development brokers

The term 'local development brokers' makes reference to the social actors implanted in a local arena who serve as intermediaries for the draining off (in the direction of the social space corresponding to this arena) of those external resources commonly referred to as 'development aid'. If we take the development project as the ideal type of the development operation, regardless of the identity of the operator, brokers represent the local social bearers of a project, those situated at the interface between the target population and the development institution, those who are supposed to represent the local population (or to express their 'needs'), the interlocutors of support and financial aid structures.[3]

Development brokers do not appear out of thin air. They are the by-products of local histories and operate within networks. What are the social processes that transform certain African actors into development brokers? There is a paucity of research on this topic.[4] The mobilization or acquisition of external resources by development brokers, for the benefit of groups or communities on whose behalf they intend to act and on whose behalf they assume the position of representatives, cannot, of course, be reduced to self-professed motivations, which are reliant on various kinds of rhetoric: concerning the public welfare, altruism or development activism. It is also a question of power or influence, if not of more basic material interests. Brokers therefore attempt, beyond their ideological declarations, to reinforce their position in the local arena (and, on occasion, in the national arena as well). A link is thus established between development brokerage and patron–client systems (which are frequently mentioned but receive little or no empirical analysis in Africa). However, the influence that brokers have is not only due to the degree of control, more or less direct or indirect, that they exercise over the modes of allocation or redistribution of the resources that development aid allows to be drained off towards the village, the neighbourhood or the region; it is also related to their capacity for negotiation and partnership with operators of the North and, consequently, on their personal integration into more or less institutionalized North–South networks. Rhetorical competence, that is to say the ability to speak the language that development institutions and donors expect, seems to be a prerequisite for integration. This is a progressively acquired competence which must allow brokers to adapt to the new, constantly emerging development 'trends' ('fundamental needs', 'sustainable development', 'self-promotion', etcetera). The fact that projects are increasingly 'localized' (in the sense that classic vertical state circuits are bypassed and replaced by a system of aid which is supposed to arrive directly into the hands of earmarked beneficiaries) results paradoxically both in an increase in the number of local brokers ('at the base', at the level of the village or of the neighbourhood), and at the same time, their progressive 'internationalization' (they enter into direct contact with their European and North American partners).

A typology of brokers in relation to their networks
An initial inventory of the types of brokers reveals four broad categories of brokerage networks:

Confessional networks
Membership of a Church, a sect, a confraternity, allows for the mobilization of social contacts on the outside of the local community, lineage and kin to which one belongs. This type of membership, connecting with former missionary

enterprises and today's philanthropic organizations, was the original form of decentralized brokerage, and is still by far the most important. It enjoys continued prosperity. The particularly interesting topic of 'religion and development' can thus be approached from the angle of the social spaces constructed by religious institutions, and the position of intermediaries that some individuals assume within them, in preference to the more classic perspective of 'religious ideologies'. Islamic confraternities, the Catholic Church, Protestant Churches and sects, syncretic movements comprise so many networks through which the brokers who adhere to these respective institutions mobilize development aid.

Civil servants from a common locality
Village member associations in towns, bringing together civil servants (public administrators, university-educated individuals, migrants, merchants) who come from the same region, district or village, have multiplied in Africa over the last few years. They impel the creation of an increasing number of development projects with the help of their professional skills and the social or political relations acquired in the town or abroad. They thus manage to maintain or to re-establish a link with their social origin, and to take up a position in the local arena.

Cultural/ethnic movements
Like village member associations, cultural/ethnic movements are often co-ordinated by high civil servants and intellectuals. They pursue a double objective. They promote the access of the populations to which they belong to a greater share of the development rent, on the claim that this population is subjected to an unfair 'ethnic' division of this rent. Their activities also allow their leaders to gain better access to positions in the national political arena. Although the ethnic question has of course been amply analysed, ethnic movements, most of them reactivated or incited by the current context of democratization, have received little attention in relation to development: yet analysis carried out in terms of mediation between the populations and the state, the capture and redistribution of aid inflows, and the strengthening of political positions and of patron–client potentials, in short, in terms of development brokerage, seems particularly promising (one might consider, for example, this dimension of the Tuareg problem in Mali and Niger).

Peasant leaders
This is an expression used by many NGOs and development agencies to designate partners originating in the agricultural milieu, and earmarked for training, in order to provide the 'barefoot' brokers that institutions from the North require. Some of these have acquired important skills which allow them

to relate directly to donors. Besides, structural adjustment provokes the return to their villages of increasing numbers of individuals who have received schooling. Having moved 'back to the land', they attempt to gain the position of peasant interlocutors of development institutions. The so-called 'communities' (co-operatives, peasant groups, village development associations) constitute one of the spaces of emerging peasant leaders (and of potential confrontations with local notables).

These four categories of brokerage network are not necessarily mutually exclusive, nor do they preclude other forms of local brokerage. But they seem to be the most interesting in terms of comparative research.

Brokers or brokerage?

Brokers are not necessarily 'professionals'. Hence, it is more appropriate to speak in terms of a 'function of brokerage' which can be accomplished by individuals who play a variety of social roles, which are sometimes more important for their social positions and in terms of their individual strategies than is their role as a broker. Brokerage roles are not always assumed by individuals; they can also be secured by an association, an institution (such as a Church or a peasant association), or, to be more precise, by the leaders of the association or institution, seeing that they often occupy a very prominent position compared to which simple members play purely figurative roles.

In fact, the disadvantage of the term 'broker' (which implies a very high degree of individualization or specialization) is merely the other side of the coin which represents its advantages: brokerage is not an abstract function but one that is embodied in specific social actors, even thought they are sometimes diffuse, exist as networks, or function only part-time. The itineraries and biographies of these brokers must be analysed in order to pinpoint their characteristics. What kind of competence is required? What is the required 'training' (travels, political activism, studies …)? How does one 'qualify', as it were, for this position? Is it possible to become a professional broker? If so, how?

Hence, it is advisable to choose between the terms 'broker' and 'brokerage' according to the circumstances at hand. Besides, a lot of interesting empirical data can be found at the interface between these two notions. The same applies to terms like 'brokerage chains' or 'brokerage networks'.

Integration of brokers into the local arena

Four broad categories can be distinguished:

- The broker is on the outside of the local political arena, and would like to get in. Implantation is a corollary of his function as broker.

- The broker is a powerless or low-status or marginalized actor in the local political arena. His role as a broker serves a strategy of upward mobilization.
- The broker is a high-status actor or occupies a central position in the local political arena. His function as a broker comprises a strategy of consolidation.
- The broker wants to get out of the local political arena. His brokerage function entails a strategy of social climbing on the outside.

In all these cases, brokerage is part of a general situation characterized by the 'multifocality' of the entire local political arena. There is never, or rarely ever, a situation of exclusive domination by one single predominant power. The situation is one of co-existence of various centres of power, whose influence and fields of competence differ, and which are more or less articulated, hierarchical or concurrent and which often arise as the result of successive layers of historical accumulation.[5] Hence, the brokerage function can constitute either a complementary resource, as sometimes occurs, or a central resource, and therefore a new centre of local power. It can also serve to consolidate acquired power or open the path to a position of power that was already in existence.

The relationships between local development brokers and traditional mediators

Many local powers of the traditional type, lineage chiefs, village chiefs, district chiefs, 'notables', served in the past[6] or continue to serve as mediators. It is a known fact that colonization made use of these indigenous intermediaries either in the administration or the improvement of territories (the forerunner of today's development), and did not hesitate to institutionalise their traditional or pseudo-traditional roles in political representation. Though these mediators benefited in their time (or still benefit now) from the financial dividends of their status (taxes, emoluments or fraud), they are often deprived of access to the development rent. In particular, as opposed to development brokers, they have not yet acquired mastery of the language spoken in the world of development. The relationships between classic political mediators and development brokers are not simple: they cut across lines of kinship and social or ethnic affiliations, and they add a new stratum to the multiple conflicts and local alliances already in place. Neverthless, is it possible to distinguish the appearance of a kind of 'historic compromise' between the traditional mediators – who manage the relationships between the state and local actors – and development brokers – who manage the relationships between development institutions and local actors?

Neo-patrimonialist forms have long since been identified in Africa. But does not the emergence of development brokers catalyse a new type of patron–client relationship, based on the broker's capacity to orient aid inflows in one direction or another, thus fuelling relationships of allegiance? Is this to be seen as a resurgence of ancient forms of clientelist relationships (for example, a reactivation of recurrent links of personal dependence between two families)? Do the rules of the development game make allowances for the emergence of original modes of affiliation (related to the new types of resources mobilized by brokers: relationships with donors, acquisition of a minimum of academic capital, integration into external networks)?

Be that as it may, in the phenomenon of modern, development-linked mediation, the capacity to serve as a go-between in the relationship between the developmentalist configuration and the local population involves a very specific factor (should this be defined as a resource or as a constraint?), namely the development language.

The development language

The main line of my argument is as follows: there is usually no communication between the linguistic world of the 'developee' (hereinafter referred to as the local language) and that of the 'developer' (which I will call the 'development language'). When these two worlds do come into contact, at the level of development projects, the development language, under the specific guise of a project language, essentially serves to reproduce projects and does not penetrate the local language. This being the case, is the current increase in the number of development brokers from the South to be interpreted as the initial stage of an 'appropriation' of the development language by local populations?

Two radically different linguistic worlds

We will begin with an observation that has been verified time and again in the field: the development language is an essential ingredient of development agencies, institutions and operators – in other words, of the developmentalist configuration – but it hardly ever penetrates into the local languages. Obviously, African languages are capable of expressing change (see Peel, 1978), if only because change was already a reality experienced by pre-colonial societies. The fact that the development language remains, as it were, on the threshold of the local languages, is not attributable to linguistic reasons. The reason is quite simple: those who use the local languages, 'developees', are not a part of the developmentalist configuration and have nothing to do with the language spoken there. 'Developees' do not have the same cultural and professional references and are not subjected to the same constraints as 'developers'. The paradoxical thing about the development language is that it is supposed to address itself to developees while, in reality, it concerns only developers.

It is true that the development language has numerous dialects. It is itself heterogeneous, marked by differences, variations and even by contradictions. Synchronic cleavages exist between 'schools', ideologies and institutions. Diachronic cleavages exist between 'trends', which can be observed by one and all. They displace one another decade by decade, if not year by year. It is impossible to ignore them, especially since these cleavages are often amplified or exacerbated by rhetorical confrontations or by competition in the same 'market'. It has even been noted that, from a diachronic point of view, the development novelties of today are erected on the forgetting of accomplishments of the recent or not-so-recent past. From a synchronic perspective, the confrontation between opposing development conceptions is constructed on a common ground of shared meta-conceptions – the altruist and the modernist paradigms (see Chapter 5).

The development language can of course be analysed in itself. We could examine its various dialects and highlight their specific or conflicting facets. This is a banal procedure, which is similar to one that various members of the developmentalist configuration use to highlight the originality of their own project, while more or less berating other members of the configuration.

A more productive procedure, however, and one that has more to do with anthropology, is to examine the possible interactions between the development language and the local languages. What happens when the development language comes into contact with a local language?

The project language

The concrete form the development language assumes in the field, once it becomes operational and embodied in an institution in contact with local populations, is what we might call the 'project language'. 'Projects' have become privileged forms of development action, each individual project being a specific and precise by-product of the development configuration, a microcosm which can be analysed as an 'organization', but also as a language system. In the same way that each organization has its own language, each project has its own project language, which is a specific and unique product of the development language, or of one of its idioms; the project language is one of the dialects of the development language. The use of the project language is limited to certain situations: the written documents produced by the project; 'project-organization' meetings; agent training sessions; but also contacts between those in charge of the project and other actors of the development configuration (national civil servants, foreign experts or evaluators). The project language is also supposed to communicate with the local language, especially when a particular emphasis is placed on participation (in reality, though projects all have participation as an objective of their relationship with the local population, an objective expressed in its rhetoric, some projects emphasize this dimension more than others, in words or in fact).

The analysis of an environmental management project, with an extremely participationist ideology, carried out in the Torodi area in Niger, is revealing in this regard (see Maman Sani, 1994). On one hand, the project language is well developed, both within the project organization itself and in its external contacts. Training sessions for its agents, permanent internal evaluation, local meetings, frequent external evaluations, visits from members of other projects (in the name of the experimental nature of the project): on all such occasions, the project language, organized around key words and phrases such as 'self-promotion', 'negotiation between partners', 'needs of the populations', 'village planning', 'appropriation', 'protection of resources', 'building responsibility', 'consensus', 'support', etcetera, is always used. The project language in question is almost always formalized through a series of illustrated posters, displayed around the project's conference room. They relate the history of the 'environmental management procedure' and highlight its participatory dimension. A tour of these posters is an exercise that no visitor to the project can escape. In the process, one learns how each village elaborates a popular development programme based on an identification of community needs and a mobilization of the entire village in the search for solutions.

But, on the other hand, the 'penetration' of this project language into the local population (in the villages concerned by the project) is almost non-existent. Ethnographic enquiry has demonstrated that the vast majority of peasants, both male and female, never use the project language, and, to tell the truth, are not at all concerned by it. The only term that is ever used is the word 'project' itself, which becomes *porze* in the Zarma (local) language. The word is in widespread use all around the country, just like projects themselves. Here, as elsewhere, the word *porze* makes direct reference to an inflow of cash which 'white' people distribute, momentarily, on certain conditions. Projects existed in the past, and will exist in the future, projects come and go, but any project is good for the taking. The particularity of the Torodi project, its strongly accentuated participationist strategy, discernible in its project language, is, moreover, seen in a negative light by peasants, who estimate that it brings in less cash than former projects: 'The project that came before was like a stranger who offers a cane to a tired old man so he can get up. The present project is like a stranger who doesn't hand the cane to the old man, but who throws it on the ground and tells the old man to make an effort to pick it up' (see Maman Sani, 1994: 14). In each village the number of peasants who have a slight notion of the project language, in its local language version, does not exceed three or four persons at the most. But they never use it except in the presence of visitors (seen, a priori, as potential donors).

Of course, this is not really a linguistic problem, related to problems of translation. The absorption of French and English words (via Ghana and Nigeria) into popular Zarma speech in an essentially pragmatic and informal manner is a current and widespread phenomenon. But the development language has not followed this bottom-up path, the word *porze* being a rare exception to the rule. Yet the development language is widely diffused and is well known under another, entirely Zarmaized form, via radio programmes aired in local languages, which have long since produced neologisms in Zarma (the invention of journalists) that are meant to translate French expressions, usually related to national or international politics. 'Development' being a major topic of the official and public speeches transmitted by radio over the last thirty years, the development language has thus been progressively translated into Zarma by this medium (hence 'development' has been translated on the radio as *jine koyan*, 'moving ahead'). But this type of language is not really a part of everyday speech. Nobody, in country or in town, ever speaks like this. This type of language is only encountered in official situations: on the radio, in the public speeches of politicians and civil servants, delivered in local languages. It is also used, as in the case of the Torodi project, during meetings organized by field agents. A project is therefore the smallest locus in which the development language is spoken, and represents the final rung on the ladder of public speeches addressed to the people. Even NGO-type projects, which distance themselves as far as possible from the state project model, even projects that aim at being alternative, with a strong emphasis on participation, relapse willy-nilly into standard official language when it comes to addressing themselves to peasant assemblies in the local languages. In Torodi, the project language is spoken in its Zarma version by project agents in the field (called in French '*animateurs*') in more or less official contexts. It makes use of all the expressions of the development language created by radio, changing a word here or there, in its effort to underline what project agents consider to be the project's unique characteristics or its identity.[7] Here, *animateurs* play a major role. They speak the French used in Niger, they speak the standard French version of the project language, they speak fluent Zarma. However, and this is a point worth noting, the project *animateurs* in question never use the project language in their everyday (practical, technical, pragmatic, phatic) interactions with peasants; on the contrary. Instead, they tend to avoid it, not necessarily consciously, but because of its total lack of relevance. But they speak it when village assemblies are called and when civil service administrators or 'strangers' come to visit. It is usually on such occasions that the rare peasant capable of reproducing this language, even partially, takes the risk of participating in the discussion.

This type of observation obviously places the project language in the same category as political clichés. Nevertheless, the project language plays a central role, not only in the relationships between the project and the local population, but also in the forms of reproduction of the project itself.

We could propose a 'model' to account for the Torodi project and projects of the same type. It is as if the project comprised three intersecting spheres. First, there is the project organization (with its personnel, its offices, its logistics, its cashflows): it is remarkably oversized and very expensive when compared to its output towards the local populations. The entire project depends, at the end of the line, on six *animateurs* in all, who do no more than could be expected of the technical services of the state in rural areas, under normal conditions. Second, there is the project language, which is omni-present, revolves around itself, and has even less of an impact on the local population than the project-organization itself. Third, there is the sphere of evaluations. These constitute a permanent reality and play the key role in the project's reproduction: its funding, prolongation, transformation, extension, survival.

The project language does not play a functional role in the relationship between the project organization and the local population involved. None-theless, it is essential for the reproduction of the project and for the continuation of its financial flows: it is the project language that defines the project's personality for the benefit of donors, and that provides at least some of the criteria needed for the continuous evaluations with which the project is confronted. It is also an essential component of the professional identity of those in charge of the project. Regular use of the project language provides them with the means of asserting their position within the local development configuration and of legitimating their competence and social worth.

Language and brokerage

Brokerage is scarcely involved in the project mentioned above. In fact, the Torodi project is an 'official' project (part of the heavy mechanism of French co-operation), and was consciously imposed on the area. Its potential media-tors between the development language and the local language hardly ever use the project language when addressing peasants. Besides, on the project organization level, they are merely agents with a task to accomplish and have very little influence. But the situation is different in other projects which share the same ideology, or, in other words, which have an identical project language but arrive through different channels, in particular NGOs. In fact, the increase in the number of NGO-type projects produces an increasing involvement of African partners originating in the 'civil society'. The result is the increase in the number of brokers referred to above.

Brokers supposedly speak the local language (since they claim to 'belong to the grassroots', to be aware of its 'needs' and to share its aspirations), but they must also master the development language (which is a prerequisite for their communication with donors). To be more precise, they must speak the specific dialect of the development language spoken by their interlocutors from the

North, a dialect which will evolve into a project language, if they manage to strike a deal. This is worlds apart from the 'notables' who served as interlocutors to the colonial power in the past. Development brokerage is a new function. The specific competence represented by the ability to speak the development language is one of its prerequisites.

As observed in the case of the Torodi project, projects reproduce themselves by means of the development language. This holds true for NGO-type projects, bilateral co-operation and international institutions alike. It is also the basis on which a project is erected, and the means by which it becomes localized.

In countries like Senegal, Mali or Burkina Faso, which have an astonishing number of NGOs per square kilometre, national interlocutors of NGOs from the North, which are increasingly organized as Southern NGOs (that is, as brokerage groups substituting for individual brokers) are on the increase. Their advent generates an extension of the development language, which is no longer used only on the radio or on television, in political speeches, or during meetings held by field agents, but which is now spoken by a new, rapidly emerging social group, namely brokers.

This social group is obviously heterogeneous, comprising urban civil servants of village origin, often in charge of 'village associations', as well as unemployed but educated persons who have returned to the land, migrants who have moved back home to the village, and even more or less self-educated local peasants. Mastery of the development language is their ticket for entry into an international network, access to the developmentalist configuration and therefore to the promise of funds and projects. Hence, young Africans from the rural milieu can be observed in the process of demonstrating their fluency in the development language at this or that colloquium, workshop or seminar held in Geneva, Montreal or Berlin.

Can this increase in the number of people capable of speaking the development language within Africa itself, through the rise of local brokerage, lead progressively to its implantation in local urban or rural milieus? To put it another way, will the development language catch on, starting with, but progressively extending beyond, its use by brokers? We should avoid giving a hasty reply to this type of question, especially in light of the fact that the diversity of local and national situations makes it difficult or even impossible to give just one answer. Can the increase of peasant associations, for example, whose leaders speak the development language with relative ease, be considered a good indicator of the 'popularization' or 'popular appropriation' of the development language, or, in other words, a certain degree of penetration of the development language into the popular language (see Jacob and Lavigne Delville, 1994; Lavigne Delville, 1994)? Or is it simply a matter of a new tool of development brokerage, in which the development language is merely a path of access through which the 'new rural elites' have to pass before entering into the development-configuration and tapping into donor aid funds? Both dynamics are possible.

Besides, is it possible to implant a new professional language into the local milieu, more or less mediated by the development language? Indeed, the development language can, on occasion, include technical or functional elements, the mastery of which indicates a certain degree of professionalization. The vocabulary needed for the writing of a rural loan proposal, or the vocabulary associated with the functioning of a co-operative (office, general assembly, treasurer, activities report, emoluments) provide two examples.

Finally, the difference between zones in which peasants' organizations generate a locally produced surplus (in zones of cotton production, for example) and those in which dependence on aid is the overriding strategy must also be taken into account. What impact does this have on the development language and, in more general terms, on brokerage?

Notes

1 See the following recent works on corruption in Africa: Olivier de Sardan 1999b; Blundo and Olivier de Sardan, 2000, 2001.

2 This part of the chapter is the result of my close collaboration with Thomas Bierschenk and is greatly indebted to him. It includes various aspects of a research programme on this topic that has now been completed: see Bierschenk, Chauveau and Olivier de Sardan, 1999.

3 Boissevain had already underscored the fact that brokers play the role of 'social manipulators', i.e. they constitute a particular type of 'entrepreneurs'. 'A broker is a professional manipulator of people and information who brings about communication for profit' (Boissevain, 1974: 148). Brokers are not themselves in control of resources (land, employment, subventions, credits, specialized knowledge etc.), but they have strategic contacts with those who control these resources. 'A broker's capital consists of his personal network of relations with people' (ibid.: 158).

4 Reference can be made to Blundo's particularly enlightening articles (Blundo, 1991, 1994).

5 See Bierschenk and Olivier de Sardan, 1998a.

6 In another context, French rural sociology underlined the mediating role that notables played between the local society and the larger society (Mendras, 1976).

7 'Controlling local development' thus becomes *mate kan aran ga hini ga koynda aran kwara jina*, literally 'how to make your village go forward', and 'participatory and consensual diagnosis' becomes *aran ma ceci waafakey bey kulu ma kaandey nga gaakasina*, literally 'you need to come to an agreement among yourselves and each person must lend a helping hand' (Maman Sani, 1994).

12
Arenas and strategic groups[1]

Local development as a political arena

Development is obviously a locus of political conflict, but not in the usual sense of the word 'political'. In the present case, I am referring neither to national nor to international politics, spheres in which politicians and high civil servants circulate, and in which 'development' is either a term of rhetoric or a politico-economic stake.

I am working at another level, for instance the one at which a development operation takes place, and which brings a series of actors, of various categories – peasants of various statuses, unemployed youth, women, rural notables, development field agents, representatives of the local administration, NGO members, visiting experts, European technical assistants, etcetera – into direct or indirect relationship with one another. These actors all develop personal and professional strategies, deployed in keeping with various criteria: in order to increase patrimonial land for some, for others in order to obtain a vehicle and the fuel to make it run, and so forth: to enhance one's position within an institution, to obtain a better contract, to increase one's network of social contacts, to become indispensable, to earn more money, to keep an eye on a neighbour or rival, to please one's friends and relations, to keep a low profile and play it safe, etcetera.

A development project (or development infrastructures, in general) thus appears to be a game in which the players involved all use different cards and play according to different rules. It could also be seen as a system of resources and opportunities which everyone tries to appropriate in his or her own way.

As Crozier and Friedberg would put it, the execution of a development project can be considered as a confrontation between several 'structures of collective action' or of 'organized action'. The 'project' itself, as an 'organization', is a specific 'structure of collective action' which others structures have

185

to contend with. Seen in the perspective of the sociology of organizations, a system of collective action is a power system because 'power is a fundamental and inescapable ingredient of all social relationships' (Crozier and Friedberg, 1977: 27). In this same perspective, power presupposes the existence of relatively autonomous actors endowed with unequal or unbalanced power resources, but who are never, or rarely ever, totally destitute of power, since even the most impoverished in this respect still have at least 'the ability, in reality and not just in theory, to refuse to do what is expected of them or to do it another way' (Friedberg, 1993: 251).

Being impenitently eclectic, I am inclined to combine this relational definition of power with another, more symbolic and more restrictive interpretation. There is also another type of power: 'instituted power', which is concentrated rather than diffuse, which can be converted into other forms of (social or economic) 'capital', in keeping with Bourdieu's perspective, for which Africa could provide myriad empirical illustrations. Gaining access to a position of power with the help of one's network of social relations, gaining personal wealth because of this position, distributing a part of this wealth to enhance one's network of 'contacts' is all part of everyday life.

The concept of the 'arena'[2] entails both these definitions of power. In an arena, heterogeneous strategic groups confront each other, driven by more or less compatible (material or symbolic) interests, the actors being endowed with a greater or lesser level or influence and power. But one also encounters centres of instituted local power: an emir, a district chief, a *sous-préfet*, an imam, the head of a fraternity, all have specific powers, linked to their functions and recognized as such.

External interventions are therefore confronted with these two kinds of power, the power everybody has and the power that only some people have, and whose intricate combination results in what we might refer to as the local arena.

The by-product of this relatively muted 'confrontation', or this relatively informal 'negotiation' (Arce, 1993; Mongbo, 1994), is what becomes of a development operation in practice: an unpredictable phenomenon. Let me say it again: the inevitable 'discrepancy' between a development operation on paper and a development operation in the field is merely the result of the different ways in which actors 'appropriate' the operation in question. In other words, certain individuals or social groups have the ability to twist the project to their own ends, either directly or indirectly.

Now, actors all over have, to varying degrees, 'resources' that enable them to influence the execution of a project (if only by ignoring or disparaging it). Some have more resources than others: more money, or more land, or more labourers, or a greater technical competence, or more energy, or more contacts, or more protection, etcetera. But this inequality in the face of a project is, obviously, not a single-faceted one: inequality is never based on just one criterion. Of course, there are persons who have multiple disadvantages, and who are therefore marginalized from the very beginning. But it is rare to encounter the target population of a project whose members have no room for manoeuvre whatsoever. Passive resistance to the project, or refusal to participate, myriad stratagems involving rumour, are some of the forms of action – which are more or less 'invisible' (viewed from the outside or by experts in a hurry) – that are available even to those who have very little influence.

The ways in which actors employ their respective visible or invisible capabilities (active or passive, action or impediment, discreet or overt) in face of the opportunities presented by a development project result in the emergence of a micro-development policy. The term 'policy' applies to the extent that there are real cases of conflict or power struggle between groups of social actors (on the part of development operators and of target populations alike), staged around the relative advantages and disadvantages (direct or indirect, material or symbolic) that development action provides.

This type of perspective obliges us both to examine the strategies that different categories of actors deploy, and to do research on the diversity of social codes and norms of behaviour which serve as references to these strategies (of developees and developers alike): the criteria based on which young men seeking emancipation from their elders regulate their behaviour in relation to a local development project are different from those of a village chief seeking to extend his network of social relationships, to say nothing of those of a European technical assistant seeking to justify his position abroad.

Moreover, not only do codes vary from one social set to another, but actors belonging to a given social set readily adopt different systems of norms and of legitimacy according to the context and their own interests. In the village milieu, one rarely encounters a game played according to just one rule with just one referee, recognized by one and all. The multifocality of power, the diversity of potential criteria of evaluation, the accumulation of 'legal' references all seem to enlarge the elbow room available to one and all. Problems related to land tenure provide the best illustration of this. In places where hydro-agricultural facilities are installed, 'in almost all case studies one observes in the ensuing years the emergence of hybrid practices about land ownership' (see Crousse, Le Bris and Le Roy, 1986). These are ambiguous and 'opportunistic'. Landowners play both on the register of modern regulations (which constitutes the rule of the official game and which in actual fact partially regulates land tenure practices) and on the register of traditional social relationships and relations to land, which are still in practice and which are just as influential in determining the rules of the game (Mathieu, 1990: 16). In more general terms, the host of authorities which can be called on in the case of land conflicts is often astounding: representatives of state administration, customary authority, Koranic judges, courts of law, the police, political parties, (see Lund, 1995). It has even been postulated, in more general terms, that permanent negotiation concerning powers, rules, prerogatives and competences is a major characteristic of contemporary rural Africa (Berry, 1994).[3]

Conflict, arena, strategic groups

'Conflict', 'arena' and 'strategic groups' are the key words of the perspective adopted in this chapter.

Some people are convinced that a village is a community united by tradition, cemented by consensus, organized around a 'world view' held in common and regulated by a shared culture. Our position is obviously very different: a village is an arena in which several 'strategic groups' enter into conflict with one another.

Conflict

The earliest works in African anthropology to accord systematic attention to social reality seen from the angle of conflicts were those of the Manchester School, of which Gluckman is irrefutably a trailblazer, as illustrated by his work revealingly entitled *Custom and Conflict in Africa* (Gluckman, 1956). However, Gluckman's use of the word 'conflict' entails three different levels of analysis which ought to be treated separately.

First, he makes an empirical observation: all societies are traversed by conflicts. Conflict is therefore a component of social life in general.

Second, he establishes a structural analysis: conflicts are indicative of a variety of social positions. Even very small societies and societies without institutionalized forms of 'government' display rifts and cleavages. These are sustained by norms, moral rules and conventions (which we could also refer to as cultural codes). Conflicts are therefore an expression of the interests linked to different social positions and are structured by culture.

Last, he employs a functionalist postulate: conflicts, which seem destined to tear societies apart and to throw them into chaos, contribute instead to their reproduction and to the reinforcement of social cohesion. They allow for the perpetuation of social ties by channelling the expression of social tension (safety valve), and by providing ritualized procedures for their resolution.

The empirical observation is still valid. The functionalist postulate is problematic. Not only has the functionalist paradigm (which was predominant in English anthropology at the time) become obsolete, but it would appear, moreover, that conflicts are also liable to result in social fragmentation and not only in social reproduction.

As for structural analysis, it needs to be nuanced (thus imitating the example set by Gluckman's own students: see Turner, 1957). Despite the fact that conflicts often reflect differences of position within the social structure, we still need to bear in mind that individuals still retain some elbow room. The emergence, management and outcome of conflicts are by no means predetermined. Interpersonal or inter-group conflicts are not only signs of opposing 'objective' interests, they are also the by-product of personal strategies and of idiosyncratic phenomena. Structural analysis must be completed by an analysis of strategies.

But our approach privileges above all the heuristic dimensions of the identification and study of conflicts: indeed, conflicts figure among the best ways of penetrating the intricacies of society, of revealing its structures, norms and codes, or of highlighting the strategies and logics of actors or of groups.[4] The postulate that consensus exists is much less productive as a research hypothesis than the postulate of conflict, if only because the analysis of conflict allows us to identify means of conflict prevention and resolution. It is clear that everyday social life is composed of consensus as well as conflict. But as far as research is concerned, conflicts are valuable indicators of the way a local society functions. Other indicators do, of course, exist. However, it would be a mistake to deprive ourselves of this avenue of research in anthropology of development, because conflicts are particularly relevant indicators of social change.

The identification of conflicts provides the means of going beyond the consensual façade, beyond the performance that local actors stage for the benefit of the intervener or foreign researcher.

Hence, our approach to societies from the angle of their conflicts should not be construed as a hunt for conflicts per se, or as an intention to place the priority on conflicts over other forms of sociability, or as the promotion of a systematically agonistic vision of societies, or as a refusal to take shared codes or conceptions into account. This is simply a methodological hypothesis which has been verified time and again, and which postulates that the identification and analysis of conflicts as an 'entry point' constitute fruitful avenues of research, which save time, while avoiding some of the snares that societies and ideologies set in the researcher's way.

Arena and field

Bailey's analyses provide the most significant use of the term 'field', which is frequently used in Anglo-Saxon literature, despite the fact that Bailey offers no explicit definition (Bailey, 1969). Bailey sees national and social political life as a 'game' in which social actors come face to face and compete with each other, grouped around leaders and in factions. The arena is basically the social space in which these confrontations and competitions occur.

The notion of an arena can be compared to other similar notions such as 'social field' (a transversal space in which institutions and multiple roles coexist), or to the French term *champ* (field), frequently employed by Bourdieu. In Bourdieu's works, *champ* remains an 'open concept', amenable to variations and opposed to unequivocal definitions. It is a market (in the metaphorical sense) in which actors possessing various types of 'capital' (economic, symbolic, social …) vie with each other. It is a particular type of autonomized social structure, with its own institutions, its specialized agents, its hierarchy of positions and its language. Its structure is, moreover, interiorized by its agents, through a 'habitus' which generates their practices. It is a space of game playing and of stakes related to a power struggle between social groups. Always, however, the term *champ* is used in a very macro, fundamentally structural sense,[5] despite the fact that the 'game' metaphor and the references to the habitus introduce a strategic dimension and aim at accounting for the stands agents take. A *champ* is above all a 'configuration of objective relations between positions' (Bourdieu, 1992: 72), 'a system of relationships which is independent of the populations which these relationships define' (ibid.: 82), and which is not to be confused with interaction. In this respect, we could define the 'developmentalist configuration' as a 'development field', comprising specific institutions, a particular language, an unequally structured market, in which competition occurs on unequal terms, one in which ideologies, salaries, competences, institutions, symbols etc. come face to face. A typical example of the progressive constitution of a field, in Bourdieu's sense of the word, can be observed in the field of health: the progressive autonomization of the medical field in Africa, in consequence of the public health apparatus introduced during the colonial era, stands in stark contrast to the relative imprecision of the borders between 'therapy', 'religion', 'power', and 'magic' that characterized pre-colonial societies (see Fassin, 1992).

Conversely, 'arena' is a more interactive notion, and also a more 'political' one (in the sense that this term has in the sociology of organizations). It refers to action on a smaller scale and presents a sharper awareness of the confrontations between actors themselves. An arena, as we understand it, is a space in which real conflicts between interacting social actors occur around common stakes. It occurs within a 'local space'. A development project is an arena. Village power is an arena. A co-operative is an arena. *Arena* has a greater descriptive content than *field*. And we prefer it. But it is of course not an explicative concept, just an exploratory one.

Strategic group

Following on Bierschenk's lead, I will now turn to Evers's (Evers and Schiel, 1988) concept of the 'strategic group'. In the works of this German sociologist, the concept of the 'strategic group' is an alternative to that of 'social class', considered to be excessively rigid, mechanical, economic and overly dependent on a Marxist analysis in terms of 'relations of production'. Hence, strategic groups appear to be social aggregates of a more empirical and variable nature, which defend common interests, especially by means of social and political action.

This more pragmatic perspective seems interesting because, instead of proposing a priori definitions of the criteria for the constitution of social groups, it deduces these criteria from the analysis of forms of action. But from Evers's point of view, strategic groups remain on the same macro level as social classes, for which they substitute, and intervene either at the national level or at the level of the society as a whole. But it would appear to me (still following on Bierschenk's lead, 1988), that the concept is most useful when applied at the level of the local society, when linked to the observation of forms of interaction between actors.

But we still have to determine whether strategic groups are 'real' groups, like 'corporate groups', relatively 'embodied', characterized by shared norms, forms of collective action or consensual procedures, or whether they are merely artificial constructs for the sake of analysis. My approach to the question is a pragmatic one: as a starting point it considers that the 'virtual' strategic group is a working hypothesis which helps us to reflect on the convergence of certain individual strategies, from which we might deduce that the individuals in question have an identical position in face of a given 'problem'. What that means is that in face of a given problem in a given social context the number of attitudes and behaviour patterns is not infinite: what we observe is a restricted number of attitudes and behaviour patterns. One of the aims of research is to determine finally whether or not these strategic groups which serve as working hypotheses at the outset *really* exist, whether actors who share a common position also share forms of interaction, informal (network, affiliation, allegiance) or formal (institution, organization, sect, faction). As opposed to classic sociological definitions of social groups, strategic groups (whether virtual or real) are not constructed once and for all and are not relevant to all types of problem: they vary according to the problem at hand, that is, according to local issues. They are linked sometimes to statutory or socio-professional characteristics (gender, caste, profession, etcetera), sometimes to lineage affiliations or to networks of solidarity or clientelism, sometimes to individual life stories and strategies.

The strategic group is a fundamentally empirical and methodological notion. It is built on the simple supposition that all actors in a given community do not share identical interests or concepts and that, depending on the problem, their interests and concepts produce different combinations, but not haphazardly so. Hypotheses can thus be postulated about the composition of strategic groups in the face of a specific 'problem': enquiry will of course determine whether or not the hypotheses were sound, or whether other strategic groups must be constructed, and the extent to which they exist in reality.

Reference will be made, by way of example, to the methodological use to which these concepts have been put, based on a framework conceptualized by Thomas Bierschenk and myself for collective enquiries in research and training (initiation to anthropology). In our opinion, this method is particularly adapted to the analysis of development projects.

The ECRIS framework

ECRIS (Enquête collective rapide pour l'identification des conflits et des groupes stratégiques) occurs in six phases. It is to be noted that this framework is a *continuous back-and-forth movement between (long) individual phases and (short) collective phases*, in contrast both to classic ethnographic enquiry, which puts the priority on long-term individual research, and to rapid enquiry methods (like Rapid Rural Appraisal, RRA, and Méthode accélérée de recherche et de planification participative, MARP), which put the priority on collective short-term enquiry.

The duration of the enquiry is not predetermined (the individual phase might vary between a fortnight and six months, depending on the themes and on previously acquired competences) and there are no ready-made tools or keys, nor are there any 'standard methods': indeed the aim of the ECRIS framework is to devise, through a phase of collective enquiry, indicators adapted to the field and to the theme, indicators which will afterwards be used for the individual enquiry which remains irreplaceable.

One of the main objectives of the ECRIS framework is to allow for a multi-site research, that is, to conduct a rigorous comparison between different sites where fieldwork will be done along unified problematics and methodologies.

Individual identificatory enquiry

This is a quick way of preparing the teamwork to come by means of a rough identification of major local issues (depending, obviously, on the type of research), in order to predetermine which are the strategic groups (that is, to propose provisional strategic groups for the local collective enquiry to come), comprising categories of actors who are presumed to have the same overall relationship to these issues.

If the research theme is about the evaluation of a local development project, the preliminary enquiry will pinpoint, for example, the existence of land tenure issues linked to the project, conflicts between cultivators and cattle breeders, rivalry between two important aristocratic families, as well as the exclusion of women as beneficiaries of the project. The following strategic groups could then be proposed: (1) ordinary cultivators, (2) ordinary cattle breeders, (3) the two aristocratic families, (4) external interveners (NGOs, technical services), (5) women.

A preparatory seminar

The preparatory seminar is aimed at familiarizing participants with the problematic and method, to review the documentation available on the research sites, to propose a series of tentative qualitative indicators that might prove helpful for later individual research (standard indicators are obviously out of the question, since each theme of enquiry requires some amount of 'working out' of specific indicators). Each indicator corresponds to the gathering of a systematic body of material, comprising a variety of data (interviews, descriptions, surveys) on a well-specified field, perceived as potentially enlightening as regards the object of study.

> In keeping with the preceding example, we could propose as tentative indicators: the history and typology of successive projects that have occurred in the village, analysis of the process of local decision-making linked to the current project, the biography of certain key actors in the project, the description of one of the co-operative's general assemblies, the inventory of places of debate and public discussion in the village …

The collective enquiry

The basic principle underlying ECRIS is the following: the entire group of enquirers makes a successive tour of each site and stays a few days on each site. While on a given site the group of enquirers splits up into several groups (two or three persons per group, at the most). During the stay, each team of enquirers concentrates on one local strategic group, and only one. It investigates only persons belonging to the strategic group assigned to the team. The composition of the enquiry groups changes from one site to another.

This collective enquiry is the very essence of ECRIS. It allows each enquiry to approach a problem via the notion of the strategic group, and provides experience on the variety and relativity of strategic groups. We do not consider the strategic group as a 'real' group, a community or a corporate group. Nor do we suppose that a strategic group should have an established position. It is not a focus group: though some interviews can be collective (usually because circumstances dictate that an individual interview speedily becomes a collective interview if it is not kept secret), individual interviews are preferred, with as great a variety of persons as possible within the strategic group assigned to the team of enquirers.

If ten enquirers are working on a given site, five groups of two enquirers per group will be formed. One group will interview only women, for instance. However, the women will not be invited to a meeting nor will female leaders be called on. The group will make successive individual calls on chiefs' wives and ordinary peasant women, elderly women and young women, female association co-ordinators and marginalized women, etcetera.

The main instruction is quite simple.

1. During the enquiry attempts must be made to identify as many conflicts and contradictions as possible, including those in which the persons being interviewed are not directly involved.

For instance, interviews with women allow us to identify not only conflicts between women and men concerning commercialization, but they also acquaint us with women's opinions on the conflicts between cattle breeders and cultivators, or concerning the conflict between two aristocratic lineages, while allowing us to identify new conflicts (related to religious or political affiliation, or concerning the election of a new executive bureau for the co-operative, or suspected pilfering …).

Two complementary instructions can be added.

2. Attempts must be made to understand, as far as possible 'from the inside', the way members of the strategic group relate to the research topic and how they perceive other groups. The strategic group must be divided into its various components, each endowed with its specific behaviour and discourse and distinguishable from other components.

How do cultivators' wives view development projects and how do they benefit from them? What opinion do they have of external interveners and of the role of the sous-préfet? Do the wives of cattle breeders express the same opinions? Do young women and elderly women appear to have similar positions and identical opinions?

3. The tentative indicators should be explored in order to discover potential fields of application.

One example of an interesting local 'decision' to be explored is the renewal of the co-operative's executive bureau; the biography of certain actors might be interesting …, the baobab tree situated in the centre of the village or the chief's house on a Saturday morning during judicial hearings are important spaces of debate to be observed, etcetera.

Each evening a collective evaluative session allows for a superposition of the different angles from which conflicts were observed. This helps the group to determine whether or not temporary working hypotheses are still relevant.

These group sessions are the groundwork for the member of the research team who will carry out subsequent work on the site. Group sessions are particularly helpful in paving the way for later individual work.

Collective discussion on site at the end of the day, based on freshly gathered empirical data collected according to a variety of perspectives and approached through the avenue of conflicts, is indeed a powerful tool for the construction of a research object and methodology. The verbalization rendered compulsory by debate as well as this collective brainstorming are not available to the individual researcher, who will consequently have the tendency to divide his research into two excessively distinct phases: data collection, on one hand; analysis and organization of data, on the other. Conversely, a collective monitoring session at the end of each day, in the 'heat of the event', makes it possible to evaluate data straightaway, prepares the next day's work, and allows for the setting up of temporary models which remain flexible because they have not become rigid by being put in writing, and which remain closely linked to field enquiry ... This is a privileged space for the generation of interpretations closely related to empirical material, in other words for the emergence of 'grounded theory' (see Glaser and Strauss, 1973). Moreover, the participants' training, their competences and their interests are all necessarily different; this variety is a form of complementarity so long as the problematic is shared, at least to some degree. On-the-spot debate and interpretation of data fresh from the field are, for this reason, more productive than the solitary and more or less intuitive reflections of an isolated researcher. One has to convince the other members of the team, substantiate one's hypotheses, take objections or counter-examples into account, face up to criticism.

An evaluation seminar of the collective enquiry
This has three objectives:

- the shared qualitative indicators, which have been tested during the collective enquiry, will finally be elaborated and will form the grounds on which each individual researcher can base his personal enquiry;
- second, the research angle appropriate to each site must be clarified;
- finally, an effort at comparison must be made in order to isolate, based on the various sites, the common elements as well as the specific characteristics of each site, the major leads and the main hypotheses.

Individual research on each site
At this point, the first phase of fieldwork has been considerably clarified and is well under way. A set method of proceeding is no longer proposed: in ECRIS, each team member is provided only with shared indicators and specific areas

to research on. It is impossible to determine a standard duration of the work. It all depends on the topics to be examined. Some topics require only a brief period of complementary individual enquiry, of the order of a week or two (the expertise of a village co-operative pharmacy, or the monitoring of a local micro-project), while others require a considerably longer period of individual enquiry, over a period of a several months (the monitoring of integrated projects or the study of forms of local power).

The closing seminar

This is prepared by the writing of individual reports by each researcher based on his enquiry on each site. It is entirely devoted to comparative analysis, through the interpretation of local data and of the results gleaned with the help of qualitative indicators based on the hypotheses proposed.

Conclusion

It goes without saying that ECRIS is particularly relevant to the field of anthropology of development. But it can also be applied to other types of studies or evaluations, for two fundamental reasons:

• Being a framework for comparative analysis carried out on several sites, ECRIS answers to the needs of studies aimed at preparation, follow-up and final evaluation of development operations. One particularly important asset of the ECRIS framework resides in the fact that it elaborates, step by step, the qualitative indicators which are often unavailable in the development universe, where usually unreliable standard statistical indicators are particularly prevalent.

• Concepts such as conflict, arena and strategic group are well adapted to the analysis of the interaction between a development project and the local society.

Notes

1 This chapter is essentially derived from a long-term collaboration with T. Bierschenk, who should be considered as its co-author. For a more elaborate version already published in English, see Bierschenk and Olivier de Sardan, 1997a.

2 The concept of the 'arena' has previously been employed in political science, but with a broader application (see Kasfir, 1976). Bierschenk (1988) and Crehan and von Oppen (1988) undoubtedly provide the clearest perspective on the development project as an 'arena'. It is also defined, in their terms, as a 'social event'.

3 'Berry argues that negotiability of rules and relationships is one of the fundamental characteristics of African societies. The apparently fixed titles, prerogatives and rules are constantly the objects of negotiation and reinterpretation. Indeed the cases

presented above seem to confirm her statement' (Lund, 1995: 19).

4 See Elwert, for example (Elwert, 1984) concerning the Ayizo people of Benin.

5 Bourdieu's first paper on a *champ* was about the *champ intellectuel* (intellectual field). He insists on the emergence of 'specific instances of selection and consecration (…) made to compete for legitimacy' (Bourdieu, 1966: 866), as the condition on which a field becomes autonomous. He also makes regular mention of other fields such as religion (Bourdieu, 1971) or art (see also Accardo and Corcuff, 1986, selected texts; and Bourdieu, 1992: 71–89).

13
Conclusion
The dialogue between
social scientists and developers

Verdicts vary on the topic of the relationship between anthropologists and developers: some people think it is a matter of isolated social scientists perched in their ivory towers, producing studies of no practical use, whose knowledge is unconnected with social reality. Others point to sociologists at the beck and call of decision makers, slapdash enquiries with no scientific value, research compromised in the cause of dubious legitimation of development ... Loss of a common idiom between 'fundamental research' and 'applied research', between the social sciences and development operators, between research institutions and research consultancies, between anthropologists and agro-economists, or several variations on this theme, all seem to constitute the various aspects of a fundamental misunderstanding. But this is not a recent phenomenon: the only novel aspect of the matter concerns the vocabulary employed, which changes according to the partners in question and in keeping with emerging intellectual fashions.

Periodic calls for dialogue are made in the attempt to surmount this difficulty, or rather to abolish it by means of incantation, in the time it takes to hold a colloquium, a training session or a conversation. Indeed, there is a strong temptation to play on a moral register, to appeal to the good will of the partners concerned, which amounts to interpreting this specific contradiction between knowledge and action in psychological terms.

Logic of knowledge and logic of action

The point of view developed in this work has nothing to do with this last position. Social scientists and developers respectively generate fundamentally distinct professional logics. It is therefore impossible to conceive how these sets of logics can be forced into interaction (creating dialogue) except by emphasizing their specific characteristics. This implies that we take our distance, from the outset, from moral presuppositions, as they tend to cloud or to bias the real nature of these logics.[1] The second implication is that these respective logics need to be approached from a historical perspective, in which they are necessarily perceived as constantly emerging social products.

As mentioned above, the developmentalist configuration can be considered as a market or as an arena, over and beyond the moral paradigm which constitutes a fundamental element of its meta-ideology. Development operators, regardless of their statuses or strategies, are professionals in this market, along with Third World activists, volunteers in non-profit organizations, co-operation personnel or local co-ordinators. By stripping the social actors in development of their moral veils, one discovers degrees of disparity which are of great interest to sociological investigation. But this also applies to social scientists; in the same way that development practices fail to correspond exactly to the discourse that legitimates them, anthropological practice cannot be taken at face value when it professes philanthropic motivations. It is a well-known fact that social science is also a 'market', thanks to Bourdieu who, after having pinpointed its various characteristics, has himself become one of the major poles around which this market is structured ... The social scientist who sets himself the task of elucidating peasant logics or of opposing them to development logics is not a mere spectator: he himself is involved in logics that influence his scientific practice (logics of professional recognition, of power, of credit 'capturing', etcetera). His scientific logics cannot simply be classified either as developers' logics or as developees' logics.

Hence, the misunderstandings that exist between anthropology of development and the developmentalist configuration are practically inevitable, seeing that social scientists and developers occupy distinct positions.

Once the moral illusion has been dispensed with, a 'disenchanted' approach to the relationship between developers and scientists can then surface, an approach that accounts for the differences in their systems of norms, of social recognition, and of legitimation, and the constraints with which they are confronted.

1.   Knowledge and action mobilize extremely dissimilar registers of legitimation. According to Bachelard's famous expression, which is still valid today, scientific knowledge in particular is constructed through a continuous, unrelenting fight against error, by means of meticulous criticism, intellectual polemic, theoretical and methodological vigilance, and of constant examination of acquired knowledge. Action, on the other hand, comprises arbitration, ambiguities, compromise, wagers, wills and emergencies. Knowledge doubts, while action needs to believe. Knowledge is purportedly disinterested, while action claims to be up to its elbows in grease. Knowledge takes time, action

hasn't got the time. Knowledge wants to observe social processes, action wants to orient and control them.

2.   The social phenomena with which social science is confronted are so complex (numerous and variable) that social science must resort to multi-dimensional rationalities, rather than linear and deterministic rationalities. Developers, on the other hand, generate a technical (or technico-economic) rationality in which decisions have to be made. The one best solution has to be found (see Crozier and Friedberg's criticism, 1977: 22). It is in this context that operators call on scientists to make 'recommendations', in other words to go beyond their field of competence.

3.   While development operators postulate and search for common interests within populations, and between the populations and themselves (since both their decision making and their execution of decisions need consensus), sociology, on the contrary, tries to detect differences and contradictions (because postulating differences is more productive from a heuristic point of view than postulating similitude). Development professionals appeal to the good will of the populations, in the name of their own good will, but social scientists cannot afford to take the good will of either at face value.

4.   Misunderstandings also arise concerning the roles each is expected to play: while development professionals take it for granted that the expert in 'human dimensions' is a natural ally or a development service provider, the expert often develops a critical and external point of view on the projects with which developers identify. Moreover, the development operators themselves are also perceived by the anthropologist as an object of study. Indeed, the scientist insists on the fact that an approach which includes developees as well as developers is required.

5.   Finally, social science and the development professions respectively are regulated by different systems of norms and different professional values. The social recognition of anthropologists depends on their publications, on their peer relationships; they have a high degree of autonomy and work on a long-term basis. However, for developers, professional identity is more problematic (expatriate status compounds the problem): the criteria that regulate their career are not really related to the quality of the 'product',[2] nor are they transparent; the time allocated is insufficient, and developers have a very hard time discerning the distinction between systems of constraint and room for manoeuvre.

As necessary as it may appear, the collaboration between social actors from two worlds as different as this is no simple matter. In face of this recurrent problem, various solutions are possible. They can be presented in the form of four 'models' (my reference here is to Boiral, 1985). Two of these models are easy to dismiss, notwithstanding the fact they are the most prevalent.

Two models to be rejected

The first concerns isolation. Social scientists and development operators rarely interact. The contacts between them are either merely rhetorical (invocations to collaboration without any subsequent effect) or financial (the commissioning of studies that remain unused, or even unusable). Social scientists remain confined to their institutional closets, enclosed in their academic logics. Development operators do not know them and haven't got the faintest idea about the research that scientists do. This is the most frequent situation, even though it is not the most to be desired.

The second model concerns submission. The anthropologist is employed by development operators who impose their terms of reference and who are bent on using scientific services to their own liking. Consultancy offices and consultants thus become a part of the internal apparatus of the developmentalist configuration. The logic of research tends to disappear in favour of the logic of development expertise. Many African social scientists are swallowed up by the expertise market and its rent, owing in part to the erosion of the state and of public research.

Third model: action research

A third model for the relationship between development and social science professionals is currently in expansion, at least in words. It aims at the fusion of these two roles, as implied by the names by which it presents itself here and there: action research, development research, participatory research. But is this a genuine epistemological break, as its disciples readily proclaim, one that should at long last allow for a reconciliation between knowledge and action, a reconciliation erected on the ruins of positivism? Is this really a case of research being piloted by and with the aid of the peasants, research which will at last put scientists at the disposal of the people? My opinion is slightly different.

Many contemporary trends originating in agronomic research have the intention, and rightly so, of breaking away from the vertical and authoritarian models which characterize the relationship between the classic tropicalist station research and rural development projects. They would like to resume dialogue with the local peasantries. But the difficulties inherent in the collaboration between research and development do not disappear, as if by magic, simply by proclaiming that there is no longer any boundary separating the two. Rhetorical cant, more or less assorted with methodological diagrams or declared programmes, is not enough, for the fundamental reason underlined above: logics of knowledge and logics of action are far removed from each other. Obviously this does not imply that isolation is a solution or that scientists have no place in development practice. What it means is that any attempt to combine these two roles, played either by one and the same person (a scientist and decision maker all in one) or by an institution or organization (associating several scientists and deciders) must respect the constraints peculiar to each of these roles. To put it another way: action research must simultaneously obey the rules of research and those of action, or incur the risk of becoming poor research and misguided action.

Action research from the angle of research

Because it is a knowledge process, action research must measure up to the same epistemological and methodological criteria as any other type of research. Let us take, for example, the relationship between 'participation' (collaborating with peasants) and 'analysis' (studying peasants): the necessity and the difficulty involved in making these two dimensions meet is not specific to action research, or even to the relationship between research and action. This is just a classic research problem, or more precisely, a constraint peculiar to prolonged *in situ* research. Since Malinowski, ethnology has recommended 'participatory observation'. The observer, whether he be an anthropologist or an agronomist, is assigned, willy-nilly, a place within the local society's system of roles. He is no longer a silent, external observer. The observer becomes a part of the phenomenon he observes. Conversely, the people he interviews are co-producers of the enquiry which they attempt to orient to their own liking. Sociological or anthropological field research constitutes an interaction between the researcher (or researchers) and the populations.

Classical positivist epistemology has long since been discredited in anthropology. The latter has in turn given up on the notion of experimentability and acknowledges that observation cannot be detached from the conditions of observation. In this respect, action research cannot claim to be an epistemological break – which would amount to flogging a dead horse. Recognizing the fact that the researcher is to a greater or lesser extent involved in the subject he studies (if only as a 'kind stranger') is hardly new. But this does not preclude the need for methodological evaluation. The bias observed in quantitative enquiries also applies to 'qualitative' enquiries based on prolonged interaction with peasants. *The researcher's 'participation' clearly implies personal and subjective slants. The role of anthropological savoir-faire is to minimize, control and use such biases.*

Close collaboration with decision makers or with peasant actors does not diminish the need for vigilance. On the contrary; the fact that one has a commissioned research report to finalize or to commence, defined by other people or in collaboration with them, serves only to compound constraints, far from alleviating them: constraints surrounding the definition of the research topic (which is narrower than usual), constraints of time (researchers normally have more time at their disposal), constraints of writing (the need to employ a register that is more accessible than academic language).

These additional constraints probably alarm some scientists. I think that those scientists are mistaken. However, those who are not frightened away are not consequently obliged to abandon their savoir-faire, or to relax their methodological vigilance. The problem with so-called 'participatory' enquiries is not that they accept certain additional constraints of time and subject definition. This is a legitimate rule of the game, in this particular instance. The question is to determine whether or not invoking 'participation' does not result in overlooking, along the way, other constraints which are just as fundamental, without which no serious or valid qualitative fieldwork can be accomplished, regardless of its duration or subject matter. Can the results obtained by means of such standardized enquiries, using the instruments they choose to employ, be deemed acceptable, reliable and plausible (see my comments on RRA on p. 210 below)?

Action research from the angle of action

By the same token, action research, if it takes the form of intervention, is subject to the same effects as other types of intervention. As we are well aware, rural development action is inevitably 'deviated', appropriated, disarticulated and reinterpreted by the various sectors of the peasant society it addresses. No matter how 'participatory' a project intends to be, it remains subjected to the two 'principles' that regulate the interaction between the population and external interveners: the principle of selection and the principle of 'sidetracking' (see Chapter 9).

But this also applies to participatory research: peasants use the opportunities and resources that researchers place at their disposal by 'selecting' those that interest them, based on objectives that do not coincide with those set by researchers. Peasants, for their part, are impervious to the illusion that there is no borderline separating the respective roles of scientists, peasants and technocrats.

Fourth model: the contractual solution

But there remains a fourth model, which I prefer, following in the wake of Boiral, namely the contractual model: social scientists and development operators agree to define a clearly circumscribed zone of interaction and collaboration without relinquishing their specific identities. The two parties decide on the terms of reference of the research through negotiation, by confronting their respective logics in a given domain. There is nothing extraordinary or revolutionary about this: this is precisely what took place in the past in the case of temporary, nonceremonial collaboration successfully carried through by operators and researchers, in the name of plain common-sense.

But could we take this a step further and suggest the definition of a few preferential zones of interaction? I will limit myself to three examples: training, sidetracking, and enquiry.

Training development agents

We need to underline the role that anthropologists can play in the training of development agents in the field.

Indeed, anthropological enquiry attempts to understand how problems appear when seen from the viewpoint of those involved, taken not as a homogeneous entity, but as an assemblage composed of differentiated elements. This knowledge is not spontaneously available to a development agent (or to a technician, agronomist or economist). It requires a certain amount of work, a certain method, a certain apprenticeship, a part of which needs to be taken out from the inner sanctum of professional anthropology and placed at the disposal of development agents. Such an adaptation/operationalization/simplification of academic anthropology, in keeping with the aims of training (rather than those of research) implies taking a certain distance from academic anthropology, which perceives anthropological enquiry only as an instrument of research to be handled by qualified, university-educated researchers, unimpeded by the contingencies of action and the pressures of time. Academic anthropology also tends to disregard the problematics of change and to regard the agents of change with contempt.

The corollary is a symmetrical opposition to the practice of certain development operators, who use the term 'sociology' to baptize the stereotypes they construct about local societies: in contrast to their approach, acquiring the instruments that produce knowledge of local African universes demands work and competence. It has nothing in common with vague notions (dialogue, needs, participation), with a 'peasant-friendly' ideologies, or with the ubiquitous ideas that many developers use to convey the impression that they take local societies into account, without taking any pains to acquire proper knowledge of these societies.

One of the advantages of possessing a minimum of anthropological competence is that development agents are thereby forearmed and forewarned against the clichés and stereotypes about local societies which abound in the development universe (see Chapter 5). Despite being seen as 'belonging' to the field, development agents are not, as a rule, immune to these. Providing development agents with genuine competence in anthropological enquiry –

this competence, though 'rudimentary', is nonetheless real – is one way of helping them to move beyond ideological or moralistic cant, which is supposed, in and by itself, to transform the development agent into a man of the people, attentive to the peasants' needs ...

Another advantage to training development agents in anthropological enquiry is that it inverts their relationships with the peasants. Indeed, the training that development agents generally receive overlooks or intensifies the problems they have in communicating with the local populations:

- The methods inherited from the colonial past, as well as the example left by the post-colonial administration, have ingrained an attitude and a tradition of contempt among civil servants and one of suspicion among peasants, which reinforce each other.
- Even when happening to be of peasant origin, a development agent is of necessity someone who has been to school, during which time he or she has been out of the field or out of the village at which children usually start to learn family skills. As a result, the development worker has little or no foundation in popular knowledge and tends instead to shun it.
- The classic methods of training development agents do not prepare them for a future role as mediators between peasant knowledge and another system of knowledge. Instead, this training inculcates in them an anti-peda-gogical attitude based on reluctance to address themselves to 'ignoramuses'.
- 'New' methods of agent training, bent on opposing traditional systems of hierarchy and training, introduce communication (meant to sensitize, 'stir' and raise the consciousness of peasants). Though ostensibly non-directive, participatory, or self-training, they in fact often involve forms of manipulation which conceal a profound ignorance concerning these peasants, even though this type of ideological rhetoric claims to rehabilitate them.

Hence the importance of showing development agents how they can learn from peasants through practical experience in the field: for a while they must become the pupils with the peasants in the role of instructors. This is indeed the principle on which anthropological enquiry is constructed. Agents will thus be better equipped for the function of mediation which is an integral part of their mission (see Chapter 11).

Adapting to sidetracking

How to adapt to 'sidetracking' can be included in the training of development agents. More generally, doing 'follow-up' on sidetracking provides an excellent opportunity for collaboration between anthropology and development institutions.

Let us return to the question of sidetracking (see Chapter 9). Of necessity, a development project implies placing a bet on the way in which the social actors involved will behave. Although preliminary sociological studies conducted prior to the execution of a project can (in the event that these are serious and taken into account, which conditions are not always fulfilled …) prevent some particularly stupid bets (which occupy numerous pages of development history), they cannot read tea leaves: they cannot annul the risk factor.[3] This is because the effective strategies deployed generate such a wide variety of variables as to become unpredictable; these include a multitude of categories of actors competing with each other in the context of a development project, endowed with a multitude of personal logics, not to mention the wide variety of stakes being vied for, and the diverse local systems of constraints (produced by the environment and by history).

Nonetheless, development operators must do all they can to minimize this risk factor. Hence, it is only natural that they call on the social sciences to do their absolute best at forecasting. A project chief is never satisfied with social science responses like 'things are a lot more difficult than you imagine'; his problem is how to reduce the chances of his project's being sidetracked. Seen from the perspective of development institutions viewed as 'organizations', the recourse to anthropology should help to improve the capacity for regulation of the established system of action and to reduce the uncertainty inherent in it (Friedberg, 1993).

The entire problem revolves around the importance attributed to sidetracking. Are they normal and essentially unpredictable effects of interactions? Or simply adverse and harmful side effects to be avoided?

Within the developmentalist configuration, these effects are usually imputed either to developees or to developers.

1. In the first case ('it's the fault of developees'), the gap between a correct understanding of the peasants' best 'interests' (as perceived by the authors of the projects) and the incomprehension the peasants themselves display has to be breached. There are only two ways of going about this, namely obligation or information. Obligation is no longer legitimate (even if in various fields – such as environment, for example, where fines are charged by hydraulic and forestry authorities – it is still practised) and has always proved itself ineffectual in the face of the multitude of far-flung levels of decision (a policemen can hardly be set on the heels of every single peasant). So that leaves us with information. This is therefore a flourishing field in the developmentalist configuration (see the rising demands for specialists in information, education, communication – IEC – whose various standard pedagogical technologies share a common overall ignorance about popular and local systems of thought and action). Their methods usually revolve around improving mass information, methods of training and communication.

2. In the second case ('it is the developers' fault'), sidetracking is attributed to the absence of preliminary studies, the overlooking of local reality, poor definition of aims, inadequate supervision, the unwieldiness of the procedures that donors stipulate, the incompetence and venality of national co-ordinators, the ethnocentrism of foreign experts, etcetera, etcetera.

Such elements can of course be observed and should not be overlooked. However, looking for this type of scapegoat (or its corollary, namely, a miracle) will not solve the problem of sidetrackings. These are usually misconstrued, in my opinion, as failures. Yet, they are, in a way, unavoidable and even indispensable. Moreover, sidetracking cannot be attributed indiscriminately either to developers or to developees. *Sidetracking is a normal phenomenon which cannot, in fact, be eliminated. It is the necessary and unintentional outcome of the intermingling of the complex variables involved in the reaction of a social milieu in the face of a voluntarist external intervention.*

We could therefore consider that, in the context of sidetracking, the anthropologist is best employed in the evaluation of the extent, nature and possible reasons behind sidetracking, or, in other words, in the *monitoring and follow-up* of development intervention.[4] Isn't this a strategic angle for rural anthropological intervention, used as action support? Indeed, the description, comprehension and interpretation of the various types of sidetracking to which development interventions are subjected can help these interventions to readjust and to adapt themselves to the selections and sidetracking that the local populations exercise, thus acting in support of the local dynamics, which, in the present case, are equally reactive and endogenous. This requires two preconditions on the part of development institutions:

(a) that projects solicit information about the sidetrackings to which they are likely to be subjected and aim at establishing frameworks for feedback;

(b) that they consider it necessary to apply to independent, competent anthropologists to do the job.

It is true that these two conditions are rarely encountered. The main problem involves the ability to adapt, by taking sidetracking into account and transforming intervention structures themselves. Institutional, political, ideological, financial and accountancy contingencies all seem to work in favour of this conclusion: integration of readjustment as an integral part of intervention structures is merely a pipe dream. The cumbersome mechanism of development aid and the conditions laid down by donors deprive projects of flexibility (in this as in other areas, NGOs are no models of virtue: see the three examples analysed by Mathieu, 1994).

However, a few examples of successful analyses of sidetracking do exist: one concerns a project for the promotion of animal (oxen) traction. Through an analysis of the sidetracking which it generated, it was revealed that peasants were in fact using credits for meat production. Consequently, the project was able to readapt by turning to fattening instead of traction (see Yung, 1985). Can we hope to discover, somewhere or other, a few reasonably open-minded, self-correcting, gradually advancing development projects, capable of reacting to feedback, of taking the reactions of their milieu into account, thereby preparing themselves to face up to the sidetracking that inevitably occurs?

We can at least hope that this role of monitoring will arouse growing interest on the part of development institutions as they search for ways of readjusting development projects to the sidetracking imposed by their clients. This might appear to be a modest ambition for anthropology of development to have. Nevertheless, it would still be an achievement if anthropology could help development projects to be more attentive to the effects induced by their interaction with the local populations and, as a result, to change their approach.

But all this depends on enquiry.

On enquiry

Pleading for an increase in anthropological enquiries is an inevitable rhetorical exercise in our profession and one in which I most willingly exert myself. It is a matter either of convincing developers that they need anthropological studies in development or of complaining that the realization of this necessity has not yet dawned on them.

The reactions of many development operators is symptomatic of the misunderstandings surrounding the notion of enquiry. On one hand, one notices an ever-increasing pile-up of studies, while 'evaluations', 'surveys', 'problem analysis', 'identification of needs', 'action enquiry', 'participative research' and all kinds of reports thrive and prosper. (And someone is suggesting still more studies?) Others are persuaded, on the contrary, that they are already engaged in anthropological studies, without the help of anthropologists. Who needs to wait for the help of an anthropologist to become acquainted with the milieu? 'We have been attentive to this for ages, and the method we elaborated makes ample room for the discovery of the local culture …'

The problem is that all enquiries are not the same. We can distinguish three types.

1.   Many people think that an 'enquiry' is a matter of questionnaires and statistics. Let's make no bones about it: this type of enquiry is extremely difficult in countries of the South and in the development universe. Questionnaires use leading questions which solicit certain answers. They are often badly put, incorrectly translated and poorly interpreted. The answers are

often biased, falsified, and ambiguous. Of course, reliable quantitative enquiries can be found in Africa (but this is rare). Demographic and socio-economic enquiries (follow-up of households, of commercial agricultural ventures, notation of commercial flows) generally enter into this category. But their cost is extremely high (since national statistical systems are not reliable and data must therefore be produced from scratch) and the quality/price ratio is not always satisfactory.

KAP (knowledge, attitudes, practices) enquiries claim to be quicker while still managing to gather discursive data. In this domain of concepts, method-ological vigilance is extremely important, as results could be invalidated by a whole range of biases. Yet the types of question asked by KAP enquiries, the method of administering questionnaires and the reliability of the results obtained are disputable, owing, in particular, to a lack of knowledge of cultural contexts and an underestimation of translation problems. Nevertheless, this type of enquiry is flourishing, in epidemiology and in project sociology alike (for a slightly critical appraisal, see Caraël, 1993; for a more radical criticism, see Pigg, 1994).

2. Yet the word 'enquiry' also has another meaning, one that refers to anthropological enquiry proper, sometimes called 'qualitative' enquiry, based on in-depth interviews, so-called participatory observation, more or less informal conversations, non-directive or semi-directive interviews, descrip-tions, surveys, case studies, etcetera (see Olivier de Sardan, 1995). This is a 'fundamental', complex, lengthy, global anthropological enquiry which is unquestionably the best approach for obtaining knowledge about the finer aspects of social knowledges and social logics, topics on which 'quantitative' sociology is not competent … But anthropological enquiry, as such, is not easily applied to development projects. And the time and professional qualification it requires do not generally correspond to the demands made by development institutions.

3. Finally, there is another type of enquiry, namely expert enquiry or the 'tour of the field'. This allows experts, consultants, researchers and decision makers to become a little more familiar with a problem or a situation, to 'get an idea', to put feelings, words, faces on files and figures. This is the favourite working method of (most) consultancy offices, NGOs, international organiza-tions, co-operation offices and national civil servants. Such enquiries respond to certain evaluative needs, but they have nothing to teach us about the logics that regulate the way populations react to the action carried out on their behalf. They are not tailored to such needs. Those who take the risk of producing appraisals in this domain usually confirm clichés, which generally reflect the play-acting ability of local actors, national officers of the state, 'resource persons', or selected local beneficiaries.[5] Expert enquiry is opposed in many respects to anthropological enquiry.

Anthropological enquiry apparently entails a lot of wasted time (like learning a language), silences and chatting, which are the necessary counterpoints of in-depth interviews. It is usually a question of interviewing individuals, repeatedly. Simple questions lead to complex answers ... Expert enquiry is carried out in a hurry, usually through 'group interviews', obtained by convening a 'village meeting' during which several problems are treated simultaneously and, obviously, superficially. Complex questions give rise to simple answers ... Anthropological enquiry seeks to discover the subtle differences between types of knowledge, modes of interpretation, and logics, and insists on the difficulty that all external interveners have in apprehending such realities. Expert enquiry usually seeks to confirm opinions or suspicions. It allows experts to convince themselves that local problems can be 'understood' at little cost.

Attempts at synthesis have been made, it is true, with the aim of adapting anthropological enquiry to the level of expertise or evaluation time available. The best-known and most widely practised is RRA (Rapid Rural Appraisal), transformed into PRA (Participatory Rural Appraisal), which has in turn given birth to a francophone offspring called MARP (Méthode accélérée de recherche et de planification participative). RRA and MARP are based on the so-called *focus group* technique, which is merely the recourse to systematic group interviews, carried out on groups defined on the basis of simple social criteria (youth, women, schoolchildren, etcetera), which enquirers combine with similarly simple tools (nomenclatures, classifications, maps, elaborated along with the members of the group). A complete evaluation of such hybrid methodologies is difficult. In the meantime, many social scientists remain sceptical (see Fall and Lericollais, 1992).[6] Yet development institutions consider that by multiplying this type of enquiry they are in some way consulting the social sciences, at a modest cost indeed, and are 'at long last' availing themselves of the required means for 'understanding the milieu'. But how can a handful of enquirers, aided only by oversimplified methodological tools and insufficient anthropological competence, in the space of a few days, possibly unearth relevant political, economic, and cultural information on the social context in which a project is to be executed? The differences opposing, on one hand, RRA–MARP type enquiries – bearing a remote resemblance to anthropology but simplified into a kit, and proposing standardized group enquiries in record time, which social scientists hold in scant esteem – and 'genuine' anthropological enquiry, on the other – with its abstract problematics, its methodological scruples and its extended time limit, remain undiminished.[7]

But we can imagine or think up alternative solutions. I have a preference for the following three:

(a) Calling to serve as 'experts' (for relatively brief evaluations) on anthropologists who are already specialists through long-term study of the region involved and/or of the theme in question: this is a means of combining previously acquired in-depth knowledge with a 'research' context marked by the characteristic constraints of time and of subject delimitation proper to the 'action' framework of development institutions;

(b) The collaborative definition of research themes between development operators, PhD students and their supervisors. Development institutions would be required to provide doctoral students working in the field of anthropology of development with the means for field enquiry;

(c) A combination of individual and collective enquiries, of medium-term and short-term enquiries, as described in Chapter 12 (the ECRIS canvass).

My position is clear: second-rate studies carried out by poorly trained anthropologists, based on ready-made methodologies, cannot provide effective action support. This can only be achieved through specialists with high-level 'fundamentalist' training, built on genuine field experience, acquired over a long period, capable of adjusting to the specific (and legitimate) requisites of expertise (limitation of subject and time) without forgoing scientific requirements.

Anthropology can help action only if it maintains high standards of quality.

Obviously, the preceding remarks constitute an overview. They do not claim to provide an exhaustive analysis of the relationship between anthropology and actors in the field of development, far from it.

For instance, this book does not broach the subject of problems of a 'political', ethical or deontological nature. Yet these are clearly at the heart of the debate on the relationship between knowledge and action. I have deliberately avoided such questions: their complexity and their symbolic and emotional facets cannot be covered in a quick overview.

Rather than making a pretence at answering questions for which no answer is available, or proposing miracle solutions in a field where it has been proved that none exist, I have found it preferable to limit myself in this concluding chapter to suggesting a few simple or even elementary levels of potential collaboration between anthropology and development operators, based on the competences specific to our discipline, and compatible to the modest, limited *operational* objective outlined at the beginning of the present work: namely, to make some contribution to improving the quality of the services that development institutions propose to populations.

Of course, we could also consider the problem from another, more ambitious perspective: are anthropologists in a position to help populations to negotiate more effectively with development institutions, for instance by informing the populations (various 'restitution' procedures can be imagined) about our findings? This kind of inversion is obviously enticing. But it suffices to ask questions like: which sectors of the populations are we talking about? Who are the persons presenting themselves as the 'representatives' of these populations, and why? With which 'local' interests is the anthropologist in league? This gives us an idea of how complex this problem is in reality.

Socio-anthropology of development and anthropology applied to development: one instance and its limit[8]

By way of a conclusion, I can, perhaps, offer our collective experience of ten years' work on this question of anthropology applied to development, its difficulties and problems. Indeed, we set up a social science research centre at Niamey, Niger: the LASDEL (Centre for Research and Study into Social Dynamics and Local Development), concerned especially with socio-anthropology. At LASDEL we initiated research programmes into themes with a direct bearing on the institutions of development; the role of development projects in the local context; the difficulties of childbearing in the rural environment; how village water pump management committees operate; hygiene and health improvements in two medium-sized towns; everyday corruption in the administration of justice, transport, health and customs; local authorities and future decentralization; interactions between health professionals and users; conflicts over credit; and so on. Many of these programmes were financed by 'funding providers', that is, development institutions active in Niger or in Africa generally.[9]

None of this was undertaken as 'applied anthropology', still less as consultancy or the provision of expertise. In every case, the programmes were based on fundamental research. We always defined the subject and its problematic ourselves. Nobody sought to set terms of reference for us. Nor did we come up with any of the 'recommendations' that expert reports usually provide, or play some operational role.

Above all, we always applied our own methodology, an anthropological or socio-anthropological or qualitative sociology approach – the label doesn't matter – along with the ECRIS methodology for the collective phases which always preceded the longer individual enquiries. All these programmes led or will lead to scientific publications.[10]

In which case, why did development institutions finance the research and give us such a free hand? The answer is twofold:

(a) We were addressing scientifically (inasmuch as this is possible in social science) themes of direct or indirect interest to funding providers, themes on which they have little or no material available. Rather than the traditional subject matter of anthropology (kinship, myth, ritual), we were tackling themes of contemporary social relevance: corruption, governance, the public arena, provision of collective services, local administration.

(b) Our approach was well documented and resolutely empirical. It required the 'qualitative rigour' that can provide precious information on how things happen in real life. Our methodology was essentially that of classical anthropology, especially the British tradition (work in local languages, the attaching of great importance to the 'emic' point of view and everyday situations, double-checking of information received …). In the development world, enquiries usually consist of 'rapid appraisal' or number-crunching, the provision of statistics – even debatable ones, as is often the case in Africa.

The socio-anthropological approach, on the other hand, allows one to draw up a detailed and credible picture of what is happening on the 'front line', where 'developers' come into contact with 'developees', and state services with their clients Neither rapid appraisal nor statistics can do as much.

In other words, we were supplying development institutions (or, more precisely, certain development professionals who were interested in our approach)[11] with a finely drawn, realistic and reliable account of what was taking place at the interface between a given social milieu and external intervention (by the state, NGOs or 'development projects').

The convergence between these development professionals and ourselves existed on the basis both of a common interest in the themes of our research and of the capacity of our methodology to satisfy that interest. As development professionals, the individuals concerned believed that these themes were particularly pertinent (essential to any political action or development activity, in their view), and as researchers we ourselves found them fascinating, of great intellectual and scientific interest.[12] For example, well-documented enquiries into everyday corruption in the local administration provide development agents, local officials or civic action movements with precious data on the way external interventions 'drift', and what local actors think about that drifting. For us, it is also both a very productive entry point for examining the day-to-day operation of the state, and one step forward towards an anthropology of African administrations, a new and stimulating subject.

Everything is not settled, for all that: what are we to do with our results? How can we turn them into reforms (reforms in both the mode of intervention and the social milieu concerned)?

The missing link

That is the whole point. Neither we – some researchers – nor our interlocutors – certain development professionals – know how to draw operational conclusions from the results. As social science researchers we derive our legitimacy from a competence in empirical research: from the initial draft of a research project and its problematic to the fieldwork and production of data, and on to the final analyses and interpretations. That is what we know how to do; our job. On the other hand, we have no particular skill in terms of institutional arrangements, organizational capacities, the formulation of practical policies, strategies for communication, and proposals for reform. One might even say that in this field our naivety is the mirror image of that of the development professionals concerning knowledge of the milieu. These development professionals, for their part, do have the skills we lack, but that does not mean that they thereby know how to make the link between the analyses we put forward and their own intervention programmes. When faced with our descriptions of the situations under investigation, they generally express both too much interest ('at last we understand how things really happen on the ground') and their embarrassment ('So what? What are we to do with this?'). Informed by our analyses of underlying realities, be they political (in the broader sense), professional, strategic or representational (the actors' perceptions), that they were previously unaware of or barely suspected, they do not know how to use this information to change their own practices and procedures. Perhaps this is because development professionals are in control of very few aspects of the reality they seek to change and are confronted both on the local and on the national level with a multitude of other actors' logics and motivations. Perhaps they have in fact no better idea than we do of the complex process of moving from knowledge to action.

If we assume that the development professionals who use our research are good at what they do, and that we are good researchers, there is still a missing link in the chain between our studies and their operational concerns. It is not enough to understand a process, a milieu, interactions, a context, misunderstandings, conflicts and contradictions; one then has to draw up a strategy, define reforms, and put a new policy into practice.

In the end we and our interlocutors in the development world share at least an assumption that it is better to act on the basis of some information about reality. But neither we nor they know how to transform knowledge of what is the case (as generated by us) into 'action to transform the case' (as put into practice by them). We are constantly confronted *in practice* with this gap between knowledge and action.

How can this gap be filled? There are many possibilities, for instance mutual collaboration between the two professions (in brainstorming sessions involving researchers and development professionals, for example, or in establishing follow-up and feedback procedures). Perhaps what we need is a new profession specializing in the interface: mediators with one foot in the development world and one foot in the social sciences. We ourselves have, sadly, yet to attempt anything noteworthy in either direction.

In fact our only experience has been the organization, whenever possible, of access to the results by the actors concerned: for instance, the data and analyses we produced on corruption in Africa were on various occasions presented to customs agents, the police, health officials (in Niger, Benin, Senegal, Burkina Faso ...) The same problem emerged. Social actors recognized that the reality they lived was as we depicted it, even if usually hidden in public. They deplored it (although they themselves were often actively involved in that reality), and they were greatly puzzled as to how to change it (expressing discouragement or fatalism).

How is this missing link to be forged, in the daily practice of serious reform initiatives rather than in comfortable rhetorical formulas? This remains one of the major challenges to present and future collaboration between social science researchers and development professionals.

Such collaboration is nothing to be ashamed of – on the contrary – but it is far more complex than is generally believed. The task is almost entirely still to be done, and demands as a preliminary condition a real professionalism on both sides, rather than good intentions and commonplace populist illusions.

We are still convinced that our own professional contribution to this desirable form of collaboration should consist in: (a) treating as worthy of investigation everything that is an important issue or a problem-in-the-making for social actors (local, national and external), giving much more emphasis to this than our discipline has done in the past; (b) approaching these issues and problems with all the methodological and theoretical seriousness that can be demanded of 'fundamental' anthropology and good-quality research.

Notes

1 Boiral insists on this point more on the strength of data originating in a European 'social' field than on data concerning 'development' in Africa. However, this problem remains, regardless of the fields in question. (See Boiral, 1985.)

2 J.P. Jacob once suggested this very caustic formula to me: 'Development is enterpreneurship without the risk'. We could go on to point out, along the same lines, that developers are entrepreneurs who let the developees assume the risks. As for scientists, they usually have no personal experience either in enterpreneurship or in risk taking.

3 The idea that prior anthropological knowledge of local societies might prevent project failure is misguided in this particular.

4 Gentil and Dufumier have already made mention of this alongside a criticism of classic agro-economic methodology: 'The methodologies underlying most systems of follow-up evaluation are founded on a number of implicit oversimplifications which make it practically impossible for them to understand the rural milieu and the real mechanisms of decision-making regarding projects' (Gentil and Dufumier, 1984: 31).

5 A good example of anthropological observation on expert enquiries (hasty enquiries) can be found in Koné (Koné, 1994). She shows how field agents selected 'peasant interlocutors' to speak the 'right language' in the presence of experts, and the strange way in which 'translators' react when peasants speak the 'wrong' language.

6 See Mosse, 1994; Bierschenk and Olivier de Sardan, 1997a; Lavigne Delville, Sellamna and Mathieu, 2000.

7 See the papers in the *Bulletin de l'APAD* , nos. 7 and 8, reporting on the Bamako workshops (January 1994) focusing on the social science/expertise relationship.

8 The following text was written in 2004 especially for this English edition. It does not appear in the original French edition.

9 Some of these programmes covered several countries and/or were assisted by researchers from other countries (amongst others T. Bierschenk, G. Blundo, Y. Jaffré, M. Koné, A. Fall, Y. Touré, Y. Diallo).

10 See Olivier de Sardan and Elhadji Dagobi, 2000; Olivier de Sardan, Moumouni and Souley, 2000; Jaffré and Olivier de Sardan (eds), 2003; Blundo and Olivier de Sardan, 2000, 2001; Olivier de Sardan, 1999a; 2001b; Hahonou, 2001; Olivier de Sardan and Tidjani Alou (eds) (forthcoming); Blundo, Hahonou and Olivier de Sardan (forthcoming). The whole LASDEL team participated in these projects (M. Tidjani Alou, A. Moumouni, A. Souley, A. Mohamadou, A. Elhadji Dagobi, E. Hahonou, H. Moussa, D. Maiga, N. Bako Arifari, A. Imorou).

11 Not all development professionals were equally interested in our work. By development professionals, I mean both national (African) actors and external actors (from the North).

12 They concern us also as citizens but, as I stated above, I will not be discussing here the political and ethical dimensions of anthropology, another debate altogether which can and should be conducted in a different way.

Bibliography

Abram, S., 1998, 'Introduction: anthropological perspectives on local development', in Abram and Waldren (eds).

Abram, S. and Waldren, J. (eds), 1998 *Anthropological Perspectives on Local Development: knowledge and sentiments in conflict*, London: Routledge.

Accardo, A. and Corcuff, P., 1986, *La sociologie de Bourdieu. textes choisis et commentés*, Bordeaux: Le Mascaret.

Aïach, P. and Fassin, D., 1992, *Sociologie des professions de santé*, Paris: Éditions de l'Espace européen.

Almond, G. and Powell, B., 1966, *Comparative Politics: a developmental approach*, Boston: Brown.

Althusser, L., 1970, 'Idéologie et appareils idéologiques d'État', *La Pensée*, 151.

Amin, S., 1972, *L'accumulation à l'échelle mondiale*, Paris: Éditions de Minuit.

Amselle, J.L., 1977, *Les négociants de la savane*, Paris: Anthropos.

Amselle, J-L. and M'bokolo, E. (eds), 1985, *Au coeur de l'ethnie. Ethnies, tribalisme et état en Afrique*, Paris: Editions La Découverte.

Ancey, G., 1975, 'Niveaux de décisions et fonction objectif en milieu rural', Paris: AMIRA, note 3 (mimeo).

Ancey, G., 1984, 'Enquêtes rurales en Afrique sur des échantillons restreints. Problèmes de méthode à travers trois analyses de cas.', Paris: AMIRA (mimeo).

Appadurai, A., 1986a, 'Introduction: commodities and the politics of value', in Appadurai (ed): 3–63.

Appadurai, A. (ed), 1986b, *The Social Life of Things: commodities in cultural perspective*, Cambridge: Cambridge University Press.

Appadurai, A., 1995, 'The production of locality', in Fardon (ed).

Appadurai, A., 1996, *Modernity at large: cultural dimensions of globalization*, Minneapolis: Univesrity of Minnesota Press.

Apter, D., 1963, *Politics of Modernisation*, Chicago: Chicago University Press.

Apthorpe, R., 1986, 'Development policy discourse', *Public Administration and Development*, 6: 377–89.

Apthorpe, R. and Gasper, D. (eds), 1996, *Arguing Development Policy: frames and discourses*, London: Frank Cass.

217

Arce, A., 1993, *Negotiating Agricultural Development. Entanglements of bureaucrats and rural producers in Western Mexico*, Wageningen: Agricultural University.

Arce, A. and Long, N. (eds), 2000, *Anthropology, Development and Modernity*, London: Routledge.

Arnfred, S., 1998, 'From quest for civilization to war against poverty: observations regarding development discourse', in Marcussen and Arnfred (eds).

Arnould, E., 1989, 'Anthropology and West African development: a political economic critique and autocritique', *Human Organization,* 48 (2): 135–48.

Augé, M., 1972, 'Sous-développement et développement: terrain d'étude et objets d'action en Afrique francophone', *Africa*, 42 (2): 205–16.

Augé, M., 1973, 'L'illusion villageoise', *Archives Internationales de Sociologie de la Coopération et du Développement*, 34.

Augé, M., 1986, 'L'anthropologie de la maladie', *L'Homme*, 26 (1–2): 81–90.

Bailey, F., 1969, *Stratagems and Spoil: a social anthropology of politics,* London: Basil Blackwell.

Bailey, F., 1973a, 'Debate, compromise and change', in Bailey (ed).

Bailey, F., 1973b, 'Promethean fire: right and wrong', in Bailey (ed).

Bailey, F. (ed), 1973c, *Debate and Compromise: the politics of innovation,* Oxford: Blackwell.

Bako-Arifari, N., 1999, 'Dynamiques et formes du pouvoir politique en milieu rural ouest-africain: étude comparative au Bénin et au Niger', PhD thesis, École des Hautes Études en Sciences Sociales, Marseille.

Bako Arifari, N., 1995, 'Démocratie et "logique du terroir" au Bénin', *Politique Africaine*, 59: 7–24.

Bako-Arifari, N. and Le Meur, P.Y., 2001, 'La chefferie au Bénin entre Etat, développement et pouvoirs locaux: une résurgence ambiguë', in H. Almeida-Topor (d') and C. H. Perrot (eds), *Rois et chefs dans les Etats africains de la veille des Indépendances à la fin du XXeme siècle. Eclipses et résurgences*, Paris: Karthala.

Balandier, G., 1963, *Sociologie actuelle de l'Afrique noire. Dynamique sociale en Afrique centrale,* Paris: Presses Universitaires de France.

Balandier, G., 1969, *Anthropologie politique,* Paris: Presses Universitaires de France.

Balandier, G., 1971, *Sens et puissance,* Paris: Presses Universitaires de France.

Barlett, P., 1980a, 'Adaptative strategies in peasant agricultural production', *Annual Review of Anthropology*, 9: 545–73.

Barlett, P. (ed), 1980b, *Agricultural Decision Making: anthropological contributions to rural development,* New York: Academic Press.

Barnett, H., 1953, *Innovation: the basis of social change,* New York: McGraw-Hill.

Barrès, J.F., Billaz, R., Dufumier, M. and Gentil, D., 1981, 'Méthode d'évaluation de projets', Paris: AMIRA-AFIRD, mimeo.

Barth, F. (ed.), 1975, *Ethnic Groups and Boundaries: the social organisation of cultural difference,* Boston: Little Brown (1st edn 1969).

Barth, F., 1981, *Process and Form in Social Life (Selected Essays of Frederic Barth:* Vol. I), London, Boston and Henley: Routledge and Kegan Paul.

Bastide, R., 1971, *Anthropologie appliquée,* Paris: Payot.

Bates, R., 1986, 'Some contemporary orthodoxies in the study of agrarian change', in Kohli (ed.): 67–86.

Bates, R., 1987, *Essays on the Political Economy of Rural Africa,* Berkeley: University of

California Press (1st edn 1983).

Bates, R., 1988a, 'Anthropology and development: a note on the structure of the field', in Bennett and Bowen (eds).

Bates, R. (ed), 1988b, *Toward a Political Economy of Development: a rational choice perspective*, Berkeley: University of California Press.

Bateson, G., 1980, *Vers une écologie de l'esprit* (Vol. 2), Paris: Seuil.

Bayart, J.F., 1989, *L'État en Afrique. La politique du ventre*, Paris: Fayart.

Bayart, J.F., Mbembe, A. and Toulabor, C., 1992, *La politique par le bas en Afrique Noire. Contributions à une problématique de la démocratie*, Paris: Karthala.

Bazin, J. and Terray, E. (eds), 1982, *Guerres de lignages et guerres d'État en Afrique,* Paris: Éditions des Archives Contemporaines.

Beek, W. van., 1993, 'Processes and limitations of Dogon agricultural knowledge', in Hobart (ed): 43–60.

Belloncle, G., 1982, *La question paysanne en Afrique noire,* Paris: Karthala.

Belloncle, G., 1985, *Participation paysanne et aménagements hydro-agricoles,* Paris: Karthala.

Bennett, J., 1966, 'Further remarks on Foster's image of limited good', *American Anthropologist,* 68 (1): 206–9.

Bennett, J., 1988, 'Anthropology and development: the ambiguous engagment', in Benett and Bowen (eds).

Bennett, J. and Bowen, J. (eds), 1988, *Production and Autonomy: anthropological studies and critiques of development,* Lanham: Society for Economic Anthropology.

Berche, T., 1998, *Anthropologie et santé publique en pays dogon,* Paris: Karthala.

Berger, P., 1978, (1976) *Pyramids of Sacrifice,* London: Allen Lane.

Berry, S., 1993, *No Condition is Permanent: the social dynamics of agrarian change in Sub-Saharan Africa,* Madison: University of Wisconsin Press.

Bierschenk, T., 1988, 'Development projects as an arena of negotiation for strategic groups: a case study from Bénin', *Sociologia Ruralis,* 28 (2–3): 146–60.

Bierschenk, T., 1991, 'Les projets et les politiques de développement sont-ils des préoccupations légitimes de l'anthropologie?', *Bulletin de l'APAD,* 1: 12–14.

Bierschenk, T., 1992, 'The ethnicisation of Fulani society in the Borgou province of Benin by the ethnologists', *Cahiers d'Etudes Africaines,* 127: 509–20.

Bierschenk, T. and Forster, R., 1991, 'Rational herdsmen: economic strategies of the agro-pastoral fulani of Northern Benin', *Applied Geography and Development,* 38: 110–25.

Bierschenk, T. and Olivier de Sardan, J.P., 1997a, 'ECRIS: Rapid collective inquiry for the identification of conflicts and strategic groups' *Human Organization,* 56 (2): 238–44.

Bierschenk, T. and Olivier de Sardan, J.P., 1997b, 'Local powers and a distant state in rural Central African Republic', *Journal of Modern African Studies,* 35 (3): 441–68.

Bierschenk, T. and Olivier de Sardan, J.P., 1998a, 'Les arènes locales face à la décentralisation et à la democratisation: analyses comparatives en milieu rural béninois', in Bierschenk and Olivier de Sardan (eds).

Bierschenk, T. and Olivier de Sardan, J.P. (eds), 1998b, *Les pouvoirs au village: le Bénin rural entre démocratisation et décentralisation,* Paris: Karthala.

Bierschenk, T. and Olivier de Sardan, J.P., 2003, 'Power in the village: rural Benin between democratisation and decentralisation', *Africa,* 73 (2): 145–73.

Bierschenk, T., Chauveau, J.P. and Olivier de Sardan, J.P. (eds), 1999, *Courtiers en développement. Les villages africains en quête de projets*, Paris: Karthala.

Binsbergen, W. van, 1998, 'Globalization and virtuality: analytical problems posed by the contemporary transformations of African societies', *Development and Change*, 29 (4): 873–904.

Binsbergen, W. van and Geschiere, P., 1985a, 'Marxist theory and anthropological practice: the application of french marxist anthropology in field-work', in Binsberger and Gerschiere (eds): 235–89.

Binsbergen, W. van and Geschiere, P. (eds), 1985b, *Old Modes of Production and Capitalist Encroachment: anthropological explorations in Africa*, London: Kegan Paul.

Bloch, M., 1948, 'Les transformations des techniques comme problèmes de psychologie collective', *Journal de psychologie normale et pathologique*, 12: 104–20.

Bloch, M. (ed), 1975, *Marxist Analysis and Social Anthropology*, London: Malaby Press.

Blundo, G., 1991, 'La brique, la terre et le puits: administration locale, "factionnalisme" et autopromotion au Sénégal', in Kwan Kaï Hong (ed), *Jeux et enjeux de l'auto-promotion. Vers d'autres formes de coopération au développement*, Paris and Geneva: Presses Universitaires de France/Cahiers de l'IUED.

Blundo, G., 1994, 'Le conflit dans "l'entente". Coopération et compétition dans les associations paysannes de Koungheul (Sénégal)', in Jacob and Lavigne Delville (eds).

Blundo, G., 1995, 'Les courtiers du développement en milieu rural sénégalais', *Cahiers d'Etudes Africaines*, 137: 73–99.

Blundo, G., 1996, 'Gérer les conflits fonciers au Sénégal: le rôle de l'administration locale dans le Sud-Est du bassin arachidier', *Cahiers Africains*, 23–24: 101–19.

Blundo, G., 1998, 'Elus locaux, associations paysannes et courtiers du développement au Sénégal. Une anthropologie politique de la décentralisation dans le Sud-Est du bassin arachidier (1974–1995)', Lausanne: Thèse de doctorat.

Blundo, G., 2000, 'La corruption entre scandales politiques et pratiques quotidiennes', *Nouveaux Cahiers de l'IUED* (Geneva), 9: 11–20.

Blundo, G. and Olivier de Sardan, J.P., 2000, 'La corruption comme terrain: pour une approche socio-anthropologique', *Nouveaux cahiers de l'IUED* (Geneva), 9: 21–46.

Blundo, G. and Olivier de Sardan, J.P., 2001a, 'La corruption quotidienne en Afrique de l'Ouest', *Politique Africaine*, 83: 8–37.

Blundo, G. et Olivier de Sardan, J.P., 2001b, 'Sémiologie populaire de la corruption', *Politique Africaine*, 83: 98–114.

Blundo, G., Hahonou, E. and Olivier de Sardan, J.P., forthcoming, 'Hygiène et assainissement dans deux villes moyennes du Niger'.

Boiral, P., 1985, 'Logiques de recherche et logiques d'action', in Boiral, Lantéri and Olivier de Sardan (eds).

Boiral, P, Lantéri, J.F, Olivier de Sardan, J.P (eds), 1985, *Paysans, experts et chercheurs en Afrique noire. Sciences sociales et développement rural*, Paris: Karthala.

Boissevain, J., 1974, *Friends of Friends. Networks, manipulators and coalition*, Oxford: Basil Blackwell.

Boissevain, J. and Mitchell, J.C. (eds), 1973, *Network analysis. Studies in social interaction*, The Hague: Mouton.

Boltanski, L. and Thévenot, L., 1991, *De la justification: les économies de la grandeur*, Paris:

Gallimard.

Bonnassieux, A., 1991, 'Petits projets villageois au Niger: rentabilité économique et rationalité sociale', in Olivier de Sardin and Paquot (eds).

Bonnet, D. 1988, 'Corps biologique, corps social. Procréation et maladies de l'enfant en pays mossi (Burkina Faso)', Paris: *Éditions de l'ORSTOM*.

Booth, D. (ed), 1994, *Rethinking Social Development: theory, research and practice*, Harlow, Essex: Longman.

Bosc, P.-M., Yung, J.-M. and Tourte, R., 1991, *Défis, recherches et innovations au Sahel*, Montpellier: CIRAD.

Bosc, P.-M. Dollé, Garin and Yung, J.-M., 1992, *Le développement agricole au Sahel* (Vol. III: *Terrains et innovations*), Montpellier: CIRAD.

Boudon, R., 1984, *La place du désordre. Critique des théories du changement social*, Paris: Presses Universitaires de France.

Boudon, R., 1988, 'Individualisme ou holisme: un débat méthodologique fondamental', in Mendras and Verret (eds).

Bouju, J., 1991, 'Pouvoirs et légitimités sur le contrôle de l'espace rural', in Olivier de Sardan and Paquot (eds).

Bouju, J., 2000, 'Clientélisme, corruption et gouvernance locale a Mopti (Mali)', *Autrepart*, 14: 143–63.

Boukharine, N., 1971, *La théorie du matérialisme historique. Manuel populaire de sociologie marxiste.*, Paris: Anthropos.

Bourdieu, P., 1966, 'Champ intellectuel et projet créateur', *Les Temps Modernes*, 246: 865–906.

Bourdieu, P. 1971, 'Genèse et structure du champ religieux', *Revue Française de Sociologie*, 12: 295–334.

Bourdieu, P. (with Wacquant, L.), 1992, *Réponses,* Paris: Seuil.

Bowen, J., 1988, 'Power and meaning in economic change: what does anthropology learn from development studies?', in Bennett and Bowen (eds).

Boyer, P., 1989, 'Pourquoi les Pygmées n'ont pas de culture?', *Gradhiva*, 7: 3–17.

Breusers, M., 1999, *On the Move: mobility, land use and livelihood practices on the central plateau in Burkina Faso*, Hamburg: Lit.

Brokensha, D., Warren, D.M. and Werner, O. (eds), 1980, *Indigenous Knowledge Systems and Development,* Lanham, New York and London: University Press of America.

Brown, D., 1989, 'Bureaucracy as an issue in Third World management: an African case study', *Public Administration and Development,* 9: 369–80.

Brown, D., 1994, 'Strategies of social development: non-governmental organizations and the limitations of the Freirean approach', Reading: The New Bulmershe Papers, mimeo.

Byres, T., 1979, 'Of neo-populist pipe-dreams: Daedalus in the Third World and myth of urban bias', *Journal of Peasant Studies*, 6 (2): 210–44.

Callon, M. (ed), 1988, *La science et ses réseaux,* Paris: La Découverte.

Caraël, M., 1993, 'Bilan des enquêtes CAP menées en Afrique: forces et faiblesses', in Dozon and Vidal (eds).

Cernea, M., 1991a, 'Preface to the second edition', in Cernea (ed).

Cernea, M. (ed), 1991b, *Putting People First. Sociological Variations in Rural Development*, (1st edn 1985), Oxford: Oxford University Press.

Cernea, M., 1996, *Social Organization and Development Anthropology*, Washington: World Bank (Environmentally Sustainable Development Studies and Monographs Series, no. 6).

Chambers, E., 1987, 'Applied anthropology in the post-Vietnam era: anticipations and irony', *Annual Review of Anthropology*, 16: 309–37.

Chambers, R., 1983, *Rural Development: putting the last first*, London: Longman.

Chambers, R., 1990, *Développement rural. La pauvreté cachée*, Paris: Karthala (1st English edn 1983).

Chambers, R., 1991, 'Shortcut and participatory methods for gaining social information for projects', in Cernea (ed).

Chambers, R., 1994, 'Participatory rural appraisal (PRA): challenges, potentials and paradigm', *World Development*, 22 (10): 1437–54.

Chambers, R., Pacey, A. and Thrupp, L.A, 1989, *Farmers first: farmer innovation and agricultural research*, London: Intermediate Technology Publications.

Chauveau, J.P., 1992, 'Du populisme bureaucratique dans l'histoire institutionnelle du développement rural en Afrique de l'Ouest', *Bulletin de l'APAD*, 4: 23–32.

Chauveau, J.P., 1994, 'Participation paysanne et populisme bureaucratique. Essai d'histoire et de sociologie de la culture du développement', in Jacob and Lavigne Delville (eds).

Chauveau, J.P., 2000a, 'Des "stratégies des agriculteurs africains". Sciences, institutions, idéologie et politique dans les études de développement en France', *Working Papers on African Societies,* 45.

Chauveau, J.P., 2000b, 'Question foncière et construction nationale en Côte d'Ivoire: les enjeux d'un coup d'Etat', *Politique Africaine*, 78: 94–125.

Chauveau, J.P. and Dozon, J.P., 1985, 'Colonisation, économie de plantation et société civile en Côte d'Ivoire', *Cahiers ORSTOM*, 21 (1): 63–80.

Chauveau, J.P., Le Pape, M. and Olivier de Sardan, J.P., 2001, 'La pluralité des normes et leurs dynamiques en Afrique', in Winter (ed).

Chayanov, A. V., 1966, *The Theory of Peasant Economy*, Homewood: Irwin (1st edn 1924).

Choquet, C., Dollfus, O., Le Roy, E., and Vernières, M., 1993, *Etat des savoirs sur le développement. Trois décennies de sciences sociales en langue française,* Paris: Karthala.

Chrétien, J.P. and Prunier, G., 1989, *Les ethnies ont une histoire,* Paris: Karthala.

Clammer, J., 1975, 'Economic anthropology and the sociology of development: "liberal" anthropology and its French critics', in Oxaal, Barnett and Booth (eds).

Clarence-Smith, G., 1985, ' "Thou shall not articulates modes of production" ', *Canadian Journal of African Studies*, 19 (1): 19–22.

Cochrane, G., 1971, *Anthropology of Development*, New York: Oxford University Press.

Cohen, A., 1993, 'Segmentary knowledge: a Whalsay sketch', in Hobart (ed).

Colin, J.P., 1990, 'Regards sur l'institutionnalisme américain', *Cahiers des Sciences Humaines*, 26 (3): 365–79.

Colin, J.P. and Crawford, E. (eds), 2000, *Research on Agricultural Systems: accomplishments, perspectives and issues*, New York: Nova Science Publishers.

Colonna, F., 1987, *Savants paysans. Éléments d'histoire sociale sur l'Algérie rurale*, Algiers: Office des Publication Universitaires.

Comaroff, J. and Comaroff, J. (eds), 1999, *Civil society and the political imagination in Africa. Critical perspectives*, Chicago: The University of Chicago Press.

Cooper, F. and Packard, R. (eds), 1997, *International development and the social sciences. Essays on the history and politics of knowledge*, Berkeley: University of California Press.

Copans, J., 1980, *Les marabouts de l'arachide*, Paris: Le Sycomore.

Copans, J., 1986, 'Mode de production: formation sociale ou ethnie? Les leçons d'un long silence de l'anthropologie marxiste française', *Revue Canadienne des Etudes Africaines*, 20 (1): 74–90.

Copans, J., 1988, 'Les modèles marxistes dans l'anthropologie économique française. Prêt-à-porter ou haute couture?', *Cahiers Internationaux de Sociologie*, 34: 161–76.

Coquery-Vidrovitch, C. 1985, *Afrique noire: Permanences et ruptures*, Paris: Payot.

Cot, J.P. and Mounier, J.P., 1974, *Pour une sociologie politique*, Paris: Seuil (2 vols).

Crehan, K and Oppen (van), A., 1988, 'Understandings of "development": an arena of struggle. The story of a development project in Zambia', *Sociologia Ruralis*, 28 (2–3): 113–45.

Croll, E. and Parkin, D. (eds), 1992, *Bush Base, Forest Farm: culture, environment and development*, London: Routledge.

Crousse, B., Le Bris, E. and Le Roy, E., 1986, *Espaces disputés en Afrique Noire: pratiques foncières locales*, Paris: Karthala.

Crozier, M., 1963, *Le phénomène bureaucratique*, Paris: Seuil.

Crozier, M. and Friedberg, E., 1977, *L'acteur et le système*, Paris: Seuil.

Crush, J. (ed), 1995, *Power of Development*, London: Routledge

Daane, J. and Mongbo, R., 1991, 'Peasant influence on development projects in Bénin: a critical analysis', *Genève-Afrique*, 29 (2): 49–76.

Dahl, G. and Hjort, A., 1985, 'Development as message and meaning', *Ethnos*, 49: 165–85.

Dalton, G., 1971, *Economic Anthropology and Development. Essays on tribal and peasant economies*, New York and London: Basic Books.

Dalton, G., 1972. 'Peasantries in anthropology and history', *Current Anthropology*, 13: 385–416 (reprinted in Dalton 1971).

Darré, J.P., 1985, *La parole et la technique. L'univers de pensée des éleveurs du Ternois*, Paris: L'Harmattan.

Darré, J.P., 1986, 'La production de connaissances dans les groupes locaux d'agriculteurs', *Agriscope*, 7: 24–36.

Darré, J.P., 1997, *L'invention des pratiques en agriculture*, Paris: Karthala.

Dartigues, L., 1997, 'La notion d'arène en anthropologie politique', *Working Papers on African Societies*, 17.

Desjeux, M., 1987, *Stratégies paysannes en Afrique noire. Le Congo. Essai sur la gestion de l'incertitude*, Paris: L'Harmattan.

Détienne, M. and Vernant, J.P., 1974, *Les ruses de l'intelligence. La métis chez les Grecs*, Paris: Flammarion.

Diawara, M., 1991, *La graine de la parole. Dimension sociale et politique des traditions orales du royaume de Jaara (Mali) du 15° au milieu du 19° siècles*, Stuttgart: Franz Steiner Verlag.

Dozon, J.P., 1978, 'Logiques des développeurs/réalité des développés: bilan d'une expérience rizicole en Côte d'Ivoire', *Mondes en Développement*, 24.

Dozon, J.P., 1985, 'Bilan d'une expérience rizicole en Côte d'Ivoire', in Boiral, Lantéri and Olivier de Sardan (eds).

Dozon, J.P., 1987, 'Ce que valoriser la médecine traditionnelle veut dire', *Politique*

Africaine, 28: 9–20.

Dozon, J.P., 1991, 'Le dilemme connaissance/action: le développement comme champ politique', *Bulletin de l'APAD*, 1: 14–17.

Dozon, J.P. and Vidal, L. (eds), 1993, 'Les sciences sociales face au sida – Cas africains autour de l'exemple ivoirien', Abidjan: Centre ORSTOM de Petit-Bassam, mimeo.

Dubet, F., 1994, *Sociologie de l'expérience*, Paris: Seuil.

Dupré, G., 1982, *Un ordre et sa destruction*, Paris: ORSTOM.

Dupré, G. (ed), 1991, *Savoirs paysans et développement*, Paris: Karthala-ORSTOM.

Easton, D., 1979, *A System Analysis of Political Life*, Chicago: University of Chicago Press.

Eisenstadt, S. and Lemarchand, R., 1981, *Political Clientelism, Patronage and Development*, Beverly Hills: Sage.

Eisenstadt, S. and Roniger, L., 1980, 'Patron–client relations as a model of structuring social exchange', *Comparative Studies in Sociology and History*, 22: 42–77.

Eisenstadt, S. and Roniger, L., 1984, *Patrons, Clients and Friends: interpersonal relations and the structure of trust in society*, Cambridge: Cambridge University Press.

Eldin, M. and Milleville, P. (eds), 1989, *Le risque en agriculture*, Paris: ORSTOM.

Elster, J., 1983, *Explaining Technical Change*, Cambridge: Cambridge University Press.

Elwert, G., 1984, 'Conflicts inside and outside the household: a West African case study', in Smith, Wallerstein, and Evers (eds).

Elwert, G. and Bierschenk, T., 1988, 'Development aid as an intervention in dynamics systems. An introduction', *Sociologia Ruralis*, 28 (2–3): 99–112.

Emmanuel, A., 1972, *L'échange inégal*, Paris: Maspéro.

Epstein, A. (ed), 1978, *The Craft of Anthropology*, London: Tavistock (1st edn 1967).

Escobar, A., 1984, 'Discourse and power in development: Michel Foucault and the relevance of his work to the Third World', *Alternatives*, X: 377–400.

Escobar, A., 1991, 'Anthropology and the development encounter: the making and marketing of anthropology of development', *American Ethnologist*, 18 (4): 658–82.

Escobar, A., 1995, *Encountering Development: the making and unmaking of the Third World*, Princeton: Princeton University Press.

Escobar, A., 1997, 'Anthropologie et développement', *Revue Internationale des Sciences Sociales*, 154: 539–59.

Esman, M. and Uphoff, N., 1984, *Local organizations: intermediaries in rural development*, Ithaca: Cornell University Press.

Evers, H. and Schiel, T., 1988, *Strategische Grupetti*, Berlin: Reimer.

Fairhead, J., 2000, 'Development discourse and its subversion: decivilisation, depoliticisation and dispossession in West Africa', in Arce and Long (eds).

Fall, A. and Lericollais, A. 1992, 'Light. Rapid rural appraisal. Des Méthodologies brillantes et légères?' *Bulletin de l'APAD*, 2.

Fardon, R., van Binsbergen, W. and van Dijk, R. (eds), 1999, *Modernity on a Shoestring: dimensions of globalization, consumption and development in Africa and beyond*, London: EIDOS.

Fassin, D., 1986, 'La vente illicite de médicaments au Sénégal. Economies "parallèles", État et société' , *Politique Africaine*, 23: 123–30.

Fassin, D., 1989, 'Les écarts de langage des guérisseurs. Systèmes de classification et modes de communication', *Colloques INSERM*, 192: 65–74.

Fassin, D., 1992a, *Pouvoir et maladie en Afrique. Anthropologie sociale dans la banlieue de Dakar*, Paris: Presses Universitaires de France.

Fassin, D., 1992b, 'Quand les traditions changent. Transformations et enjeux actuels des médecines du Tiers Monde', in Aïach and Fassin.

Fassin, D. and Jaffré, Y. (eds), 1990, *Sociétés, développement et santé*, Paris: Ellipses.

Fay, C., 2000, 'La décentralisation dans un cercle (Tenenkou, Mali)' *Autrepart*, 14: 121–42.

Ferguson, J., 1990, *The Anti-politics Machine: 'development', depoliticization and bureaucratic power in Lesotho*, Cambridge: Cambridge University Press.

Ferguson, J., 1997, 'Anthropology and its evil twin: "development" in the constitution of a discipline', in Cooper and Packard (eds).

Ferguson, J., 1998, 'Transnational topographies of power: beyond "the State" and "civil society" in the study of African politiques', in Marcussen and Arnfred (eds).

Ferks, G. and Ouden, J. den (eds), 1995, *In Search of the Middle Ground: essays on the sociology of planned development*, Wageningen: Agricultural University.

Foster, G., 1962, *Traditional Cultures: the impact of technological change*, New York: Harper and Brothers.

Foster, G., 1965, 'Peasant society and the image of limited good', *American Anthropologist*, 67: 293–315.

Foster, G., 1966, 'Reply', *American Anthropologist*, 68 (1): 210–14.

Foster, G., 1972, 'A second look at limited good', *Anthropological Quarterly*, 45 (2): 57–64.

Frank, A.G., 1972, *Le développement du sous-développement*, Paris: Maspéro.

Freire, P., 1980 (1970), *Pedagogy of the Oppressed*, London and New York: Continuum.

Freud, C., 1985, 'Projets de coopération', in Boiral, Lantéri and Olivier de Sardan (eds).

Freud, C., 1986, 'La mission d'évaluation du ministère des relations extérieures (Service de la Coopération et du Développement)', in *L'exercice du développement*: 207–26.

Freud, C., 1988, *Quelle coopération? Un bilan de l'aide au développement*, Paris: Karthala.

Freyssinet, J., 1966, *Le concept de sous-développement*, Paris: Mouton.

Friedberg, E., 1993, *Le pouvoir et la règle. Dynamique de l'action organisée*, Paris: Seuil.

Gardner, K. and Lewis, D., 1996, *Anthropology, Development and the Post-modern Challenge*, London: Pluto Press.

Geertz, C., 1986, *Savoir local, savoir global. Les lieux du savoir*, Paris: Presses Universitaires de France.

Gentil, D., 1984, *Les pratiques coopératives en milieu rural africain*, Paris: L'Harmattan.

Gentil, D. and Dufumier, M., 1984, 'Le suivi évaluation dans les projets de développement rural. Orientations méthodologiques', AMIRA, working paper no. 44 (mimeo).

Geschiere, P., 1984, '‘La paysannerie africaine est-elle captive? Sur la thèse de Goran Hyden et pour une réponse plus nuancée', *Politique Africaine*, 14: 13–33.

Geschiere, P. and Gugler, J., 1998, 'Introduction. The rural–urban connection. Changing issues of belonging and identification', *Africa*: 68 (3): 309–19.

Geschiere, P. and Schlemmer, B., 1987, *Terrains et perspectives*, Leyde: ORSTOM.

Giddens, A., 1979, *Central Problems in Social Theory: action, structure and contradiction in social analysis*, London: Macmillan.

Giddens, A., 1984, *The Constitution of Society*, Cambridge: Polity Press.

Giddens, A., 1987, *Social Theory and Modern Sociology*, Stanford: Stanford University Press.

Glaser, B.G. and Strauss, A.L., 1973 (1967), *The Discovery of Grounded Theory. Strategies for qualitative research*, Chicago: Aldine.

Gluckman, M., 1956, *Custom and Conflict in Africa*, London: Blackwell.

Gould, J., 1997, *Localizing Modernity: action, interests and association in rural Zambia*, Helsinki: Transactions of the Finnish Anthropological Society (40).

Granovetter, M., 1973, 'The strength of the weak ties', *American Journal of Sociology*, 78 (6): 1360–80.

Granovetter, M., 1985, 'Economic action and social structure: the problem of embeddedness', *American Journal of Sociology*, 91 (3): 481–510.

Green, E. (ed), 1986, *Practicing Anthropology of Development*, Boulder: Westview Press.

Grégoire, E. and Labazée, P., 1993, *Grands commerçants d'Afrique de l'Ouest. Logiques et pratiques d'un groupe d'hommes d'affaires contemporains.*, Paris: Karthala-ORSTOM.

Gregory, J., 1975, 'Image of limited good or expectation of reciprocity?', *Current Anthropology*, 16 (1): 73–92.

Grignon, C. and Passeron, J.-C., 1989, *Le savant et le populaire. Misérabilisme et populisme en sociologie et en littérature*, Paris: Seuil.

Grillo, R., 1985, 'Applied anthropology in the 1980s: retrospect and prospect', in Grillo, R. and Rew, A. (eds): 1–36.

Grillo, R., 1997, 'Discourses of development: the view from anthropology', in Grillo and Stirrat (eds).

Grillo, R. and Rew, A. (eds), 1985, *Social Anthropology and Development Policy*, London and New York: Tavistock.

Grillo, R. and Stirrat, L. (eds), 1997, *Discourses of Development: anthropological perspectives*, Oxford: Berg.

Guha, R. and Spivak, G.C., 1988, *Selected Subaltern Studies*, Oxford: Oxford University Press.

Guichaoua, A. and Goussault, Y., 1993, *Sciences sociales et développement*, Paris: Cursus.

Gupta, A. and Ferguson, J., 1997a, 'Discipline and practice: "the field" as site, method, and location in anthropologie', in Gupta and Ferguson (eds).

Gupta, A. and Ferguson, J. (eds), 1997b, *Anthropological Locations: boundaries and grounds for a field science*, Berkeley: University of California Press.

Hahonou, E., 2001, 'Service des urgences. Les interactions entre usagers et agents de santé à l'hôpital national de Niamey (Niger)', *Working Papers on African Societies*, 51 (Berlin: Das Arabische Buch).

Hill, P., 1986, *Development Economics on Trial: the anthropological case for a prosecution*, Cambridge: Cambridge University Press.

Hirschmann, A., 1967, *Development Projects Observed*, Washington: The Brookings Institution.

Hobart, M., 1993a, 'Introduction: the growth of ignorance?' in Hobart (ed).

Hobart, M. (ed.), 1993b, *An Anthropological Critique of Development: the growth of ignorance*, London: Routledge.

Hoben, A., 1982, 'Anthropologists and Development', *Annual Review of Anthropology*, 11: 349–75.

Horowitz, M., 1996, 'On not offending the borrower: (self?)-ghettoization of anthropology at the World Bank' *Development Anthropologist*, 14 (1–2).

Horowitz, M. and Painter, T., 1986, *Anthropology and Rural Development in West Africa*, Boulder: Westview Press.

Hoselitz, B., 1962, *Sociological Aspects of Economic Growth*, Glencoe: Free Press.

Hunt, D., 1988, 'From the millenium to the everyday: James Scott's search for the essence of peasant politics', *Radical History Review*, 42: 155–72.

Hutton, C. and Robin, C., 1975, 'African peasants and resistance to change: a reconsideration of sociological approaches', in Oxaal, Barnett and Booth (eds).

Hyden, G., 1980, *Beyond Ujamaa in Tanzania, underdevelopment and an uncaptured peasantry*, London: Heinemann.

Hyden, G., 1983, *No Shortcuts to Progress: African development management in perspective*, Berkeley: University of California Press.

Hyden, G., 1985, 'La crise africaine et la paysannerie non capturée', *Politique africaine*, 18: 93–113.

Hyden, G., 1986, 'The anomaly of the African peasantry', *Development and Change*, 17: 677–705.

Hyden, G., 1987, 'Final rejoinder', *Development and Change*, 18: 661–67.

Ionescu, G. and Gellner, E. (eds), 1969, *Populism: its meaning and national characteristics. Introduction*, London: Weidenfeld and Nicolson.

Jacob, J.P., 1989, *Bibliographie sélective et commentée d'anthropologie du développement*, Geneva: IUED.

Jacob, J.P. (ed), 2000, *Sciences sociales et coopération en Afrique: les rendez-vous manqués*, Geneva: Nouveaux Cahiers de l'IUED (10).

Jacob, J.P. and Blundo, G., 1997, *Socio-anthropologie de la décentralisation en milieu rural africain. Bibliographie sélective et commentée*, Geneva: IUED.

Jacob, J.P. and Lavigne Delville, P. (eds), 1994, *Les associations paysannes en Afrique – Organisation et dynamiques*, Paris: APAD–Karthala–IUED.

Jacquemot, P. (ed), 1981, *Economie et sociologie du Tiers Monde. Un guide bibliographique et documentaire*, Paris: L'Harmattan.

Jaffré, Y., 1991, 'Anthropologie de la santé et éducation pour la santé', *Cahiers Santé*, 1: 406–14.

Jaffré, Y., 1993, 'Anthropologie et santé publique. Naître, voir et manger en pays songhay-zarma', PhD thesis, Université Francois Rabelais, Tours.

Jaffré, Y., 1999, 'Les services de santé "pour de vrai". Politiques sanitaires et interactions quotidiennes dans quelques centres de santé (Bamako, Dakar, Niamey)', *Bulletin de l'APAD*, 17: 3–17.

Jaffré, Y. and Olivier de Sardan J.P., 1995, 'Tijiri: la naissance sociale d'une maladie', *Cahiers des Sciences Humaines*, 31 (4): 773–95.

Jaffré, Y. and Olivier de Sardan, J.P. (eds), 1999, *La construction sociale des maladies. Les entités nosologiques populaires en Afrique de l'Ouest*, Paris: PUF.

Jaffré, Y. and Olivier de Sardan, J.P. (eds), 2003, *Une médecine inhospitalière. Soignants et soignés dans cinq capitales d'Afrique de l'Ouest*, Paris: Karthala.

Jewsiewicki, B., 1986, 'Anthropologie marxiste et recherche empirique', *Cahiers d'Etudes Africaines*, 101–2: 266–9.

Jewsiewicki, B. and Letourneau, J. (eds), 1985, *Mode of Production: the challenge of Africa*, Sainte-Foy: Editions Safi.

Jollivet, M. and Mendras, H., 1971, *Les collectivités rurales françaises*, Paris: Armand Colin.

Kaplan, D. and Saler, B., 1966, 'Foster's image of the limited good: an example of anthropological explanation', *American Anthropologist*, 68 (1): 202–5.

Kasfir, N., 1976, *The Shrinking Political Arena*, Berkeley: University of California Press.

Kasfir, N., 1986, 'Are african peasants self-sufficient? A review of Goran Hyden's "Beyond Ujamaa in Tanzania" and "No Shortcuts to Progress"', *Development and Change*, 17 (2): 335–57.

Katz, E. and Lazarsfeld, F., 1955, *Personal Influence. The part played by people in the flow of communications*, New York: The Free Press.

Katz, E., Levin, M. and Hamilton, H., 1971, 'Tradition of research on the diffusion of innovation', *American Sociological Review*: 237–52.

Kay, C., 1989, *Latin American Theories of Development and Underdevelopment*, London: Routledge.

Kellermann, L., 1992, *La dimension culturelle du développement. Bibliographie sélective et annotée 1985–1990*, Paris: L'Harmattan.

Kilani, M., 1994, 'Anthropologie du développement ou développement de l'anthropologie? Quelques réflexions critiques', in Rist (ed).

Kintz, D., 1987, De l'art peul de l'adultère, *Bulletin de l'AFA*, 29–30: 119–43.

Kintz, D., 1991, 'L'environnement comme écosystèmes: thème peul de pointe', in Olivier de Sardan and Paquot (eds).

Kitching, G., 1982, *Development and Underdevelopement in Historical Perspective: populism, nationalism and industrialisation*, London and New York: Methuen.

Kohli, A. (ed), 1986, *The State and Development in the Third World*, Princeton: Princeton University Press.

Koné, M., 1994, 'Être encadreur agricole en Côte d'Ivoire: principes et pratiques (le cas de Sakassou)', PhD thesis, École des Hautes Études en Sciences Sociales, Marseille.

Koné, M. and Chauveau, J.P. , 1998, 'Décentralisation de la gestion foncière et "petits papiers": pluralisme des règles, pratiques locales et régulation politique dans le Centre-Ouest ivoirien', *Bulletin de l'APAD*, 16: 41–64.

Kroeber, A.L. and Kluckhohn, C.K., 1952, *Culture: a critical review of concepts and definitions*, Cambridge, MA: Harvard University Press.

Kuhn, T., 1970, *La structure des révolutions scientifiques*, Paris: Flammarion.

Kwan-Kai-Hong (ed), 1991, *Jeux et enjeux de l'auto-promotion. Vers d'autres formes de coopération au développement*, Paris and Geneva: Presses Universitaires de France– Cahiers de l'IUED.

Labazée, P., 1994, 'Producteurs, consommateurs et marchands du Nord ivoirien', *Cahiers des Sciences Humaines*, 30 (1–2): 211–27.

Labov, W., 1976, *Sociolinguistique*, Paris: Editions de Minuit.

Last, M., 1981, 'The importance of knowing about non-knowing', *Social Science and Medicine*, 15 B: 387–92.

Latouche, S., 1986, *Faut-il refuser le développement?*, Paris: Presses Universitaires de France.

Latour, B., 1989, *La science en action*, Paris: La Découverte.

Laurent, P.J. and Mathieu, P., 1994, 'Migrations, environnement et projet de développement. Récit d'un conflit foncier entre Nuni et Mossi au Burkina Faso', *Cahiers du CIDEP*, 20: 87–133.

Laurent, P.J., 1993, 'Un "mâle" nécessaire pour le programme de la Fédération Wend-Yam (Burkina Faso)', *Bulletin de l'APAD*, 6: 19–24.

Laurent, P.J., 1995, 'Les pouvoirs locaux et la décentralisation au Burkina Faso', *Cahiers du CIDEP*, 26.

Laurent, P.J., 1997, *Une association de développement en pays mossi. Le don comme ruse*, Paris: Karthala.

Lavigne Delville, P., 1994, 'Migrations internationales, restructurations agraires et dynamiques associatives en pays soninké et haalpulaar (1975–1990)'. Essai d'anthropologie du changement social et du développement, PhD thesis, École des Hautes Études en Sciences Sociale, Marseille.

Lavigne Delville, P., 2000, 'Impasses cognitives et expertises en sciences sociales. Réflexions à propos du développement rural en Afrique', in Jacob (ed).

Lavigne Delville P., Sellamna N. and Mathieu M. (eds), 2000, *Les enquêtes participatives en débat: ambitions, pratiques, enjeux*, Paris: Karthala.

Lavigne Delville, P. , Bouju, J. and Le Roy, E., 2000, *Prendre en compte les enjeux fonciers dans une démarche d'aménagement, les bas-fonds au Sahel*, Paris: GRET.

Le Meur, P.Y., 1999, 'Coping with institutional uncertainty. Contested local public spaces and power in rural Benin', *Afrika Spectrum*, 34 (2): 187–211.

Leach, M. and Mearns, R. (eds), 1996, *The Lie of the Land: challenging received wisdom on the African environment*, Oxford: James Currey.

Lemarchand, R., 1989, 'African peasantries, reciprocity and the market', *Cahiers d'Etudes Africaines*, 113: 33–67.

Lemarchand, R., 1992, 'Uncivil states and civil societies: how illusion became reality', *Journal of Modern African Studies*, 30 (2): 177–91.

Lenin, V.I., 1968, *Que Faire?*, in *Oeuvres Choisies*, Moscou: Editions du Progrès.

Leroi-Gourhan, A., 1964, *Le geste et la parole. Technique et langage*, Paris: Albin Michel.

Lévy-Bruhl, L., 1931, *Le surnaturel et la nature dans la mentalité primitive*, Paris: Alcan.

Lewis, O., 1969, *La Vida: Une famille porto-ricaine dans une culture de pauvreté*, Paris: Gallimard (1st English edn 1965).

Lipton, M., 1977, *Why Poor People Stay Poor: a study of urban bias in world development*, London: Temple Smith.

Lloyd, G., 1993, *Pour en finir avec les mentalité primitive*, Paris: Alcan.

Long, N., 1968, *Social Change and the Individual: a study of social and religious responses to innovation in a Zambian rural community*, Manchester: Manchester University Press.

Long, N., 1975, 'Structural dependency, modes of production and economic brokerage in rural Peru', in Oxaal, Barnett and Booth (eds).

Long, N., 1977, *An Introduction to the Sociology of Rural Development*, London and New York: Tavistock.

Long, N., 1984, 'Creating space for change. A perspective on the sociology of development', *Sociologia Ruralis*, 24: 168–83.

Long, N. (ed), 1989, *Encounters at the Interface: a perspective on social discontinuities in rural development*, Wageningen: Agricultural University.

Long, N., 1992a, 'Conclusion', in Long and Long (eds).

Long, N., 1992b, 'From paradigm lost to paradigm regained? The case for an actor-oriented sociology of development', in Long and Long (eds).

Long, N., 1992c, 'Introduction', in Long and Long (eds).

Long, N. 1994, 'Du paradigme perdu au paradigme retrouvé? Pour une sociologie du développement orientée vers les acteurs', *Bulletin de l'APAD*, 7: 11–34.

Long, N., 1996, 'Globalization and localisation: new challenge to rural research', in Moore (ed).

Long, N., 2000, 'Exploring local/global transformations: a view from anthropology', in Arce and Long (eds).

Long, N. and Long, A. (eds), 1992, *Battlefields of Knowledge: the interlocking of theory and practice in social research and development*, London: Routledge.

Long, N. and Ploeg (van der) J.D., 1994, 'Heterogeneity, actor and structure: towards a reconstitution of the concept of structure', in Booth (ed).

Long, N. and Ploeg (van der) J.D., 1997, *Socio-anthropologie de la décentralisation en milieu rural africain. Bibliographie sélective et commentée*, Geneva: IUED.

Lund, C., 1995, Competition over jurisdictions and political manoeuvering in Niger, *Bulletin de l'APAD*, 9.

Lund, C., 1998, *Law, power and politics in Niger*, Hamburg: Lit Verlag.

Maïzi, P., 1991, 'Le groupement féminin 6S à Gourga (Burkina Faso): pratiques et discours', in Olivier de Sardan and Paquot (eds).

Malinowski, B., 1970, *Les dynamiques de l'évolution culturelle* (published in English in 1945: The dynamic of culture change, an inquiry into race relations in Africa), Paris: Payot.

Maman Sani, S., 1994, 'Socio-anthropologie d'une expertise: cas d'une évaluation externe d'un projet au Niger', Niamey: Mission de Coopération (mimeo).

Marcussen, H.S. and Arnfred, S. (eds), 1998, *Concepts and Metaphors: ideologies, narratives and myths in development discourse*, Rotskilde: Rotskilde University (Occasional Paper 19).

Martinelli, B., 1987, 'La fin et les moyens. L'ethnologie et l'intervention technologique', *L'Uomo*, 11 (2): 319–41.

Marty, A., 1986, 'Une approche de la classifiation sociale en milieu rural sahélien', Paris: AMIRA (mimeo no. 50).

Marty, A., 1990, Les organisations coopératives en milieu pastoral: héritages et enjeux, *Cahiers des Sciences Humaines*, 26 (1–2): 121–36.

Mathieu, M. L., 1994, 'Interaction entre population tamacheq de Tin Aouker, Tlemsi, en 70 Région du Mali et trois interventions d'ONG. Les stratégies personnalisées et invisibles qui se développent dans le cadre des projets de développement', Mareille: Mémoire de l'EHESS (mimeo).

Mathieu, P., 1990, 'Culture, rapports sociaux et efficacite de l'irrigation en Afrique sub-saharienne', Brussels: Institut d'étude des pays en voie de développement (Studies and documents).

Médart, J.F., 1981, 'L'État clientéliste transcendé', *Politique Africaine*, 1: 120–4.

Médart, J.F. (ed), 1991, *Etats d'Afrique noire: formation, mécanismes et crise*, Paris: Karthala.

Médart, J.F., 1992, 'Le "big man" en Afrique. Esquisse d'une analyse du politicien entrepreneur', *L'Année Sociologique*, 42: 167–92.

Meillassoux, C., 1964, *Anthropologie économique des Gouro de Côte d'Ivoire*, Paris: Mouton.

Meillassoux, C. (ed), 1971, *The Development of Indigenous Trade and Markets in West Africa*, London: Oxford University Press.

Meillassoux, C., 1975a, *Femmes, greniers et capitaux*, Paris: Maspéro.

Meillassoux, C. (ed), 1975b, *L'esclavage en Afrique pré-coloniale*, Paris: Maspéro.

Meillassoux, C., 1977, *Terrains et théories*, Paris: Maspéro.

Meillassoux, C., 1986, *Anthropologie de l'esclavage. Le ventre de fer et d'argent*, Paris: Presses Universitaires de France

Mendras, H., 1976, *Sociétés paysannes*, Paris: Armand Colin.

Mendras, H., 1984, *La fin des paysans, suivi d'une réflexion sur la fin des paysans vingt ans après*, Arles: Actes-Sud.

Mendras, H. and Forsé, M., 1983, *Le changement social*, Paris: Armand Colin.

Mendras, H. and Verret, M. (eds), 1988, *Les champs de la sociologie française*, Paris: A. Colin.

Meyer B. and Geschiere, P. (eds), 1999, *Globalization and Identity. dialectics of flow and closure*, Oxford: Blackwell.

Miller, D. (ed), 1995, *Worlds Apart: modernity through the prism of local*, London: Routledge.

Mills, D., 1999, '"Progress" as discursive spectacle: but what comes after development?', in Fardon, van Binsbergen and van Dijk (eds).

Mitchell, J.C. (ed), 1969, *Social Networks in Urban Situations: analysis of personal relationships in Central African towns*, Manchester: Manchester University Press.

Mitchell, J.C., 1983, 'Case and situation analysis', *Sociological Review*, 31 (2): 187–211.

Mongbo, R., 1994, 'La dynamique des associations paysannes et la négociation quotidienne: du développement rural à la base, une étude de cas au Bénin', in Jacob and Lavigne Delville (eds).

Mongbo, R., 1995, 'The appropriation and dismembering of development intervention: policy, discourse and pratice in the field of rural development in Benin', PhD thesis, Wageningen: Agricultural University of Wageningen.

Mongbo, R. and Floquet, A., 1994, 'Systèmes de connaissances agricoles et organisations paysannes' (mimeo), Montpellier: CIRAD.

Monteil, C., 1932, *Une cité soudanaise, Djenné*, Paris: Anthropos.

Moore, D. and Schmitz, G. (eds), 1995, *Debating Development Discourse: institutional and popular perspectives*, New York: St Martin's Press.

Mosse, D., 1994, 'Authority, gender, and knowledge: theoretical reflections on the practice of participatory rural appraisal', *Development and Change*, 25 (3): 497–525.

Mosse, D., 1998, 'Process-oriented approaches to development practice and social research', in D. Mosse, Farrington, and A. Rew (eds.), 1998, *Development as Process: working with complexity*, London: Routledge/ODI.

Olivier de Sardan, J.P., 1969, *Système des relations économiques et sociales chez les Wogo (Niger)*, Paris: Institut d'Ethnologie.

Olivier, J.P., 1975, 'Qui exploite qui? (à propos de Samir Amin et des nouvelles bourgeoisies africaines)', *Les Temps Modernes*, 346: 1507–51; 347: 1744–75.

Olivier de Sardan, J.P., 1984, *Les sociétés songhay-zarma. Chefs, esclaves, guerriers, paysans…*, Paris: Karthala.

Olivier de Sardan, J.P., 1991, 'Paysannerie', in P. Bonte and M. Izard (eds), *Dictionnaire de l'ethnologie et de l'anthropologie*, Paris: PUF (2nd edn 2000): 565–8.

Olivier de Sardan, J.P., 1993, 'L'espace wébérien des sciences sociales', *Genèses*, 10: 146–60.

Olivier de Sardan, J.P., 1994, 'La logique de la nomination. Les représentations fluides et prosaïques de deux maladies au Niger', *Sciences Sociales et Santé*, 12 (3): 15–45.

Olivier de Sardan, J.P., 1995a, *Anthropologie et développement. Essai en socio-anthropologie du changement social*, Paris: Karthala.

Olivier de Sardan, J.P., 1995b, 'La politique du terrain. La production des données en anthropologie', *Enquête*, 1: 71–112.

Olivier de Sardan, J.P., 1999a, 'L'espace public introuvable. Chefs et projets dans les villages nigériens', *Revue Tiers Monde*, 157: 139–67.

Olivier de Sardan, J.P., 1999b, 'A moral economy of corruption in Africa?', *The Journal of Modern African Studies*, 37 (1): 25–52, reprinted in R. Williams (ed.), *Explaining Corruption* (Vol. 1 of *The Political Corruption*).

Olivier de Sardan, J.P., 2001a, 'Populisme idéologique et populisme méthodologique en anthropologie', in Fabiani (ed), *Le goût de l'enquête. Pour Jean-Claude Passeron*, Paris: L'Harmattan.

Olivier de Sardan, J.P., 2001b, 'La sage-femme et le douanier. Cultures professionnelles locales et culture bureaucratique privatisée en Afrique de l'Ouest', *Autrepart*, 20: 61–73.

Olivier de Sardan, J.P., and Bierschenk, T., 1993, 'Les Courtiers locaux du développement', *Bulletin de l'APAD*, 5: 71–6.

Olivier de Sardan, J.P. and Elhadji Dagobi, A., 2000, 'La gestion communautaire sert-elle l'intérêt public? Le cas de l'hydraulique villageoise au Niger', *Politique africaine*, 80: 153–68.

Olivier de Sardan, J.P. and Paquot, E. (eds), 1991, *D'un savoir à l'autre. Les agents de développement comme médiateurs*, Paris: GRET–Ministère de la Coopération.

Olivier de Sardan, J.P., Moumouni, A. and Souley, A., 2000, '"L'accouchement, c'est la guerre". Accoucher en milieu rural nigérien', *Afrique Contemporaine*, 195: 136–54.

Olivier de Sardan, J.P. and Tidjani Alou, M. (eds), forthcoming, *Les pouvoirs locaux au Niger*.

ORSTOM 1979, *Maîtrise de l'espace agraire et développement en Afrique tropicale. Logique paysanne et rationalité technique*, Paris: Office de recherche scientifique et technique d'outre mer.

Ouedraogo, A., 1998, 'Enseignement agricole et formation des ruraux', PhD thesis, École des Hautes Études en Sciences Sociales, Paris.

Ouedraogo, J.B., 1997, *Violences et communautés en Afrique Noire*, Paris: Karthala

Oxaal, I., Barnett, T. and Booth, D. (eds), 1975, *Beyond the Sociology of Development: economy and society in Latin America and Africa*, London: Routledge and Kegan Paul.

Painter, T., 1986, 'In search of peasant connection: spontaneous cooperation, introduced cooperatives and agricultural development in Niger', in Horowitz and Painter (eds).

Painter, T., 1987, 'Making migrants: Zarma peasants in Niger, 1900–1920', in Cordell and Gregory (eds).

Parsons, T., 1976, *Elément pour une sociologie de l'action* , Paris: Plon.

Partridge, W., 1984, *Training Manual in Development Anthropology*, Washington DC: American Association for Applied Anthropology.

Passeron, J.C., 1991, *Le raisonnement sociologique. L'espace non-poppérien du raisonnement naturel*, Paris: Nathan.

Peel, J.D., 1968, *Aladura: a religious movement among the Yoruba*, London: Oxford University Press.

Peel, J.D., 1978, 'Olaju: a Yoruba concept of development', *Journal of Development Studies*, 14: 135–65.

Pélissier, P., 1979, 'Le paysan et le technicien: quelques aspects d'un difficile face à face', in ORSTOM, *Maîtrise de l'espace agraire et developpement en Afrique tropicale*.

Pelto, P. and Pelto, G., 1975, 'Intra-cultural diversity: some theoretical issues', *American Ethnologist*, 2: 1–18.

Piker, S., 1966, 'The image of limited good: comments on an exercise in description and interpretation', *American Anthropologist*, 68 (5): 1202–11.

Pitt, D., 1976, 'Introductrion to Development from Below', in Pitt (ed), 1–5.

Pitt, D. (ed.), 1976, *Development from Below: anthropologists and development situations*, The Hague: Mouton.

Polanyi, K., 1983, *La grande transformation. Aux origines politiques et économiques de notre temps*, Paris: Gallimard (first published in English in 1944).

Pollet, E. and Winter, G. 1971, La Société Soninké (Dyamhunu, Mali), Brussels: Université de Bruxelles (Etudes ethnologiques).

Pontié, G. and Ruff, T., 1985, 'L'opération de rénovation de la caféière et de la cacaoyère togolaises', in Boiral, Lantéri and Olivier de Sardan (eds).

Popkin, S., 1979, *The Rational Peasant: the political economy of rural society in Vietnam*, Berkeley: University of California Press.

Pottier, J. (ed), 1993, *Practising Development: social science perspective*, London: Routledge.

Pottier, J., 1997, 'Towards an ethnography of participatory appraisal and research', in Grillo and Stirrat (eds).

Poutignat, P. and Streiff-Fenart, J., 1995, *Théories de l'ethnicité*, Paris: Presses Universitaires de France.

Pye, L., 1966, *Aspects of Political Development*, Boston: Brown.

Quiminal, C., 1991, *Gens d'ici, gens d'ailleurs. Migrations Soninké et transformations villageoises*, Paris: Christian Bourgeois.

Radcliffe-Brown, A.R., 1972, *Structure et fonction dans la société primitive*, Paris: Seuil.

Rahnema, M. and Bawtree, V. (eds), 1997, *The Post-development Reader*, London: Zed Books.

Rancière, J., 1983, *Le philosophe et ses pauvres*, Paris: Fayard.

Raynaut, C., 1986, 'Compte-rendu de "Seeds of famine" (Franke and Chasin, ed.)', *Africa*, 56 (1): 105–111.

Raynaut, C., 1989, 'L'opération de développement et les logiques du changement: la nécessité d'une approche holistique. L'exemple d'un cas nigérien', *Genève Afrique*, 27 (2): 8–38.

Redfield, R., 1956, *Peasant Society and Culture: an anthropological approach to civilization*, Chicago: University of Chicago Press.

Revel, J. (ed), 1995, *Jeux d'échelles. La microanalyse à l'expérience*, Paris: Gallimard–Le Seuil.

Rey, P.P., 1971, *Colonialisme, néo-colonialisme et transition au capitalisme*, Paris: Maspéro.

Rice, R. and Rogers, E., 1980, 'Re-invention in the innovation process', *Knowledge*, 1: 499–514.

Richards, P., 1985, *Indigenous Agricultural Revolution*, London: Hutchinson.

Richards, P., 1986, *Coping with Hunger: hazard and experiment in an African rice farming system*, London: Allen and Unwin.

Richards, P., 1993, 'Cultivation: knowledge or performance?', in Hobart (ed).

Rist, G. (ed), 1994, *La culture otage du développement?*, Paris: L'Harmattan.

Robertson, A.F., 1984, *People and the State: an anthropology of planned development*, Cambridge: Cambridge University Press.

Roe, E., 1991, 'Development narratives or making the best of blueprint development', *World Development*, 19: 287–300.

Roe, E., 1995, 'Except Africa: postscript to a special section on development narratives', *World Development*, 23 (6): 1065–69.

Rogers, E. and Kincaid, L., 1981, *Communications Networks: toward a new paradigm for research*, New York: Free Press.

Rogers, E.M., 1983, *Diffusion of Innovations*, New York: Free Press (3rd edition).

Röling, N., 1987, *Extension Science: information systems for agricultural development*, Cambridge: Cambridge University Press.

Röling, N., 1991, 'Institutional knowledge systems and farmers' knowledge systems. Lessons for technology development', in Dupré (ed).

Rouch, J., 1956, 'Migrations au Ghana', *Journal de la Société des Africanistes*, 26 (1–2): 33–196.

Sachs, W. (ed), 1992, *The Development Dictionary: a guide to knowledge as power*, London: Zed Books.

Sahlins, M., 1989, *Des îles dans l'histoire*, Paris: Gallimard-Le Seuil.

Sautter, G., 1978, 'Dirigisme opérationnel et stratégie paysanne, ou l'aménageur aménagé', *L'Espace Géographique*, 4: 223–43.

Schelling, T., 1980, *La tyrannie des petites décisions*, Paris: PUF (first published in English in 1978 as *Micro-motives and Macro-behavior*).

Schelling, T., 1973 (1960), *The Strategy of Conflicts*, Oxford: Oxford University Press.

Schmidt, S., Scott, J., Lande C., and Guasti L. (eds), 1977, *Friends, Followers and Factions: a reader on political clientelism*, Berkeley: University of California Press.

Schneider, H., 1975, 'Economic development and anthropology', *Annual Review of Anthropology*, 4: 271–92.

Schneider, H., 1987, 'Anthropology's contribution to understanding development', *L'Uomo*, 11 (2): 252–63.

Schumacher, E., 1978, *Small is beautiful. Une société à la mesure de l'homme*, Paris: Seuil (first published in English in 1973).

Schumpeter, J., 1934, *The Theory of Economic Development*, Cambridge, Mass.: Harvard University Press.

Schutz, A., 1987, *Le chercheur et le quotidien. Phénoménologie des sciences sociales*, Paris: Méridiens-Klincksieck.

Scoones, I. and Thompson, J. (eds), 1994, *Beyond Farmer First: rural knowledge in agricultural research and extension practices*, London: Intermediate Technology Publications.

Scott, J., 1976, *The Moral Economy of the Peasant: rebellion and subsistence in Southeast Asia*, New Haven and London: Yale University Press.

Scott, J., 1977, 'Patronage or exploitation', in Gellner and Waterbury (eds): 21–39.

Scott, J., 1985, *Weapons of the Weak*, Yale: Yale University Press.

Scott, J., 1986, 'Everyday forms of peasant resistance', *The Journal of Peasant Studies*, 13 (2): 5–35.

Scott, J., 1990, *Domination and the Arts of Resistance: hidden transcripts*, London: Yale University Press.

Scott, J., 1998, *Seeing like a State: how certain schemes to improve the human condition have failed*, New Haven: Yale University Press.

Silverman, S., 1974, 'Bailey's politics', *Journal of Peasant Studies*, 2: 11–120.

Simon, H., 1957, *Models of Man: social and rational*, New York: Wiley.

Smith, J., Wallerstein, I. and Evers, H.D. (eds), 1984, *Households and the World Economy* (3 vols), London: Sage Publications.

Spittler, G., 1979, 'Peasants and the state in Niger', *Peasant Studies*, 8 (1): 30–47.

Spittler, G., 1984, 'Peasants, the administration and rural development', *Sociologia Ruralis*, 24: 7–9.

Strauss, A., 1987, *Qualitative Analysis for Social Scientists*, New York: Cambridge University Press.

Strauss, A., 1993, *La trame de la négociation. Sociologie qualitative et interactionnisme*, Paris: L'Harmattan.

Tauxier, L., 1932, *Religion, moeurs et coutumes des Agnis de Côte d'Ivoire*, Paris: Geuthner.

Terray, E., 1972, *Le marxisme devant les sociétés primitives*, Paris: Maspéro.

Thompson, E.P., 1971, 'The moral economy of the English crowd during the eighteenth century', *Past and Present*, 50: 76–117.

Tidjani Alou, M., 1994, 'Les projets de développement sanitaire face à l'administration publique au Niger', *Santé Publique*, 4.

Touraine, A., 1984, *Le retour de l'acteur*, Paris: Fayart.

Turner, V., 1957, *Schism and Continuity in an African Society*, Manchester: Manchester University Press.

Velsen, J. van, 1978, 'Situational analysis and the extended case methods', in Epstein (ed).

Watts, M., 1994, 'Development II: the privatization of everything?', *Progress in Human Geography*, 18 (3): 371–84.

Williams, G., 1987, 'Primitive accumulation: the way to progress?', *Development and Change*, 18: 637–59.

Winter, G. (ed), 2001, *Inégalités et politiques publiques en Afrique. Pluralité des normes et jeux d'acteurs*, Paris: Karthala.

Wolf, E., 1988, 'Afterword: indigenous responses to economic development', *Urban Anthropology and Studies of Cultural Systems and World Economies*, 17: 103–6.

Yung, J.M., 1985, 'Evaluation de la filière arachide au Sénégal', in Boiral, Lantéri and Olivier de Sardan (eds).

Yung, J.M. and Zaslavsky, J., 1992, *Pour une prise en compte des stratégies des producteurs*, Montpellier: Cirad.

Index